international
guide
to mixed
drinks

Publishing Pty Limited.

International Guide to Mixed Drinks (A special Borders
Edition)

ISBN 1 740221 06 0
First published in Australia 2000
4cPublishing Pty Limited
Copyright © 4cPublishing Pty Limited
Enquiries should be addressed to the publisher.
4cPublishing Pty Ltd
154 Upper Washington Drive,
Bonnet Bay, NSW. 2226. Australia.
Printed and bound in Singapore by Tat Wei Printing Packaging Pte Ltd

METHODS OF MIXING COCKTAILS

The four methods below are the most common processes of mixing cocktails:-

1. Shake   **2.** Stir

3. Build   **4.** Blend

1. SHAKE: To shake is to mix a cocktail by shaking it in a cocktail shaker by hand. First, fill the glass part of the shaker three quarters full with ice, then pour the ingredients on top of the ice. Less expensive ingredients are more frequently poured before the deluxe ingredients. Pour the contents of the glass into the metal part of the shaker and shake vigorously for ten to fifteen seconds. Remove the glass section and using a Hawthorn strainer, strain contents into the cocktail glass.

Shaking ingredients that do not mix easily with spirits is easy and practical (juices, egg whites, cream and sugar syrups).

Most shakers have two or three parts. In a busy bar, the cap is often temporarily misplaced. If this happens, a coaster or the inside palm of your hand is quite effective. American shakers are best.

To sample the cocktail before serving to the customer, pour a small amount into the shaker cap and using a straw check the taste.

2. STIR: To stir a cocktail is to mix the ingredients by stirring them with ice in a mixing glass and then straining them into a chilled cocktail glass. Short circular twirls are most preferred. (NB. The glass part of the American

Introduction

shaker will do well for this.) Spirits, liqueurs and vermouths that blend easily together are mixed by this method.

3. BUILD: To build a cocktail is to mix the ingredients in the glass in which the cocktail is to be served, floating one on top of the other.

Hi-Ball, long fruit juice and carbonated mixed cocktails are typically built using this technique. Where possible a swizzle stick should be put into the drink to mix the ingredients after being presented to the customer. Long straws are excellent substitutes when swizzle sticks are unavailable.

4. BLEND: To blend a cocktail is to mix the ingredients using an electric blender/mixer. It is recommended to add the fruit (fresh or tinned) first. Slicing small pieces gives a smoother texture than if you add the whole fruit. Next, pour the alcohol. Ice should always be added last. This order ensures that the fruit is blended freely with the alcoholic ingredients allowing the ice to gradually mix into the food and beverage, chilling the flavour. Ideally, the blender should be on for at least 20 seconds. Following this procedure will prevent ice and fruit lumps that then need to be strained.

If the blender starts to rattle and hum, ice may be obstructing the blades from spinning. Always check that the blender is clean before you start. Angostura Bitters is ammonia based which is suitable for cleaning. Fill 4 to 5 shakes with hot water, rinse and then wipe clean.

TECHNIQUES IN MAKING COCKTAILS

1. SHAKE AND POUR: After shaking the cocktail, pour the contents straight into the glass. When pouring into Hi-Ball glasses and sometimes old fashioned glasses the ice cubes are included. This eliminates straining.

2. SHAKE AND STRAIN: Using a Hawthorn strainer (or knife) this technique prevents the ice going into the glass. Straining protects the cocktail ensuring melted ice won't dilute the flavour and mixture.

3. FLOAT INGREDIENTS: Hold the spoon right way up and rest it with the lip slightly above the level of the last layer. Fill spoon gently and the contents will flow smoothly from all around the rim. Use the back of the spoons dish only if you are experienced.

4. FROSTING (sugar and salt rims): This technique is used to coat the rim of the glass with either salt or sugar. First, rub lemon/orange slice juice all the way around only the glass rim. Next, holding the glass by the stem upside down, rest on a plate containing salt or sugar and turn slightly so that it adheres to the glass. Pressing the glass too deeply into the salt or sugar often results in chunks sticking to the glass. A lemon slice is used for salt and an orange slice is used for sugar.

To achieve colour affects, put a small amount of grenadine or coloured liqueur in a plate and coat the rim of the glass, then gently place in the sugar. The grenadine absorbs the sugar and turns it pink. This is much easier than mixing grenadine with sugar and then trying to get it to stick to the glass.

Introduction

HELPFUL HINTS

Cocktail mixing is an art which is expressed in the preparation and presentation of the cocktail.

HOW TO MAKE A BRANDY ALEXANDER CROSS

Take two short straws and, with a sharp knife, slice one of the straws half way through in the middle and wedge the other uncut straw into the cut straw to create a cross.

STORING FRUIT JUICES

Take a 750ml bottle and soak it in hot water to remove the label and sterilise the alcohol. The glass has excellent appeal and you'll find it easier to pour the correct measurement with an attached nip pourer.

SUGAR SYRUP RECIPE

Fill a cup or bowl (depending on how much you want to make) with white sugar, top it up with boiling water until the receptacle is just about full and keep stirring until the sugar is fully dissolved. Refrigerate when not in use. Putting a teaspoon of sugar into a cocktail is being lazy, it does not do the job properly as the sugar dissolves.

JUICE TIPS

Never leave juices, Coconut Cream or other ingredients in cans. Pour them into clean bottles, cap and refrigerate them. All recipes in this book have been tested with Berri fruit juices.

ICE

Ice is probably the most important part of cocktails. It is used in nearly all cocktails. Consequently ice must be clean and fresh at all times.

The small squared cubes and flat chips of ice are superior for chilling and mixing cocktails. Ice cubes with holes are inefficient. Wet ice, ice scraps and broken ice should only be used in blenders.

CRUSHED ICE

Take the required amount of ice and fold into a clean linen cloth. Although uncivilised, the most effective method is to smash it against the bar floor. Shattering with a bottle may break the bottle. Certain retailers sell portable ice crushers. Alternatively a blender may be used. Half fill with ice and then pour water into the blender until it reaches the level of the ice. Blend for about 30 seconds, strain out the water and you have perfectly crushed ice. Always try and use a metal scoop to collect the ice from the ice tray.

Never pick up the ice with your hands. This is unhygienic. Shovelling the glass into the ice tray to gather ice can also cause breakages and hence should be avoided where possible.

Introduction

It is important that the ice tray is cleaned each day. As ice is colourless and odourless, many people assume wrongly it is always clean. Taking a cloth soaked in hot water, wipe the inside of the bucket warm. The blenders used for all of our bar requirements are Moulinex blenders with glass bowls. We have found these blenders to be of exceptional quality.

GLASSES

Cordial (Embassy):	30ml	Fancy Hi-Ball Glass:	220ml, 350ml, 470ml
Cordial (Lexington):	37ml	Hurricane Glass:	230ml, 440ml, 650ml
Tall Dutch Cordial:	45ml	Irish Coffee Glass:	250ml
Whisky Shot:	45ml	Margarita Glass:	260ml
Martini Glass:	90ml	Hi-Ball Glass:	270ml, 285ml, 330ml
Cocktail Glass:	90ml, 140ml	Footed Hi-Ball Glass:	270ml, 300ml
Champagne Saucer:	140ml	Salud Grande Glass:	290ml
Champagne Flute:	140ml, 180ml	Fiesta Grande Glass:	350ml, 490ml
Wine Goblet:	140ml, 190ml	Poco Grande Glass:	380ml
Old Fashioned Spirit:	185ml, 210ml, 290ml	Brandy Balloon:	650ml
Fancy Cocktail:	210ml, 300ml		

A proven method to cleaning glasses is to hold each glass individually over a bucket of boiling water until the glass becomes steamy and then with a clean linen cloth rub in a circular way to ensure the glass is polished for the next serve

Cocktails can be poured into any glass but the better the glass the better the appearance of the cocktail.

One basic rule should apply and that is, use no coloured glasses as they spoil the appearance of cocktails. All glasses have been designed for a specific task, e.g.,

1. Hi-Ball glasses for long cool refreshing drinks.

2. Cocktail glasses for short sharp, or stronger drinks.

3. Champagne saucers for creamy after-dinner style drinks, etc.,

The stem of the glass has been designed so you may hold it whilst polishing, leaving the bowl free of marks and germs so that you may enjoy your drink. All cocktail glasses should be kept in a refrigerator or filled with ice while you are preparing the cocktails in order to chill the glass. An appealing affect on a 90ml cocktail glass can be achieved by running the glass under cold water and then placing it in the freezer.

GARNISHES AND JUICES

Banana	Onions
Celery	Oranges
Cucumber	Pineapple
Lemons	Red Maraschino Cherries
Limes	Rockmelon
Mint leaves	Strawberries
Olives	Canned fruit
Celery salt	Nutmeg
Chocolate flake	Pepper, Salt

Introduction

Cinnamon

Fresh eggs

Fresh single cream

Fresh milk

Apple

Carbonated waters

Coconut Cream

Lemon – pure

Orange

Jelly Babies

Almonds

Apricot Conserve

Vanilla Ice Cream

Tomato

Sugar and sugar cubes

Tabasco sauce

Worcestershire sauce

Orange and Mango

Pineapple

Sugar syrup

Canned nectars

Canned pulps

Crushed Pineapple

Blueberries

Red Cocktail Onions

Flowers (assorted)

Simplicity is the most important fact to keep in mind when garnishing cocktails. Do not overdo the garnish; make it striking, but if you can't get near the cocktail to drink it then you have failed. Most world champion cocktails just have a lemon slice, or a single red cherry.

Tall refreshing Hi-Balls tend to have more garnish as the glass is larger. A swizzle stick should be served nearly always in long cocktails. Straws are always served for a lady, but optional for a man.

Plastic animals, umbrellas, fans and a whole variety of novelty goods are now available to garnish with, and they add a lot of fun to the drink.

ALCOHOL RECOMMENDED FOR A COCKTAIL BAR

Spirits

Aphrodite Ouzo

Bourbon – Rebel Yell

Brandy – Milne

Campari

Canadian Club

Gin – Gilbey's

Malibu

Pernod

Rum – Bacardi

Rum – Bundaberg

Scotch – Ballantine's

Scotch – Bell's

Scotch – Johnnie Walker

Southern Comfort

Tennessee Whiskey – Jack Daniel's

Tequila – El Toro

Tequila – Pepe Lopez

Vandermint

Vodka – Smirnoff

Liqueurs

Advocaat

Amaretto

Bailey's Irish Cream

Benedictine

Blue Curacao

Galliano

Grand Marnier

Kahlúa

Kirsch

Lena Banana

Cassis

Chartreuse – Green

Chartreuse – Yellow

Cherry Advocaat

Cherry Brandy

Clayton's Tonic (Non-alcoholic)

Cointreau

Creme de Menthe Green

Dark Creme de Cacao

Drambuie

Frangelico

Mango

Midori

Peach

Pimm's

Sambuca – di Galliano

Sambuca – Lago Nera

Sambuca – Opal Nera

Sambuca – Romana

Strawberry

Tia Maria

Vermouth

Cinzano Bianco Vermouth

Cinzano Dry Vermouth

Cinzano Rosso Vermouth

Martini Bianco Vermouth

Martini Dry Vermouth

Martini Rosso Vermouth

ESSENTIAL EQUIPMENT FOR A COCKTAIL BAR

Cocktail shaker

Hawthorn Strainer

Waiter's friend corkscrew

Bottle openers

Mixing glass	Ice scoop
Spoon with muddler	Ice bucket
Moulinex Electric blender	Free pourers
Knife, cutting board	Swizzle sticks, straws
Measures (jiggers)	Coasters and napkins
Can opener	Scooper spoon (long teaspoon)
Hand cloths for cleaning glasses	

DESCRIPTION OF LIQUEURS AND SPIRITS

Advocaat: A combination of fresh egg whites, yolks, sugar, brandy and spirit. Limited shelf life, Recommend shelf life 12-15 months from manufacture.

Amaretto: A rich subtle liqueur with a unique almond flavour.

Angostura Bitters: An essential part of any bar or kitchen. A unique additive whose origins date back to 1824. A mysterious blend of natural herbs and spices, both a seasoning and flavouring agent, in both sweet and savoury dishes and drinks. Ideal for dieters as it is low in sodium and calories.

Baileys Irish Cream: The largest selling liqueur in the world. It is a blend of Irish Whiskey, softened by Irish Cream and other flavourings. It is a natural product.

Benedictine: A perfect end to a perfect meal. Serve straight, with ice, soda, or as part of a favourite cocktail.

Bourbon – Rebel Yell: Has a deep flavour of one of America's authentic bourbon whiskies.

Campari: A drink for many occasions, both as a long or short drink, or as

Introduction

a key ingredient in many fashionable cocktails.

Cassis: Deep, rich purple promises and delivers a regal and robust flavour and aroma. Cassis lends itself to neat drinking or an endless array of delicious sauces and desserts.

Chartreuse: A liqueur available in either yellow or green colour. Made by the monks of the Carthusian order. The only world famous liqueur still made by monks.

Cherry Advocaat: Same as Advocaat, plus natural cherry flavours and colour is added.

Cherry Brandy: Is made from concentrated, morello cherry juice. Small quantity of bitter almonds and vanilla is added to make it more enjoyable as a neat drink before or after dinner. Excellent for mixers, topping, ice cream, fruit salads, pancakes, etc.

Coconut: A smooth liqueur, composed of exotic coconut, heightened with light-bodied white rum.

Cointreau: Made from a neutral grain spirit, as opposed to Cognac. An aromatic flavour of natural citrus fruits. A great mixer or delightful over ice.

Creme de Cacao Dark: Rich, deep chocolate. Smooth and classy. Serve on its own, or mix for all kinds of delectable treats.

Creme de Cacao White: This liqueur delivers a powerfully lively, full bodied chocolate flavour. Excellent ingredient when absence of colour is desired.

Creme de Grand Marnier: A blend of Grand Marnier and smooth French cream. A premium product, a very smooth taste with the orange/cognac flavour blending beautifully with smooth cream.

Creme de Menthe Green: Clear peppermint flavour, reminiscent of a fresh, crisp, clean winter's day in the mountains. Excellent mixer, a necessity in the gourmet kitchen.

Creme de Menthe White: As Creme de Menthe Green, when colour is not desired.

Curacao Blue: Same as Triple Sec, brilliant blue colour is added to make some cocktails more exciting.

Curacao Orange: Again, same as above, but stronger in orange, colouring is used for other varieties of cocktail mixers.

Curacao Triple Sec: Based on natural citrus fruits. Well known fact is citrus fruits are the most important aromatic flavour constituents. Interesting to know citrus fruit was known 2,000 years before Christ. As a liqueur one of the most versatile. Can be enjoyed with or without ice as a neat drink, or used in mixed cocktails more than any other liqueur. Triple Sec – also known as White Curacao.

Galliano: The distinguished taste! A classic liqueur that blends with a vast array of mixed drinks.

Gin – Gilbey's: The number one selling Gin in Australia. Its aroma comes from using the highest quality juniper berries and other rare and subtle herbs. Perfect mixer for both short and long drinks.

Kirsch: A fruit brandy distilled from morello cherries.

Delicious drunk straight and excellent in a variety of food recipes.

Drambuie: A Scotch whisky liqueur. Made from a secret recipe dating back to 1745. "Dram Buidheach" the drink that satisfies.

Introduction

Frangelico: A precious liqueur imported from Italy. Made from wild hazelnuts with infusions of berries and flowers to enrich the flavour.

Grand Marnier: An original blend of fine old Cognac and an extract of oranges. The recipe is over 150 years old

Kahlúa: A smooth, dark liqueur made from real coffee and fine clear spirits. Its origins are based in Mexico.

Lena Banana: Fresh ripe bananas are the perfect base for the definitive daiquiri and a host of other exciting fruit cocktails.

Malibu: A clear liqueur based on white rum with the subtle addition of coconut. Its distinctive taste blends naturally with virtually every mixer available.

Midori: Soft green, exudes freshness. Refreshing and mouthwatering honeydew melon. Simple yet complex. Smooth on the palate, serve on the rocks, or use to create summertime cocktails.

Ouzo: The traditional spirit aperitif of Greece. The distinctive flavour is derived mainly from the seed of the anise plant. A neutral grain spirit, flavoured with anise.

Peach: The flavour of fresh peaches and natural peach juice make this cocktail lover's dream.

Peachtree Schnapps: Crystal clear, light liqueur, bursting with the taste of ripe peaches. Drink chilled or on the rocks or mix with any soft drink or juice.

Pineapple: A just ripe, sun-filled delight. Delicious neat, a necessity for summertime cocktails.

Rum – Bacardi: A smooth, dry, light bodied rum, especially suited for drinks in which you require subtle aroma and delicate flavour.

Rum – Bacardi Gold: Matured in charred oak barrels to give a dry smooth taste and a clear golden colour. Use in Bacardi drinks where you want a fuller, mellow flavour.

Rum – Bundaberg: The most popular Australian rum, mixes well with all juices and splits.

Rye Whiskey – Canadian Club: The largest selling Canadian Whiskey in North America and Australia. Distilled from corn, rye and malted barley. A light, mild and delicate Whiskey, ideal for drinking straight or in mixed cocktails.

Sabra: A unique flavour which comes from tangy jaffa oranges, with a hint of chocolate.

Sambuca: The Italian electric taste experience. Made from elderberries with a touch of anise.

Sambuca – Lago Nera: An exciting encounter between Sambuca di Galliano and extracts of black elderberry.

Sambuca – Opal Nera: The black Sambuca. Perfect after dinner or as an aperitif. The delicate oil from the Elderbush. The rich flavour of anise, with the subtle essence of lemon. Mingled, they are the dark secret of Opal Nera's delightful flavour.

Scotch Whisky – Ballantine's: One of the top three Scotch whiskies in the world. It is a blended whisky and is one of the very few "bottled in Scotland" products available in Australia.

Introduction

Scotch Whisky – Johnnie Walker: Established 1820, distilled, blended and bottled in Scotland. Australia's largest selling Scotch whisky.

Southern Comfort: A liqueur not a bourbon as often thought. It is unique, full-bodied liquor with a touch of sweetness. Its recipe is a secret, but it is known to be based on peaches and apricots. It is the largest selling liqueur in Australia.

Strawberry: Fluorescent red, unmistakable strawberry bouquet. Natural liqueur delivers a true to nature, fresh strawberry flavour.

Tennessee Whiskey – Jack Daniel's: Contrary to popular belief, Jack Daniel's is not a bourbon, it is a distinctive product called Tennessee Whiskey. Made from the 'old sour mash' process. Leached through hard maple charcoal, then aged in charred white oak barrels, at a controlled temperature, acquiring its body, bouquet and colour, yet remaining smooth.

Tequila – El Toro: A clear tequila imported from Mexico, with a scented clean character and slight burn, perfect for drinking straight, and is also a great mixer.

Tequila – Pepe Lopez: Distilled from the Mexcal variety of the agave plant – not Cacti. Pepe Lopez was named after a 19th Century Mexican bandit. A perfect mixer or drink straight with salt and lemon.

Tia Maria: A liqueur with a cane spirit base, and its flavour derived from the finest Jamaican coffee. It is not too sweet with a subtle taste of coffee.

Vandermint: A rich chocolate liqueur with the added zest of mint.

Vermouth: By description, Vermouth is a herbally infused wine.

Three styles are most prevalent, these are:

Rosso: A bitter sweet herbal flavour, often drunk as an aperitif.

Bianco: Is light, fruity and refreshing. Mixes well with soda, lemonade and fruit juices.

Dry: Is crisp, light and dry and is used as a base for many cocktails.

Vodka: The second largest selling spirit in the world. Most Vodkas are steeped in tanks containing charcoal, but Smirnoff is pumped through ten columns of best hardwood charcoal for seven hours, removing all odours and impurities, making a superior quality product

A.R.B.D.

20 mL Southern Comfort
20 mL Tia Maria
20 mL blue curaçao
20 mL cherry advocaat

Method
Layer in a Test Tube or shot glass
and serve.

ABBEY

60mL/2oz gin
1 dash sweet vermouth
30 mL/1oz orange juice
garnish:
maraschino cherry
1 dash Angostura bitters

Method
Shake and strain into a 140mL/5oz
cocktail glass and serve.

ABC

5 ice cubes
champagne or sparkling white
wine
20 mL (3/4 oz) Armagnac
garnish:
lemon slice
20 mL (3/4 oz) Benedictine
orange segments
1 dash Angostura bitters
maraschino cherries

Method
Crack 2 ice cubes and place them
into a shaker with Armagnac,
Benedictine and Angostura bitters
and shake well. Crush remaining ice
cubes and empty into a goblet.
Drain contents of shaker of the
crushed ice and top with
champagne. Serve garnished
with lemon slice, orange segments
and cherries.

ABERDEEN ANGUS

Ingredients
Glass:
130 ml Cocktail Glass
Mixers:
30 ml Ballantine's Scotch Whisky
10 ml Drambuie
1 tablespoon honey
10ml fresh lime juice

Method
Mix honey into Ballantine's Scotch
Whisky and add lime then warm
Drambuie over a low flame and
pour. Garnish with a plastic bull.
Comments: A traditional flambé.

ABORTION

30 mL (1 oz) vodka
30 mL (1 oz) sambuca
30 mL (1 oz) Bailey's Irish cream
3 drops grenadine

Method
Layer into an 85 mL (3 oz) cocktail
glass and serve.

ABSINTH

50 mL (13/4 oz) Pernod
1 tsp anisette
2 tbsp water
1 dash orange bitters

Method
Shake ingredients with ice and strain into a chilled cocktail glass.

ACAPULCO I

30 mL (1 oz) tequila
30 mL (1 oz) dark rum
30 mL (1 oz) Tia Maria
150 mL (51/2 oz) coconut cream

Method
Shake ingredients and strain over ice into a 285 mL (10 oz) cocktail glass and serve.

ACAPULCO II

30 mL (1 oz) light rum
1 tsp sugar
15 mL (¹/₂ oz) Cointreau or triple sec
¹/₂ egg white
15 mL (¹/₂ oz) lime juice
garnish:
mint leaves

Method
Shake all ingredients except mint leaves and strain over ice into an 85 mL (3 oz) cocktail glass and serve. Garnish with mint.

ADAM & EVE OLD-FASHIONED

1 sugar cube
3 ice cubes
1 dash Angostura bitters
40 mL (1¹/₂ oz) Tennessee whiskey
soda water
15 mL (¹/₂oz) Galliano Liverno

Method
Place the sugar cube in the bottom of an Old Fashioned glass. Add bitters and cover sugar cube with soda water. Add ice, whiskey, Galliano Liverno, and serve.

ADIOS MOTHER

60 mL (2 oz) vodka
1 dash triple sec
60 mL (2 oz) white rum
90 mL (3 oz) lemon juice
60 mL (2 oz) melon liqueur
3 tsp sugar
1 dash blue curaçao

Method
Pour ingredients over ice into a 285 mL (10 oz) tulip champagne glass and serve.

ADMIRAL CANNON

45 mL (1¹/₂ oz) bourbon
15 mL (¹/₂ oz) lemon juice
30 mL (1 oz) white rum
1 tsp maple syrup

Method
Shake and strain into a 140 mL (5 oz) cocktail glass over cracked ice and serve.

ADONIS

30 mL (1 oz) sweet sherry
1 dash Angostura bitters
20 mL (3/4 oz) sweet vermouth
3 ice cubes

Method
Shake and strain into an 85 mL
(3 oz) cocktail glass.

AFFINITY

60 mL (2 oz) Scotch whiskey
2 dashes Angostura bitters
30 mL (1 oz) dry vermouth
cracked ice
30 mL (1 oz) sweet vermouth
garnish:
twist lemon peel

Method
Half fill a mixing glass with cracked
ice, add liquid ingredients and stir.
Strain into a 140 mL (5 oz)
champagne glass, garnish with
lemon peel and serve.

AFRICAN COFFEE

hot black coffee
sugar (optional)
30 mL (1 oz) Afrikoko
marshmallow cream

Method
Fill a goblet with hot coffee and
add Afrikoko. Add sugar, if desired,
stirring well. Float marshmallow
cream on top and serve.

AFRICAN NIGHTS

20 mL (3/4 oz) melon liqueur
20 mL (3/4 oz) cream
20 mL (3/4 oz) Kahlúa
20 mL (3/4 oz) milk
20 mL (3/4 oz) Afrikoko
garnish:
grated chocolate

Method
Shake ingredients and strain into
a 140 mL (5 oz) cocktail glass.
Sprinkle with grated chocolate
and serve.

AFRICAN NIPPLE

30 mL (1 oz) vodka
1 tsp grenadine
30 mL (1 oz) Afrikoko
60 mL (2 oz) cream

Method
Shake and strain into a champagne
saucer and serve.

AFTER EIGHT

15 mL ($^{1}/_{2}$ oz) Kahlúa
20 mL (3/4 oz) Bailey's Irish cream
10 mL (1/3 oz) crème de menthe

Method
Layer ingredients in order into a
tall Dutch cordial glass or shot
glass and serve.

A

AGENT 99

15mL/¹/₂oz parfait amour
15mL/¹/₂oz ouzo
15mL/¹/₂oz Bailey's Irish cream

Method
Layer ingredients in order into a
tall Dutch cordial glass or shot glass
and serve.

AIDA'S CURSE

30 mL (1 oz) melon liqueur
45 mL (12/3 oz) pineapple juice
30 mL (1 oz) Cointreau
10 mL (1/3 oz) banana liqueur
15 mL (1/2 oz) lemon juice

Method
Shake first 4 ingredients. Pour
banana liqueur in side of a 140 mL
(5 oz) cocktail glass. Add shaken
ingredients and serve.

ALABAMA SLAMMER

30 mL (1 oz) amaretto
15 mL sloe gin
30 mL (1 oz) Southern Comfort
1 dash orange juice

Method
Shake and strain into a 3 oz
cocktail glass and serve.

ALASKA

60 mL (1 oz) gin
3 ice cubes
20 mL yellow Chartreuse
garnish:
lemon peel

Method
Mix ingredients in a mixing glass.
Strain into a 3 oz cocktail glass.
Garnish with lemon peel and serve.

ALEXANDER

45 mL gin
3 ice cubes
20 mL crème de cacao
nutmeg
15 mL (1/2 oz) fresh cream

Method
Shake liquid ingredients and strain
into a 3 oz cocktail glass. Cross two
straws over glass, sprinkle nutmeg
over the top. Remove straws and
serve.

ALFONSO

15 mL (1/2 oz) dry gin
4 dashes sweet vermouth
15 mL (1/2 oz) French vermouth
1 dash Angostura bitters
30 mL (1 oz) Grand Marnier
4 ice cubes

Method
Shake and strain into a 3 oz
cocktail glass and serve.

ALICE

30 mL (1 oz) Scotch whiskey
30 mL (1 oz) kümmel liqueur
30 mL (1 oz) sweet vermouth
cracked ice

Method
Half fill mixing glass with ice and add liquid ingredients. Stir and strain into 5 oz champagne glass. Garnish with lemon peel and serve.

ALICE IN WONDERLAND

Glass:
170ml Champagne Flute
Mixers:
100ml grapefruit juice
30ml green tea
20ml lemon juice
15ml sugar syrup
top up with soda

Method
Build over ice and top up with soda. Garnish with white grapes.

ALL NIGHT

30 mL (1 oz) tequila
1 dash grenadine
20 mL lime juice
3 ice cubes
1 egg white
garnish:
1 maraschino cherry

Method
Shake ingredients and strain into a 3 oz cocktail glass. Garnish with cherry and serve.

ALMOND ORANGE FROST

Glass:
240ml Champagne Sherbert Glass
Mixers:
15ml Amaretto di Galliano
15ml Frangelico
15ml Chambord
10ml fresh lime juice
10ml fresh lemon juice
1 teaspoon chopped almonds
2 scoops orange sherbert

Method
Blend with ice. Garnish with orange slice and chopped almonds.

ALMOND JOY

30 mL (1 oz) amaretto
90 mL milk
1 dash crème de cacao
30 mL (1 oz) coconut syrup
1 scoop ice cream
garnish:
1 pineapple wedge

Method
Blend ingredients and pour into a 10 oz tulip glass, garnish with a pineapple wedge, straws and serve.

ALTERED STATES SHOOTER

15 mL (1/2 oz) Kahlúa
15 mL (1/2 oz) peach liqueur
15 mL (1/2 oz) Bailey's Irish cream

Method
Layer in a shot glass and serve.

A

AMARETTO CHOCO CREAM

Glass:
240ml Champagne Sherbert Glass
Mixers:
30ml Amaretto di Galliano
30ml Kahlúa
30ml Chocolate Syrup
2 scoops of vanilla ice cream

Method
Blend without ice and pour over ice. Garnish with aerosol whipping cream.

AMARETTO SOUR

45 mL amaretto
1/2 lemon, squeezed
soda water
3 ice cubes

Method
Shake amaretto, lemon juice and ice, pour into a sour glass and top with soda. Garnish with a strip of lemon peel and serve.

AMARETTO STINGER

45 mL amaretto
3 ice cubes
25 mL white crème de menthe

Method
Shake well, strain into a 3 oz cocktail glass and serve.

AMERICAN BEAUTY

15 mL (1/2 oz) brandy
15 mL (1/2 oz) grenadine
15 mL (1/2 oz) dry vermouth
15 mL (1/2 oz) orange juice
port wine
3 dashes white crème de menthe

Method
Shake all ingredients except port wine. Strain into a 5 oz glass, top with port wine and serve.

AMERICANO

30 mL (1 oz) Campari
soda water
60 mL (1 oz) sweet vermouth
garnish:
1 twist lemon
3 ice cubes

Method
Place all ingredients except soda into a 10 oz highball glass and stir well. Top with soda and serve.

AMSTERDAM

30 mL (1 oz) gin
4 dashes orange bitters
15 mL (1/2 oz) orange juice
15 mL (1/2 oz) Cointreau
cracked ice

Method
Shake ingredients and strain into a 3 oz cocktail glass and serve.

ANABOLIC STEROID SHOOTER

30 mL (1 oz) Midori
30 mL (1 oz) Cointreau
30 mL (1 oz) blue curaçao

Method
Layer in a shot glass and serve.

ANDY WILLIAMS

60ml Clayton's Tonic
15ml lime juice
dash sugar syrup
top up with soda water

Method
Shake with ice and pour.
Garnish with a thin lime slice
floated in the drink.

ANGEL DEW

15 mL (1/2 oz) Benedictine
15 mL (1/2 oz) Bailey's Irish cream

Method
Layer in a shot glass and serve.

ANGEL TIP SHOOTER

15 mL (1/2 oz) crème de cacao
15 mL (1/2 oz) Bailey's Irish cream

Method
Layer in a shot glass. Garnish with
an Impaled cherry and serve.

ANGEL PUNCH

100ml apple juice
30ml green tea
20ml lemon juice
15ml sugar syrup
top up with soda

Method
Build over ice and top up with soda.
Garnish with sprinkled tea leaves.

ANGEL WING SHOOTER

15 mL (1/2 oz) crème de cacao
15 mL (1/2 oz) Bailey's cream
15 mL (1/2 oz) brandy

Method
Layer in order in a shot glass
and serve.

ANGEL'S DELIGHT

30 mL (1 oz) Cointreau
50 mL cream
30 mL (1 oz) gin
1 dash grenadine

Method
Shake and strain into a 5 oz
cocktail glass and serve.

ANGEL'S FACE

20 mL apricot brandy
10 mL Calvados
20 mL gin
3 ice cubes

Method
Shake and strain into 3 oz cocktail
glass and serve.

A

ANGEL'S KISS NO. 1

20 mL apricot liqueur
1 tsp Thickened cream

Method
Place apricot liqueur in a
90 mL cocktail glass, float cream
and serve.

ANGEL'S KISS NO. 2

10 mL crème de cacao
10 mL Prunelle
10 mL crème de Violette
10 mL fresh cream

Method
Layer in a liqueur glass and serve.

ANGEL'S KISS NO. 3

10 mL maraschino liqueur
10 mL Benedictine
10 mL parfait amour
10 mL cognac
10 mL yellow Chartreuse
10 mL cream

Method
Layer in order in a Mousse Cafe
glass and serve.

ANGEL'S KISS NO. 4

30 mL (1 oz) crème de cacao
30 mL (1 oz) gin
30 mL (1 oz) cream
30 mL (1 oz) brandy

Method
Layer in order in a 150 mL cocktail
glass and serve.

ANGELIQUE

30 mL (1 oz) ouzo
30 mL (1 oz) fresh cream
30 mL (1 oz) advocaat
30 mL (1 oz) orange juice
30 mL (1 oz) Strega
garnish:
1 maraschino cherry

Method
Shake and strain into a champagne
saucer. Garnish with cherry and serve.

ANGRY FIJIAN

30 mL (1 oz) banana liqueur
30 mL (1 oz) Bailey's Irish cream
30 mL (1 oz) Malibu

Method
Layer in a 3 oz cocktail glass and
serve.

ANWAR SADAT

30 mL (1 oz) Sabra liqueur
mineral water
30 mL (1 oz) advocaat

Method
Place Sabra and advocaat in a 5 oz
cocktail glass. Top with mineral water.
Garnish with Umbrella and serve.

APOLLO 13

60 mL (1 oz) white rum
1 dash grenadine
15 mL (1/2 oz) Galliano Liverno
60 mL (1 oz) fresh cream
15 mL (1/2 oz) Grand Marnier
cracked ice

Method
Shake and strain into a 5 oz
champagne saucer. Garnish with a
maraschino cherry and serve.

APOTHEKE

20 mL brandy
15 mL (1/2 oz) Fernet-Branca
15 mL (1/2 oz) crème de menthe

Method
Place ingredients in a 3 oz cocktail
glass and serve.

APPEASE ME

30 mL (1 oz) mango liqueur
60 mL (1 oz) orange juice
20 mL advocaat
30 mL (1 oz) cream
20 mL vodka
2 slices mango

Method
Blend ingredients with ice and pour
into a 10 oz highball glass. Garnish
with the pulp of half a passionfruit
and serve with straws.

APPLE À LA MODE

Glass:
285ml Tulip Wine Glass
Mixers:
30ml Bacardi
2 sprinkles Cinnamon powder
1/2 ripe apple (seedless)
60ml apple cider
2 scoops vanilla ice cream

Method
Blend without ice and pour into
glass over ice. Garnish with apple
slice and sprinkle of cinnamon.

APPLE ANGEL

30 mL (1 oz) brandy
1 maraschino cherry
30 mL (1 oz) Calvados
garnish:
1 slice apple
1 dash grenadine
3 ice cubes
15 mL (1/2 oz) lemon juice

Method
Shake and strain into a 3 oz
cocktail glass. Garnish with apple,
cherry and serve.

APPLE JACK

Glass:
210 Old Fashioned Spirit Glass
Mixers:
30ml Jack Daniel's
top up with fresh apple juice

Method
Build over ice. Garnish with an
apple slice.

A

APPLE JACKRABBIT

30 mL (1 oz) Calvados

1 tsp sugar syrup

20 mL orange juice

1 dash orange bitters

10 mL lemon juice

2-3 ice cubes

Method
Shake and strain into a 3 oz cocktail glass and serve.

APPLE MAGIC

30 mL (1 oz) Midori

10 mL orange

15 mL (1/2 oz) Southern Comfort

90 mL apple juice

15 mL (1/2 oz) Grand Marnier

Method
Blend and pour into a colada glass. Garnish with a slice of apple and strawberry and serve.

APPLE SPECIAL

60 mL (1 oz) brandy

1 slice apple

15 mL (1/2 oz) Cointreau

3 ice cubes

dry apple cider (top up)

garnish:

1 apple slice

Method
Shake ice, brandy and Cointreau. Strain into a 10 oz highball glass and top with soda. Garnish with apple slice and serve with straws.

APPLE STRAWBERRY CORDIAL

1 apple, peeled and cored

3 strawberries

30ml Ballantine's Scotch Whisky

1 teaspoon brown sugar

allspice, nutmeg

Method
Blend over ice and pour into a 210ml Old Fashioned Spirit Glass. Garnish with a strawberry and sprinkle of nutmeg

APRES SKI

30 mL (1 oz) crème de menthe

15 mL (1/2 oz) Pernod

15 mL (1/2 oz) vodka

lemonade

Method
Third fill a 10 oz highball glass with ice and pour ingredients over ice. Top with lemonade and serve with straws.

APRICOT

30 mL (1 oz) gin

2 drops Angostura bitters

15 mL (1/2 oz) apricot brandy

1/2 tsp lemon juice

2 dashes grenadine

Method
Shake and strain into a 3 oz cocktail glass and serve.

APRICOT MARIA

30 mL (1 oz) Tia Maria
60 mL (1 oz) apricot nectar
15 mL (1/2 oz) vodka
3 ice cubes

Method
Blend and pour into a 5 oz cocktail glass and serve.

APRICOT RICKEY

30ml Apricot Liqueur
top up with soda
squeeze of lime, optional

Method
Build over ice and top up with soda. Garnish with a slice of lime.

APRIL SHOWER

30 mL (1 oz) brandy
60 mL (1 oz) orange juice
30 mL (1 oz) Benedictine
2 ice cubes
soda water (top up)

Method
Pour ingredients except soda into a 10 oz highball glass. Stir, top with soda and serve with straws.

AQUAVIT FIZZ

45ml Aquavit
30ml lemon juice
15ml Cherry Heering
10ml sugar syrup
1 egg white
top up with soda

Method
Shake over ice and strain then top up with soda. Garnish with a red cherry.

AQUA THUNDER

10 mL blue curaçao
10 mL lemon juice
10 mL banana liqueur
soda water (top up)
30 mL (1 oz) Midori

Method
Build ingredients over ice in a 5 oz cocktail glass. Garnish with swizzle stick, a slice of lemon and serve.

ARCADIA No. 1

25 mL Lochan Ora
garnish:
1 spiral lemon peel
60 mL (1 oz) saki (hot)
1 spiral orange peel
15 mL (1/2 oz) boiling water

Method
Pour Lochan Ora into a 4 oz cocktail glass. Stir and Ignite, pour remaining ingredients over the top. Garnish with a spiral of orange peel and lemon peel and serve.

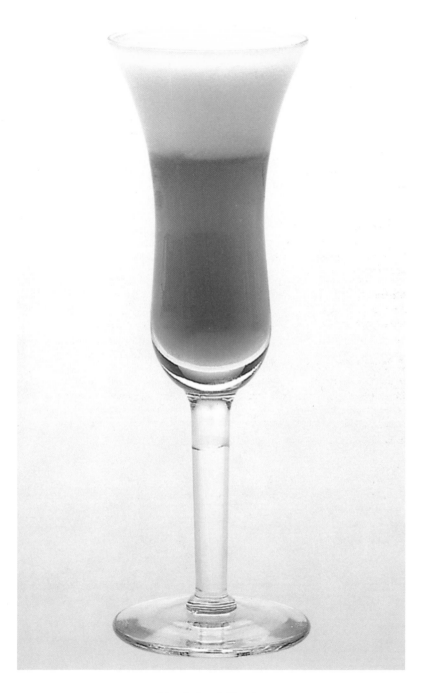

Atomic Bomb Shooter

After Eight

Bananarama

Banana Split

Bee Sting

B&B

A

ARCADIA No. 2

45 mL Midori
1 dash grenadine
15 mL (1/2 oz) lemon juice
30 mL (1 oz) orange juice

Method
In a 10 oz highball glass place a
scoop of crushed ice. Blend
ingredients except grenadine and
pour over ice. Add grenadine and
serve with straws.

ARGYLE TAVERN

60 mL (1 oz) brandy
15 mL (1/2 oz) almond liqueur
15 mL (1/2 oz) Galliano Liverno
garnish: 1 maraschino cherry
30 mL (1 oz) dry vermouth
cracked ice

Method
Half fill a mixing glass with cracked
ice and add ingredients. Stir and
strain into a 5 oz cocktail glass,
garnish with cherry and serve.

ASPIRATION

30 mL (1 oz) Midori
30 mL (1 oz) pineapple juice
15 mL (1/2 oz) Galliano Liverno
[?] kiwifruit
5 mL white curaçao
1 dash coconut cream

Method
Blend and pour into a colada glass.
Garnish with a slice of kiwifruit
and serve.

ASTRONAUT

30ml Coruba Rum
30ml Smirnoff Vodka
10ml fresh lemon juice
6 drops of passionfruit pulp

Method
Shake over ice and strain. Garnish
with 1/2 scoop of passionfruit.

ATOMIC BOMB SHOOTER

30 mL (1 oz) Tia Maria
15 mL (1/2 oz) gin

Method
Layer in a shot glass and serve.

AUSSIE SLINGER

45 mL any white Spirit
lemonade
30 mL (1 oz) grenadine
1 dash Angostura bitters
60 mL (1 oz) lemon juice
1 cracked ice

Method
Half fill a 10 oz highball glass with cracked ice, add ingredients and top with lemonade. Garnish with 1/2 orange slice, 1/2 lemon slice, 1 maraschino cherry, swizzle stick, straws and serve.

AUSTRALIA III

30 mL (1 oz) Midori
1 egg yolk
15 mL (1/2 oz) Grand Marnier
1/2 kiwifruit
15 mL (1/2 oz) pineapple juice
4 ice cubes

Method
Blend ingredients and pour into a 5 oz tulip glass. Garnish with a slice of kiwifruit and serve.

AUSTRALIAN CRAWL

15 mL (1/2 oz) Bundaberg rum
15 mL (1/2 oz) Scotch whiskey
15 mL (1/2 oz) gin
Coca-Cola
15 mL (1/2 oz) vodka
cracked ice

Method
Build ingredients except Coca-Cola over ice in a 10 oz highball glass. Top with Coca-Cola, garnish with a lemon wheel, straws and serve.

AUSTRALIAN GOLD

30 mL (1 oz) Bundaberg rum
30 mL (1 oz) Galliano Liverno
30 mL (1 oz) mango liqueur
garnish:
pineapple wedge

Method
Build over ice in a 5 oz cocktail glass. Garnish and serve.

AUSTRALIS

20 mL white rum
15 mL (1/2 oz) cream
20 mL melon liqueur
20 mL pineapple juice
20 mL blue curaçao
garnish:
1 slice pineapple
3 ice cubes
1 maraschino cherry

Method
Shake and strain into a 5 oz cocktail glass. Garnish and serve.

AUTUMN LEAF

30 mL (1 oz) Arrak

30 mL (1 oz) Dazzinger goldwasser

30 mL (1 oz) crème de cacao

Method

Mix in mixing glass with cracked ice, strain into 3 oz cocktail glass and serve.

AVALANCHE

30 mL (1 oz) Cointreau

30 mL (1 oz) orange juice

30 mL (1 oz) Tia Maria

50 mL cream

Method

Shake and strain into a champagne glass and serve.

B&B

30 mL (1 oz) brandy
30 mL (1 oz) Benedictine

Method
Pour over ice in a brandy Balloon
and serve.

B&G

30 mL (1 oz) Benedictine
30 mL (1 oz) Grand Mariner

Method
Pour over ice in an Old Fashioned
glass.

B&P

30 mL (1 oz) Benedictine
60 mL (1 oz) port

Method
Pour over ice in a brandy Balloon
and serve.

B.B.C. SHOOTER

15 mL (1/2 oz) Benedictine
15 mL (1/2 oz) Cointreau
15 mL (1/2 oz) Bailey's Irish cream

Method
Layer in order in a shot glass and
serve.

B.B.G. SHOOTER

15 mL (1/2 oz) Benedictine
15 mL (1/2 oz) Grand Marnier
15 mL (1/2 oz) Bailey's Irish cream

Method
Layer in order in a shot glass and
serve.

B52

30 mL (1 oz) Kahlúa
30 mL (1 oz) Bailey's Irish cream
30 mL (1 oz) Grand Marnier
crushed ice

Method
Place a scoop full of crushed ice in
a 5 oz cocktail glass. Layer
ingredients and serve.

B53 SHOOTER

10 mL Kahlúa
10 mL tequila
10 mL Bailey's Irish cream

Method
Layer in order in a shot glass and
serve.

B

B54 SHOOTER

10 mL Kahlúa
10 mL Grand Marnier
15 mL (1/2 oz) Bailey's Irish cream
10 mL tequila

Method
Layer in order in a shot glass and serve.

BACARDI

45 mL Bacardi rum
1 dash egg white
1 dash grenadine
3 ice cubes
15 mL (1/2 oz) lemon juice
garnish:
1 maraschino cherry

Method
Shake and strain into a 3 oz cocktail glass. Garnish with cherry on a toothpick and serve.

BACARDI BLOSSOM

40 mL Bacardi rum
3 ice cubes
10 mL orange juice
10 mL lemon juice
1 tsp sugar

Method
Shake and strain into a 3 oz cocktail glass and serve.

BACARDI NO. 2

60 mL (1 oz) Bacardi rum
1 egg white
5 mL grenadine
ice
20 mL lemon or lime juice

Method
Shake and strain into a 5 oz cocktail glass and serve.

BACCILE BALL

30 mL (1 oz) amaretto
30 mL (1 oz) soda water
60 mL (1 oz) orange juice

Method
Pour ingredients over ice in a rocks glass and serve.

BAD GIRL

15 mL (1/2 oz) Malibu
10 mL Galliano Liverno
15 mL (1/2 oz) banana liqueur
30 mL (1 oz) cream
15 mL (1/2 oz) advocaat

Method
Blend ingredients, pour into a 5 oz champagne glass and serve.

BAHAMA MAMA

Bacardi Gold Rum

15ml Malibu

15ml Banana Liqueur

15ml Grenadine

100ml orange juice

60ml pineapple juice

Method
Blend over ice. Garnish with a
pineapple wedge and leaves.

BAILEY'S COCONUT CREAM

30 mL (1 oz) Bailey's Irish cream

30 mL (1 oz) cream

15 mL (1/2 oz) Malibu

60 mL (1 oz) orange juice

Method
Shake ingredients and pour over
cracked ice in a 5 oz wine glass.
Add a dash of grenadine and serve
with straws.

BALALANKA

40 mL vodka

garnish:

1 spiral orange peel

15 mL (1/2 oz) Cointreau

3 ice cubes

15 mL (1/2 oz) lemon juice

Method
Shake and strain into a 3 oz
cocktail glass. Garnish with orange
peel and serve.

BALI HI

30 mL (1 oz) advocaat

orange soft drink

10 mL orange curaçao

garnish:

1 slice orange

10 mL Mandarin liqueur

1 maraschino cherry

Method
Mix ingredients except Soft drink
with cracked ice in a 10 oz highball
glass. Top with soft drink, garnish
and serve with straws.

BALL OF FIRE

50 mL white rum

lemonade

60 mL (1 oz) advocaat

cracked ice

30 mL (1 oz) Pernod

garnish:

maraschino cherry

grenadine

Method
Half fill a 10 oz highball glass with
cracked ice. Add rum, Pernod and
advocaat. Top with lemonade and
float grenadine. Garnish with cherry,
swizzle stick. straws and serve.

B

BALLET RUSSE

30ml Smirnoff Vodka

15ml Creme de Cassis

15ml fresh lime juice

15ml fresh lemon juice

Method
Shake with ice and strain. Garnish with an orange slice and a red cherry.

BALTIMORE ZOO

15ml Coruba Rum

15ml Gilbey's Gin

15ml Cointreau

60ml cranberry juice

top with draft beer

Method
Shake with ice and strain then top with draft beer.

BAMBOO

30 mL (1 oz) dry vermouth

2 ice cubes

30 mL (1 oz) dry sherry

1 dash orange bitters

2 dashes Angostura bitters

garnish:

1 maraschino cherry

Method
Mix ingredients in a mixing glass, strain into a 5 oz cocktail glass. Garnish with cherry and serve.

BANANA BENDER

30 mL (1 oz) Cointreau

60 mL (1 oz) cream

30 mL (1 oz) banana liqueur

1/2 banana

Method
Blend ingredients until smooth, pour into a 5 oz champagne glass and serve.

BANANA BENDER NO. 2.

30 mL (1 oz) banana liqueur

30 mL (1 oz) cream

30 mL (1 oz) Cointreau

2 slices banana

30 mL (1 oz) pineapple juice

1/2 Scoop crushed ice

Method
Blend until smooth, pour into a 6 oz flute glass and serve.

BANANA BLISS

30 mL (1 oz) cognac

crushed ice

30 mL (1 oz) banana liqueur

Method
Fill a 6 oz Old Fashioned glass with crushed ice, Build liquid ingredients and serve.

BANANA COLADA

45 mL Bacardi light rum
1 dash cream
15 mL (1/2 oz) banana liqueur
1/2 banana
15 mL (1/2 oz) Malibu
60 mL (1 oz) pineapple juice
30 mL (1 oz) coconut cream
1 Scoop ice cream

Method
Blend until smooth and pour into
a colada glass. Garnish with a
pineapple wedge, straws and serve.

BANANA JAFFA

15 mL (1/2 oz) Kahlúa
30 mL (1 oz) cream
15 mL (1/2 oz) brandy
1/2 banana
30 mL (1 oz) orange juice

Method
Blend until smooth, pour into a 10
oz highball glass. Garnish with an
orange wheel. pineapple wedge,
straws and serve.

BANANA COW

30 mL (1 oz) white rum
45 mL cream
30 mL (1 oz) crème de banana
garnish:
nutmeg
1 dash grenadine

Method
Shake and pour into a 5 oz cocktail
glass. Sprinkle with nutmeg and
serve.

BANANA MARGARITA

30 mL (1 oz) tequila
30 mL (1 oz) lemon juice
15 mL (1/2 oz) Cointreau
1/2 small banana
15 mL (1/2 oz) banana liqueur
cracked ice

Method
Blend until smooth, pour into a salt
rimmed margarita glass and serve.

BANANA PEEL

45 mL vodka
60 mL (1 oz) orange juice
45 mL banana liqueur

Method
Shake and strain over ice in a 5 oz
Old Fashioned glass and serve.

BANANA CREAMY

30 mL (1 oz) banana liqueur
15 mL (1/2 oz) cream
90 mL milk
1 banana

Method
Blend until smooth, pour into a
5 oz champagne glass and serve.

B

BANANA SPLIT

30 mL (1 oz) banana liqueur
15 mL (1/2 oz) cream
30 mL (1 oz) crème de cacao

Method
Shake and strain into a 3 oz
cocktail glass. Garnish with a
banana wheel and serve.

BANANA SPLIT
SHOOTER

15 mL (1/2 oz) Kahlúa
10 mL grenadine
15 mL (1/2 oz) banana liqueur
whipped cream

Method
Layer in order in a cordial glass and
serve.

BANANA WONDER

20 mL Kahlúa
30 mL (1 oz) cream
20 mL Bailey's Irish cream
1/2 banana

Method
Blend until smooth, pour into a 5
oz cocktail glass. Garnish with a
slice of banana and serve.

BANANARAMA

30 mL (1 oz) vodka
1 banana
30 mL (1 oz) Kahlúa
60 mL (1 oz) cream
15 mL (1/2 oz) Bailey's Irish cream

Method
Blend with ice and pour into a 5 oz
cocktail glass. Garnish with two
banana wheels and serve.

BANGER

30 mL (1 oz) Bacardi rum
180 mL orange juice
15 mL (1/2 oz) Galliano Liverno
cracked ice

Method
Pour into 10 oz highball glass.
Garnish with orange wheel, straws
and serve.

BANGO

45 mL mango liqueur
slice pineapple
20 mL Malibu
1/2 banana
60 mL (1 oz) pineapple juice

Method
Blend until smooth, pour into a
flute glass and serve.

BANSHEE

30 mL (1 oz) rum
60 mL (1 oz) cream
20 mL crème de cacao
1 banana
15 mL (1/2 oz) banana liqueur

Method
Blend until smooth, pour into a
brandy Balloon and serve.

BANSHEE NO. 2

30 mL (1 oz) banana liqueur
60 mL (1 oz) cream
30 mL (1 oz) white crème de cacao
ice

Method
Shake and strain into a 5 oz
cocktail glass. Garnish with a cherry
and serve.

BEAR HUG

30 mL (1 oz) Bailey's Irish cream
60 mL (1 oz) cream
20 mL vodka.

Method
Shake and strain into a 5 oz
cocktail glass and serve.

BEE STING SHOOTER

20 mL tequila
10 mL yellow Chartreuse

Method
Layer in order in a shot glass, Ignite
and serve.

BELLINI

champagne
1 large peach
1 dash amaretto
garnish:
1 slice peach

Method
Liquidise the peach in a blender,
pour into a flute glass. Add dash of
amaretto and top with chilled
champagne. Garnish with peach
slice, straws and serve.

BELLINI NO. 2

45 mL peach juice
90 mL champagne (chilled)

Method
Place peach juice in a tulip flute,
lop with champagne and serve.

B

BELLY DANCER

Ingredients
Glass:
90ml Cocktail Glass – Frosted
Mixers:
30ml cream
15ml lime juice
60ml coconut cream
15ml Grenadine

Method
Shake over ice and strain. Garnish
with grated coconut.

BERMUDA ROSE

Ingredients
Glass:
90ml Cocktail Glass
Mixers:
30ml Gilbey's Gin
10ml lime juice
5ml Grenadine
4-5 drops of Apricot Brandy

Method
Shake over ice and strain. Garnish
with a slice of lime.

BERLIN

20 mL gin
20 mL orange juice
20 mL Madeira
3 ice cubes
1 dash Angostura bitters

Method
Crush ice and shake with other
ingredients. Pour into a 5 oz
cocktail glass and serve with straws.

BERMUDA TRIANGLE

30 mL (1 oz) blue curaçao
60 mL (1 oz) pineapple juice
30 mL (1 oz) Bacardi rum
crushed ice
20 mL amaretto
garnish:
pineapple wedge

Method
Blend until smooth, pour into a
5 oz cocktail glass.
garnish with pineapple wedge
and serve.

BERLIN BINGE

30 mL (1 oz) bourbon
30 mL (1 oz) vodka
30 mL (1 oz) gin
garnish:
1 green olive
30 mL (1 oz) cognac

Method
Mix ingredients in a 4 oz cocktail
glass, garnish with olive and serve.

BERRY A RET TO

30 mL (1 oz) amaretto

60 mL (1 oz) milk

1 scoop ice cream

3-6 strawberries

Method
Blend and pour into a 6 oz tulip glass.
garnish with a strawberry, straws and serve.

BESSIE & JESSIE

60 mL (1 oz) Blended whiskey

180 mL milk

30 mL (1 oz) advocaat

ice

Method
Shake ice, whiskey and milk. Pour into a 10 oz highball glass, Float advocaat and serve with straws.

BETWEEN THE SHEETS

10 mL brandy

juice 1/2 lemon

10 mL rum

ice

10 mL triple sec

Method
Shake ingredients, strain into a 3 ox cocktail glass and serve.

BETWEEN THE SHEETS. NO. 2

30 mL (1 oz) brandy

15 mL (1/2 oz) lemon juice

30 mL (1 oz) white rum

cracked ice

30 mL (1 oz) Cointreau

Method
Shake and strain into a 5 oz cocktail glass and serve.

BIKINI

90 mL vodka

30 mL (1 oz) milk

15 mL (1/2 oz) lemon juice

Method
Shake and strain into a 5 oz cocktail glass and serve.

BILL BAILEY

60 mL (1 oz) Bailey's Irish cream

soda water

30 mL (1 oz) vodka

ice

Method
Pour ingredients over ice in a colada glass and serve.

BILL BRONX

45 mL gin
15 mL (1/2 oz) orange juice
15 mL (1/2 oz) sweet vermouth
garnish:
orange and lemon slices
15 mL (1/2 oz) dry vermouth
ice

Method
Shake ingredients and strain into 5
oz cocktail glass, garnish with
orange and lemon and serve.

BLACK DREAM SHOOTER

20 mL Opal Nera
10 mL Bailey's Irish cream

Method
Layer in a shot glass and serve.

BLACK FOREST

30 mL (1 oz) vodka
90 mL apple juice
30 mL (1 oz) Cointreau
1 tbsp Raspberries
15 mL (1/2 oz) Blackberry liqueur

Method
Blend until smooth, pour over ice
in a 10 oz highball glass.
Serve with straws.

BLACK HELL SHOOTER

30 mL (1 oz) Opal Nera
30 mL (1 oz) strawberry liqueur
30 mL (1 oz) Midori

Method
Layer in a shot glass and serve.

BLACKJACK

30ml Kirsch
40ml ice coffee
5ml Milne Brandy

Method
Stir with ice and pour into a 130ml
Cocktail Glass. Garnish with coffee
granules.

BLACK JACK SHOOTER

30 mL (1 oz) Kahlúa
25 mL ouzo

Method
Layer in a shot glass and serve.

BLACK MAGIC

30 mL (1 oz) Jamaican rum
30 mL (1 oz) pineapple juice
15 mL (1/2 oz) Kahlúa
15 mL (1/2 oz) lemon juice
30 mL (1 oz) mango liqueur
2 slices mango
30 mL (1 oz) orange juice
1 Scoop ice

Method
Blend and pour into a brandy
Balloon, add two black straws and
serve.

BLACK NIPPLE SHOOTER

45 mL Opal Nera
45 mL Bailey's Irish cream

Method
Layer in a shot glass and serve.

BLACK NUTS

30 mL (1 oz) Frangelico
crushed ice
30 mL (1 oz) Opal Nera

Method
Build ingredients over ice in a 3 oz cocktail glass and serve.

BLACK ON BLUE SHOOTER

15 mL (1/2 oz) Opal Nera
15 mL (1/2 oz) Blue sambuca

Method
Layer in a shot glass and serve.

BLACK ON GREEN SHOOTER

15 mL (1/2 oz) Opal Nera
15 mL (1/2 oz) green sambuca

Method
Layer in a shot glass and serve.

BLACK ON RED SHOOTER

15 mL (1/2 oz) Opal Nera
15 mL (1/2 oz) red sambuca

Method
Layer in a shot glass and serve.

BLACK ON WHITE SHOOTER

15 mL (1/2 oz) Opal Nera
15 mL (1/2 oz) sambuca

Method
Layer in a shot glass and serve.

BLACK OPAL

1 Mug hot coffee
30 mL (1 oz) Galleon Liverno
whipped cream

Method
Float Galleon Liverno over the top of the coffee and ignite. When serving extinguish the flame by putting cream on top.

BLACK RUSSIAN

30ml Smirnoff Vodka
30ml Kahlúa

Method
Build over ice. Place a swizzle stick in the glass. Add milk to make a White Russian.

B

BLACK VELVET

champagne

stout

Method
Half fill a champagne flute with chilled stout. Top with chilled champagne and serve.

BLACK WIDOW SHOOTER

30 mL (1 oz) Opal Nera

30 mL (1 oz) cream

30 mL (1 oz) strawberry liqueur

Method
Layer in a shot glass and serve.

BLINKER

15 mL (1/2 oz) Canadian whiskey

25 mL grapefruit juice

7 mL grenadine

cracked ice

Method
Shake and strain into a 3 oz cocktail glass and serve.

BLOOD AND SAND

30 mL (1 oz) Scotch whiskey

30 mL (1 oz) orange juice

30 mL (1 oz) cherry brandy

cracked ice

30 mL (1 oz) sweet vermouth

garnish:

1 twist orange peel

Method
Half fill mixing glass with cracked ice, add liquid ingredients and stir. Strain into a 5 oz champagne saucer, garnish with orange peel and serve.

BLOOD CLOT SHOOTER

30 mL (1 oz) sambuca

30 mL (1 oz) cream

30 mL (1 oz) Opal Nera

3-4 drops grenadine

Method
Layer in a shot glass and serve.

BLOOD SHOT

30 mL (1 oz) vodka

15 mL (1/2 oz) lemon juice

60 mL (1 oz) condensed consommé

15 mL (1/2 oz) tomato sauce (catsup)

15 mL (1/2 oz) Worcestershire sauce

Method
Shake and strain into a 5 oz cocktail glass. Garnish with a sprinkle of celery salt and a slice of Cucumber and serve.

BLOOD TYPE 0-NEGATIVE SHOOTER

30 mL (1 oz) strawberry liqueur
30 mL (1 oz) gin
30 mL (1 oz) red crème de menthe

Method
Layer in a shot glass and serve.

BLOOD TYPE 0-POSITIVE SHOOTER

30 mL (1 oz) triple sec
30 mL (1 oz) strawberry liqueur
30 mL (1 oz) sambuca

Method
Layer in order in a 3 oz shot or port glass and serve.

BLOOD TYPE A-POSITIVE SHOOTER

30 mL (1 oz) red crème de menthe
30 mL (1 oz) sambuca
30 mL (1 oz) strawberry liqueur

Method
Layer in a shot glass and serve.

BLOODBATH SHOOTER

30 mL (1 oz) tequila
30 mL (1 oz) strawberry liqueur

Method
Layer in a shot glass and serve.

BLOODHOUND

15 mL (1/2 oz) dry vermouth
3 dashes strawberry liqueur
15 mL (1/2 oz) gin
4 strawberries (TWO FOR GARNISH)
15 mL (1/2 oz) sweet vermouth
4 ice cubes

Method
Blend two ice cubes. gin, vermouths, strawberry liqueur and two strawberries. Pour into a 5 oz cocktail glass over remaining ice cubes. Garnish with remaining strawberries and serve.

BLOODHOUND NO. 2

15 mL (1/2 oz) gin
15 mL (1/2 oz) Rubis
15 mL (1/2 oz) dry vermouth
5 strawberries (TWO FOR GARNISH)
15 mL (1/2 oz) sweet vermouth
1 scoop crushed ice

Method
Blend all ingredients except 3 strawberries until smooth. Pour into an old fashioned glass, garnish with remaining strawberry and serve.

B

BLOODY LOVELY

30 mL (1 oz) Midori
30 mL (1 oz) cream
30 mL (1 oz) Bailey's Irish cream
4 strawberries
30 mL (1 oz) Malibu
ice

Method
Blend and pour into a 6 oz tulip glass and serve.

BLOODY MARY

60 mL (1 oz) vodka
1 dash Worcestershire Sauce
10 mL lemon juice
2-3 drops Tabasco Sauce
tomato juice
3 ice cubes
Salt
pepper

Method
In a 10 oz highball glass or equivalent place vodka, Sauces, lemon juices and a sprinkle of salt and pepper. Top with tomato juice and serve with swizzle stick and straws. (white rum or tequila may be used instead of vodka)

BLOSSOM

30 mL (1 oz) white rum
15 mL (1/2 oz) orange juice
15 mL (1/2 oz) apple juice
cracked ice
15 mL (1/2 oz) sugar syrup

Method
Half fill shaker with cracked ice, add ingredients, shake and strain into a 5 oz champagne saucer and serve.

BLOW JOB SHOOTER

15 mL (1/2 oz) Kahlúa
15 mL (1/2 oz) Bailey's Irish cream
10 mL banana liqueur
whipped cream

Method
Layer in order in a shot glass and serve.

BLOW UP

30 mL (1 oz) Bacardi rum
5 drops green crème de menthe
30 mL (1 oz) Chartreuse
5 drops grenadine
15 mL (1/2 oz) parfait amour
cracked ice

Method
Half fill a mixing glass with cracked ice and add Bacardi rum, Chartreuse and parfait amour. Stir and strain into a 5 oz cocktail glass, add other ingredients and serve.

BLUEBERRY DELIGHT

20 mL Opal Nera
60 mL (1 oz) cream
20 mL strawberry liqueur
ice
20 mL Malibu

Method
Shake and strain into a 5 oz cocktail glass and serve.

BLUEBERRY DELIGHT NO. 2

15 mL (1/2 oz) Galleon Liverno
15 mL (1/2 oz) blue curaçao
15 mL (1/2 oz) dry vermouth
lemonade
30 mL (1 oz) gin

Method
Shake ingredients except lemonade and strain into a 10 oz highball glass. Top with lemonade, garnish with an lemon wheel, mint leaves, straws and serve.

BLUE DAY

40 mL vodka
garnish:
1 lemon slice
20 mL blue curaçao
peel 1/2 lemon
3 ice cubes

Method
Crack ice and place in shaker with liquid ingredients, shake and strain into a 3 oz cocktail glass. Squeeze 1/2 lemon peel over the top, garnish with the lemon slice and serve.

BLUE BLAZER

60 mL (1 oz) Scotch whiskey
garnish:
lemon peel
60 mL (1 oz) boiling water
2 Mugs (silver or copper)
sugar

Method
Pour whiskey into one mug and water into the other. Ignite whiskey and pour into water mug. Pour ingredients from one mug to the other a few times. Add sugar to taste, garnish with lemon peel and serve.

BLUE DOVE

30 mL (1 oz) blue curaçao
lemonade
20 mL vodka
whipped cream

Method
Pour blue curaçao and vodka over ice in a 10 oz highball glass. Top with lemonade, add whipped cream to top and serve.

BLUE FRENCH

30 mL (1 oz) Pernod
5 mL lemon juice
5 mL blue curaçao
Bitter lemon soft drink

Method
Build over ice in a 10 oz highball glass. Top with Bitter lemon soft drink. Garnish with lemon wheel, straws and serve.

B

BLUE HAWAIIAN

15 mL (1/2 oz) white rum
90 mL pineapple juice
15 mL (1/2 oz) blue curaçao
3 tbsp cream
3 tbsp coconut milk
ice

Method
Mix ingredients in a 10 oz highball glass, top with cream. Add straws and serve.

BLUE HAZE

30 mL (1 oz) Bacardi rum
15 mL (1/2 oz) Cointreau
15 mL (1/2 oz) sweet vermouth
15 mL (1/2 oz) Rossi vermouth
4 drops blue curaçao
15 mL (1/2 oz) parfait amour

Method
Add all ingredients except blue curaçao in mixing glass. Strain into a 5 oz champagne saucer, add blue curaçao and serve.

BLUE HEAVEN

60 mL (1 oz) vodka
150 mL lemonade
30 mL (1 oz) blue curaçao

Method
Shake vodka and blue curaçao. Pour over ice in a 10 oz highball glass. Top with lemonade and serve with straws.

BLUE LADY

25 mL gin
garnish:
1 maraschino cherry
15 mL (1/2 oz) blue curaçao
3 ice cubes
15 mL (1/2 oz) lemon juice

Method
Shake and strain into a 3 oz cocktail glass. Garnish with cherry and serve.

BLUE LAGOON

30 mL (1 oz) blue curaçao
lemonade
Galleon Liverno
cracked ice

Method
Pour blue curaçao over ice in a 10 oz highball glass. Top with lemonade, float Galleon Liverno. Serve with straws.

BLUE LAGOON NO. 2

30 mL (1 oz) vodka
15 mL (1/2 oz) lemon juice
5 mL blue curaçao
ice

Method
Shake and strain into a 5 oz cocktail glass and serve.

BLUE LAGOON NO. 3

30 mL (1 oz) vodka
lemonade
15 mL (1/2 oz) blue curaçao
ice

Method
Half fill a 10 oz highball glass with
ice. Add vodka and blue curaçao,
top with lemonade and serve.

BLUE MALLET

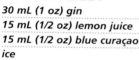

30 mL (1 oz) gin
15 mL (1/2 oz) lemon juice
15 mL (1/2 oz) blue curaçao
ice

Method
Shake and strain into a 3 oz
cocktail glass and serve.

BLUE MONDAY

30 mL (1 oz) vodka
ice
15 mL (1/2 oz) Blue Curaco

Method
Shake and strain into a 3 oz
cocktail glass and serve.

BLUE MOON

30 mL (1 oz) dry gin
15 mL (1/2 oz) lemon juice
15 mL (1/2 oz) crème Yvette
cracked ice

Method
Shake and strain into a 3 oz
cocktail glass and serve.

BLUE NEGLIGÉE

15 mL (1/2 oz) ouzo
garnish:
1 maraschino cherry
15 mL (1/2 oz) Chartreuse
ice
15 mL (1/2 oz) Parfait Armour

Method
Shake and strain into a 3 oz
cocktail glass. Garnish with cherry
and serve.

BLUE PACIFIC

60 mL (1 oz) dry gin
cracked ice
30 mL (1 oz) blue curaçao
1 tsp castor sugar
1 dash orange bitters
garnish:
1 orange wheel

Method
Half fill shaker with ice, add liquid
ingredients and shake. Rim a 5 oz
champagne saucer with sugar.
Strain liquid ingredients into
glass. Garnish with orange wheel
and serve.

BLUE SEAS

15 mL (1/2 oz) blue curaçao
lemonade
30 mL (1 oz) vodka
Galliano Liverno (float)

Method
Build over ice in a 10 oz highball
glass. Top with lemonade.
Float Galleon Liverno and serve
with straws.

BLUE SEAS NO. 2

30 mL (1 oz) vodka
lemonade
15 mL (1/2 oz) Blue sambuca
Galliano Liverno (float)

Method
Build over ice in a 10 oz highball
glass. Top with lemonade.
Float Galleon Liverno and serve
with straws.

BLUE TRAIN

45 mL brandy
45 mL pineapple juice
30 mL (1 oz) blue curaçao
champagne
cracked ice
garnish:
1 maraschino cherry

Method
Layer brandy, curaçao and
pineapple juice over cracked ice.
Top with champagne, garnish with
cherry and serve.

BLUE VEIN

30 mL (1 oz) Malibu
30 mL (1 oz) blue curaçao
30 mL (1 oz) Cointreau

Method
Layer in a 3 oz cocktail glass and
serve.

BOBBY BURNS

15 mL (1/2 oz) Scotch whiskey
1 dash Benedictine
7 mL sweet vermouth
garnish:
lemon peel
7 mL dry vermouth
ice

Method
Stir ingredients in a mixing glass,
strain into a 3 oz cocktail glass.
Garnish with lemon peel and serve.

BODY HEAT

30 mL (1 oz) Malibu
30 mL (1 oz) pineapple juice
30 mL (1 oz) banana liqueur
30 mL (1 oz) orange juice
1 dash grenadine
8 mL lemon juice

Method
Blend all ingredients with ice until
smooth, pour into a 10 oz highball
glass. Add grenadine and serve
with straws.

BOILERMAKER

Serve 30-60 mL (1 oz) Scotch
Whiskey with a beer Chaser.

BOLSHOI PUNCH

30ml Smirnoff Vodka
10ml Coruba Rum
10ml Creme de Cassis
15ml lime juice
15ml lemon juice
top up with bitter lemon

Method
Blend with ice and strain then top up with bitter lemon. Garnish with an orange slice and red cherry.

BONDI BLUE

45 mL Bacardi rum
1/2 egg white
30 mL (1 oz) blue curaçao
cracked ice
30 mL (1 oz) banana liqueur
lemonade

Method
Shake all ingredients except lemonade, strain over ice in a 10 oz highball glass. Top with lemonade, add straws and serve.

BOMBAY

60 mL (1 oz) brandy
3 dashes crème de cacao
7 mL dry vermouth
ice
7 mL sweet vermouth

Method
Shake and strain into a 3 oz cocktail glass and serve.

BOOMERANG

30 mL (1 oz) Canadian whiskey
23 mL Swedish punch
23 mL dry vermouth
2 dashes lemon juice
ice

Method
Shake and strain into 3 oz cocktail glass and serve.

BOND 7 & JAMES

30 mL (1 oz) Bond 7 whiskey
garnish:
orange peel
1 dash sweet vermouth
1 maraschino cherry
Spa water

Method
Pour whiskey and vermouth into highball glass over ice.
Top with spa water, garnish with orange peel and cherry and serve.

BORN TO BE ALIVE

30 mL (1 oz) Bacardi rum
15 mL (1/2 oz) Peter Herring
15 mL (1/2 oz) advocaat
15 mL (1/2 oz) blue curaçao
15 mL (1/2 oz) green Chartreuse
5 mL Galliano Liverno
15 mL (1/2 oz) yellow Chartreuse

Method
Gently layer ingredients in a 5 oz cocktail glass with advocaat in the centre. Serve.

B

BOSOM CARESSER

45 mL brandy

1 egg yolk

15 mL (1/2 oz) blue curaçao

1 tsp grenadine

Method
Shake and strain into 3 oz cocktail glass and serve.

BOSOM CARESSER NO. 2

30 mL (1 oz) brandy

1 egg yolk

15 mL (1/2 oz) orange curaçao

ice

5 mL grenadine

Method
Shake and strain into a 5 oz cocktail glass and serve.

BOSSA NOVA

30 mL (1 oz) Galleon Liverno

60 mL (1 oz) pineapple juice

30 mL (1 oz) light dark rum

10 mL lemon juice

10 mL apricot brandy

15 mL (1/2 oz) egg white

Method
Shake and pour over ice in a highball glass.
garnish with fruit and serve.

BOSTON COCKTAIL

30ml Gilbey's Gin

30ml Apricot Brandy

5ml lemon juice

5ml Grenadine

Method
Shake over ice and strain then add Grenadine. Garnish with a red cherry.

BOSTON CREAM

30ml cream

15ml lime juice

30ml coconut cream

15ml Grenadine

Method
Shake over ice and strain. Garnish with a chocolate cross.

BOURBON BANANA

30 mL (1 oz) bourbon

30 mL (1 oz) orange juice

30 mL (1 oz) Kahlúa

30 mL (1 oz) cream

1 banana

Method
Blend ingredients with ice and serve in a brandy Balloon.

BRAIN DEAD BLASTER SHOOTER

10 mL Southern Comfort
10 mL tequila
10 mL Galliano Liverno
10 mL Tia Maria
10 mL blue curaçao

Method
Layer in a Test Tube or shot glass and serve.

BRANDY ALEXANDER

30 mL (1 oz) crème de cacao
30 mL (1 oz) fresh cream
30 mL (1 oz) brandy
garnish:
Ground nutmeg

Method
Shake ingredients and strain into a champagne saucer. Cross two straws over glass and sprinkle with nutmeg. Remove straws and serve.

BRANDY BOOSTER

30 mL (1 oz) brandy
30 mL (1 oz) orange juice
2 tsp lemon juice
1 egg yolk
1/2 tsp Icing sugar
ice

Method
Blend and pour into a rocks glass and serve.

BRANDY BOSS

30 mL (1 oz) brandy
15 mL (1/2 oz) Tia Maria
15 mL (1/2 oz) Vandermint
60 mL (1 oz) cream

Method
Shake and strain into a champagne saucer and serve.

BRANDY CIDER

60 mL (1 oz) brandy
apple cider

Method
Pour brandy over ice in a 10 oz brandy Balloon. Top with cider and serve.

BRANDY DAISY

60 mL (1 oz) brandy
6 dashes grenadine
30 mL (1 oz) lemon juice
fruit & mint for garnish
soda water
cracked ice

Method
Fill a Goblet with cracked ice, shake brandy, lemon juice and grenadine. Strain into Goblet, top soda. Garnish and serve.

B

BRANDY EGG NOG

30 mL (1 oz) brandy

1 egg yolk

5 mL sugar syrup

milk

Method
Shake all ingredients except milk, strain into a 10 oz highball glass. Top with milk, sprinkle with nutmeg, add straws and serve.

BRANDY FIX

30 mL (1 oz) brandy

30 mL (1 oz) lemon juice

30 mL (1 oz) cherry brandy

1 tsp water

1 tsp sugar

garnish:

1 lemon wheel

Method
Stir ingredients in a 5 o^ cocktail glass, garnish with lemon wheel and serve.

BRANDY FLIP

60 mL (1 oz) brandy

ice

1 tsp sugar

garnish:

nutmeg

l egg

Method
Shake ingredients and strain into a champagne saucer. Sprinkle with nutmeg and serve.

BRANDY ICE

30ml Milne Brandy

15ml vanilla extract

2 scoops vanilla ice cream

15ml lemon juice

top up with bitter lemon

Method
Blend with ice and strain then top up with bitter lemon. Garnish with an orange slice and a cherry

BRANDY KISS

30 mL (1 oz) brandy

30 mL (1 oz) lemon juice

30 mL (1 oz) Grand Marnier

Method
Shake and strain into a 3 oz cocktail glass and serve.

BRANDY, LIME & SODA

45 mL brandy

ice

15 mL (1/2 oz) lime juice

garnish:

1 lime or lemon wheel

soda water

Method
Pour brandy and lime juice over one scoop of ice in a 10 oz highball glass. Top with soda water, garnish with lime or lemon wheel, straws and serve.

BRANDY RIVIERA

30 mL (1 oz) brandy
30 mL (1 oz) Vandermint
30 mL (1 oz) banana liqueur
cracked ice

Method
Pour ingredients over ice in a champagne saucer and serve.

BRANDY SMASH

60 mL (1 oz) brandy
2 Spring mint
1 tsp sugar
cracked ice
water

Method
Dissolve sugar in a little water. Muddle with ice and mint in Old Fashioned glass. Pour brandy over the top and serve.

BRANDY SNAPS

10ml Milne Brandy
10ml Peach Schnapps
10ml apple juice

Method
Layer Brandy onto Peach Schnapps, then pour apple juice. Garnish with floated cream (optional).

BRANDY TODDY

60 mL (1 oz) brandy
1 tsp sugar
water
cracked ice

Method
Dissolve sugar in a little water in a 3 oz cocktail glass. Acid ice, brandy and serve.

BRAVE BULL

60 mL (1 oz) Kahlúa
60 mL (1 oz) tequila

Method
Place two ice cubes in a 3 oz cocktail glass and pour ingredients over ice. Serve with two short straws.

BRAZILIAN MONK

30ml Kahlúa
15ml Frangelico
15ml Dark Creme de Cacao
2 scoops vanilla ice cream

Method
Blend with ice. Garnish with a wild flower or flower petals.

B

BREAK SHOOTER

10 mL Kahlúa

10 mL ouzo

10 mL banana liqueur

Method

Layer in order in a shot glass
and serve.

BREATHALYSER BUSTER

12 mL crème de menthe

12 mL vodka

12 mL Cointreau

Method

Pour into a 3 oz cocktail glass
and serve.

BRITTANY

30ml Gilbey's Gin

15ml Amer Picon

10ml orange juice

10ml lemon juice

Method

Build over ice. Garnish with
lemon peel.

BRONX

30 mL (1 oz) gin

15 mL (1/2 oz) orange juice

1 dash French vermouth

cracked ice

1 dash Italian vermouth

Method

Shake and strain into 3 oz cocktail
glass and serve.

BRONX DISCO

30 mL (1 oz) dry gin

15 mL (1/2 oz) dry vermouth

30 mL (1 oz) Galliano Liverno

30 mL (1 oz) orange juice

15 mL (1/2 oz) sweet vermouth

Method

Shake and strain into a 5 oz
cocktail glass and serve.

BROWN BETTY

60 mL (1 oz) beer or ale

1 tbsp Brown sugar

15 mL (1/2 oz) brandy

1 lemon wheel (GARNISHED)

1 pinch cinnamon

30 mL (1 oz) water

nutmeg

Pinch Ground Cloves

1/2 slice toasted bread

1/2 fresh ginger Root

Method

Dissolve sugar in water and allow
to stand for 15 minutes. Add
Cloves, brandy and beer or ale and
stir well. Pour into a 10 oz brandy
Balloon, break toasted bread into
it. Sprinkle with nutmeg and grate
ginger root over top and serve.

BROWN BOMBER

45 mL Kahlúa

45 mL Bailey's Irish cream

Method

Pour over ice in a sherry glass and
serve.

BROWN COW

45 mL Tia Maria

milk

Method
Pour Tia Maria over ice in a 10 oz highball glass, top with milk. Add straws and serve.

BROWN SMOOTHIE

45 mL Kahlúa

30 mL (1 oz) cream

1 banana

ice

Method
Blend until smooth, pour into a flute glass and serve.

BROWN SQUIRREL

30 mL (1 oz) amaretto

30 mL (1 oz) heavy cream

15 mL (1/2 oz) crème de cacao

Method
Shake and strain into a 5 oz champagne saucer and serve.

BRUISE SHOOTER

30 mL (1 oz) Kahlúa

30 mL (1 oz) Bailey's Irish cream

30 mL (1 oz) crème de menthe

Method
Layer in order in a shot glass and serve.

BUBBLE YUM

30 mL (1 oz) Cointreau

10 mL raspberry cordial

30 mL (1 oz) banana liqueur

60 mL (1 oz) cream

Method
Shake and strain into a 5 oz cocktail glass and serve.

BUCCANEER

45 mL Bundaberg rum

dry ginger ale

15 mL (1/2 oz) advocaat

Method
Shake rum and advocaat and strain over ice in a 10 oz highball glass. Top with dry ginger ale and serve with straws.

BUCKS

60 mL (1 oz) champagne

60 mL (1 oz) orange juice

Method
Mix together in a flute glass and serve.

Blue Hawaii

Black Russian

Blue French

Brandy Alexander

Between the Sheets

Black Widow

B

BULLSHOT

40 mL vodka

1 Beef Stock Cube

60 mL (1 oz) hot water

1/4 tsp Celery salt or salt

1 squeeze lemon juice

ice

garnish: 1 strip lemon peel

Method

In a mixing glass dissolve stock cube in water, add salt, squeeze of lemon and vodka, Stir rapidly and pour into an Old Fashioned glass. Garnish with lemon peel and serve.

BULLSHOT SHOOTER

10 mL Kahlúa

10 mL tequila

10 mL Bacardi rum

Method

Layer in order in a shot glass and serve.

BURNING DESIRE

30 mL (1 oz) Cointreau

50 mL orange juice

15 mL (1/2 oz) Galleon Liverno

5 mL grenadine

1 dash egg white

Method

Shake and strain into a 5 oz cocktail glass and serve.

BUSH PEAK

20 mL Cointreau

20 mL Galleon Liverno

20 mL Grand Marnier

90 mL orange juice

20 mL brandy

grenadine [??]

Method

Shake all ingredients except grenadine and pour into a 10 oz highball glass. Add grenadine, flexible straws and serve.

BUTTERFLY FLIP

30 mL (1 oz) brandy

1 egg yolk

30 mL (1 oz) crème de cacao

2-3 ice cubes

1/2 tsp castor sugar

garnish:

nutmeg

25 mL cream

Method

Shake and strain into a 5 oz cocktail glass, sprinkle with nutmeg and serve.

BYRRH FREEZER

60 mL (1 oz) Byrrh

garnish:

1 lemon wheel

15 mL (1/2 oz) lemon cordial

1 maraschino cherry

soda water

Method

Pour Byrrh and cordial over ice in a 10 oz highball glass. Top with soda, garnish with lemon wheel, cherry and serve.

CAFÉ DE PARIS

60ml Gilbey's Gin

10ml double cream

5ml Pernod

1 egg white

Method
Shake over ice and strain. Garnish with half a slice of lemon.

CAFÉ NERO

30ml Galliano

black coffee

fresh cream

sugar

Method
Firstly, sprinkle white sugar inside the glass after coating with Galliano. Set Galliano alight and twirl the glass so that flames burn brightly. Pour black coffee gently into glass then layer cream on top of the burning coffee. Sprinkle grated chocolate over the coffee.

CAFÉ OSCAR

20ml Kahlúa

20ml Amaretto di Galliano

top up with hot coffee

layer double cream

2 scoops vanilla ice cream

Method
Pour in order then float cream. Garnish with ice cream.

CAFÉ ROYALE

1 cup black coffee

1 Lump sugar

1 tbsp brandy

Method
Place sugar in spoon and hold over coffee, fill spoon with brandy and ignite. When flame starts to fade place spoon in coffee and serve.

CAFÉ SOCIETY

30 mL (1 oz) Cadbury cream liqueur

60 mL (1 oz) cream

30 mL (1 oz) Frangelico

garnish:

grated chocolate

15 mL (1/2 oz) Kahlúa

strawberry

Method
Blend with ice and pour into a 5 oz colada glass. Garnish with Flake chocolate and a strawberry, serve with straws.

CALVADOS

30 mL (1 oz) Calvados

garnish:

apple slices

15 mL (1/2 oz) Cointreau

1 maraschino cherry

30 mL (1 oz) orange juice

Method
Shake liquid ingredients and strain into 3 oz cocktail glass, garnish with apple slices and cherry and serve.

C

CAMERON CANNON

30 mL (1 oz) Kahlúa

30 mL (1 oz) Bailey's Irish cream

90 mL vodka

dash crème de menthe

3 drops green Chartreuse

crushed ice

Method

Shake and strain into 5 oz cocktail glass and serve.

CAMPARI

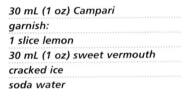

30 mL (1 oz) Campari

garnish:

1 slice lemon

30 mL (1 oz) sweet vermouth

cracked ice

soda water

Method

Half fill a 10 ox highball glass with ice, pour Campari and vermouth over ice. Top with soda water, garnish with lemon slice, straws and serve.

CAMPINO

15 mL (1/2 oz) Campari

2 dashes crème de cassis

15 mL (1/2 oz) sweet vermouth

garnish:

1 spiral orange peel

15 mL (1/2 oz) dry vermouth

soda water

15 mL (1/2 oz) gin

Method

Mix all ingredients except soda water and peel in mixing glass. Pour into small Tumbler and top with soda. Garnish with peel and serve.

CANADIAN DAISY

30ml Canadian Club Whisky

10ml Milne Brandy

10ml lemon juice

5ml raspberry syrup

top up with soda

Method

Shake over ice and strain then top up with soda. Garnish with assorted colourful cherries.

CANADIAN SHERBET

30 mL (1 oz) Canadian whiskey

30 mL (1 oz) lemon juice

15 mL (1/2 oz) Tia Maria

30 mL (1 oz) sugar syrup

Method

Blend and pour into chilled margarita glass, garnish with banana slice and strawberry and serve.

CANDY CANE

15 mL (1/2 oz) grenadine

15 mL (1/2 oz) vodka

15 mL (1/2 oz) crème de menthe

Method

Layer in order in shot glass and serve.

CAPE KENNEDY

5 mL dark rum

20 mL lemon juice

5 mL Scotch whiskey

20 mL orange juice

5 mL Benedictine

2-3 ice Cubes

5 mL sugar syrup

Method
Shake and strain into 3 oz cocktail glass and serve.

CAPER'S CAPER

30 mL (1 oz) advocaat

1/4 Avocado

30 mL (1 oz) Frangelico

1 scoop ice cream

4-5 strawberries

garnish:

coffee Bean

Method
Blend ingredients with ice and pour into a 10 oz colada glass. Float coffee Bean and serve with straws.

CAPER'S CAPER NO. 2

30 mL (1 oz) Frangelico

90 mL cream

30 mL (1 oz) vodka

3-4 strawberries

15 mL (1/2 oz) Cointreau

Method
Blend ingredients with ice and pour into an 8 oz colada glass.
garnish with strawberries and straws and serve.

CAPER'S TRAFFIC LIGHT

30 mL (1 oz) strawberry liqueur

30 mL (1 oz) Midori

6 strawberries

1 slice honeydew melon

30 mL (1 oz) banana liqueur

1/2 banana

Method
Blend each liqueur and corresponding fruit with ice and layer in a 10 oz colada glass in recipe order. Garnish with fruits and straws and serve.

CARDINAL

45 mL gin

1 twist lemon

45 mL dry vermouth

cracked ice

45 mL Campari

Method
Shake and strain into 5 oz cocktail glass, garnish with lemon peel and serve.

CARELESS WHISPER

30 mL (1 oz) strawberry liqueur

10 mL cream

10 mL Cheri-Suisse

garnish:

grated chocolate

20 mL Amanda

1 maraschino cherry

Method
Shake and strain into a 3 oz cocktail glass, garnish with chocolate, cherry and serve.

C

CARIBBEAN CHAMPAGNE

100ml Champagne
10ml Bacardi
10ml Banana Liqueur
5ml Orange Bitters

Method
Stir without ice and strain. Garnish with a slice of banana.

CARLTON

30 mL (1 oz) Canadian whiskey
10 mL orange juice
15 mL (1/2 oz) Cointreau
cracked ice

Method
Shake and strain into a 3 oz cocktail glass and serve.

CAT WALK

30 mL (1 oz) Bacardi rum
15 mL (1/2 oz) lemon juice
20 mL Cointreau
4 strawberries
15 mL (1/2 oz) Malibu

Method
Blend until smooth, pour into a 3 oz cocktail glass and serve.

CATCH ME

45 mL vodka
30 mL (1 oz) lemon juice
15 mL (1/2 oz) red curaçao

Method
Shake and strain into a 3 oz cocktail glass and serve.

CATERPILLAR

15 mL (1/2 oz) gin
15 mL (1/2 oz) yellow Chartreuse
15 mL (1/2 oz) blue curaçao
ice

Method
Pour ingredients over ice in a 3 oz cocktail glass and serve.

CHA CHA

30 mL (1 oz) Frangelico
15 mL (1/2 oz) cream
30 mL (1 oz) crème de cacao

Method
Float ingredients in a 3 oz cocktail glass and serve.

CHABLIS CUP

20ml Grand Marnier

15ml Kirsch

1 peach slice

1 bananas slice

1 orange slice

1 lemon slice

1 mint sprig

top 60ml Chablis wine

Method

Blend over ice and then top up with Chablis. Garnish with an assorted fruit arrangement.

CHAMPAGNE 69

15 mL (1/2 oz) Cointreau

chilled champagne

15 mL (1/2 oz) Grand Marnier

Method

Build Cointreau and Grand Marnier in a champagne saucer. Top with champagne and serve.

CHAMPAGNE COCKTAIL

15 mL (1/2 oz) brandy

1 sugar Cube

chilled champagne

garnish:

1 twist lemon

Angostura bitters

Method

Place sugar Cube in a champagne saucer and saturate with Angostura bitters. Add brandy and fill with champagne, stir until sugar is dissolved. Garnish with twist of lemon and serve.

CHAMPAGNE COCKTAIL NO. 2.

15 mL (1/2 oz) brandy

1 sugar Cube

chilled champagne

1 dash Angostura bitters

1 dash orange curaçao

garnish:

1 strip orange peel

Method

Place sugar Cube in a champagne saucer, add Angostura bitters and curaçao. Fill almost to top with champagne, float brandy on top. Garnish with orange peel and serve.

CHAMPAGNE COCKTAIL NO. 3

30 mL (1 oz) cognac

10 mL Angostura bitters

chilled champagne

garnish:

1 strawberry

1 sugar Cube

Method

Place sugar Cube in a champagne saucer and saturate with Angostura bitters. Add cognac and top with champagne. Garnish with strawberry and serve.

C

CHAMPAGNE COCKTAIL NO. 4

15 mL (1/2 oz) Grand Marnier
20 mL orange juice
chilled champagne
1 egg yolk

Method
Shake Grand Marnier, orange juice and egg yolk with ice. Strain into a champagne saucer, top with champagne and serve.

CHAMPAGNE PICK-ME-UP

30 mL brandy
30 mL (1 oz) orange juice
chilled champagne
ice
5 mL
grenadine

Method
Shake ingredients except champagne and strain into a flute glass. Top with champagne and serve.

CHAMPAGNE ST. MORITZ

10ml Beefeater Dry Gin
10ml Apricot Brandy
10ml orange juice
top up with Champagne

Method
Shake over ice and strain then top up with Champagne. Garnish with a slice of orange.

CHAMPAGNE TORY

15 mL (1/2 oz) Midori
15 mL (1/2 oz) Rubis
15 mL (1/2 oz) banana liqueur
chilled champagne

Method
Pour ingredients into a champagne saucer, top with champagne and serve.

CHANNEL 64 SHOOTER

10 mL advocaat
10 mL Bailey's Irish cream
10 mL banana liqueur

Method
Layer in order in a shot glass and serve.

CHASTITY BELT SHOOTER

20 mL Tia Maria
10 mL Bailey's Irish cream
10 mL Frangelico
5 mL cream

Method
Layer in order in a shot glass and serve.

CHEE CHEE

30 mL (1 oz) vodka
60 mL (1 oz) pineapple juice
30 mL (1 oz) coconut milk
garnish:
1 pineapple wedge

Method
Shake and strain into a champagne
saucer, garnish with pineapple
wedge and serve.

CHERRIES JUBILEE

30 mL (1 oz) cherry advocaat
15 mL (1/2 oz) milk
30 mL (1 oz) white crème de cacao
grated chocolate (GARNISH
15 mL (1/2 oz) Malibu
garnish:
1 strip coconut Rind
40 mL cream
1 maraschino cherry

Method
Shake and strain into a 5 oz
cocktail glass. Garnish and serve.

CHERRY

15 mL (1/2 oz) cherry brandy
15 mL (1/2 oz) Double cream
1 tsp white rum
garnish:
2 small sprigs mint
90 mL Sparkling white wine

Method
Stir all ingredients except wine in a
10 oz highball glass. Top with wine,
garnish with mint, straws and serve.

CHERRY ALEXANDER

30 mL (1 oz) cherry brandy
60 mL (1 oz) cream
30 mL (1 oz) crème de cacao
ice

Method
Shake and strain into a 5 oz
cocktail glass and serve.

CHERRY BOMB

30ml Smirnoff Vodka
15ml Cherry Brandy
5ml Grenadine
top up with lemonade

Method
Colour sugar with Grenadine and
prepare glass by sugar coating rim.
Blend over ice and pour then top
up with lemonade. Garnish with an
orchid.

CHERYL

30 mL (1 oz) vodka
1 scoop vanilla ice cream
30 mL (1 oz) Galleon Liverno
garnish:
1 maraschino cherry

Method
Shake and strain into a 5 oz
cocktail glass, garnish with cherry
and serve.

C

CHEVRON'S MOON LANDING

1 pineapple
15 mL (1/2 oz) cherry brandy
30 mL (1 oz) vodka
1 dash Angostura bitters
30 mL (1 oz) dark rum
12 maraschino Cherries
15 mL (1/2 oz) apricot brandy
2 lemon slices
2 olives
3 ice cubes

Method
Cut the top off the pineapple approximately two inches from the top and hollow out the bottom section of the pineapple. Cut half the fruit into cubes and replace it in the hollowed shell. In a shaker, place ice cubes, vodka, rum, apricot brandy, cherry brandy and bitters. Shake rapidly and pour unstrained over fruit in pineapple. Place four Toothpicks around top of pineapple Shell and place three Cherries on each toothpick. Place four more toothpicks in top of pineapple so that they match the ones in the shell and replace the top so that the toothpicks line up through the Cherries. Place a slice of lemon on each side of the pineapple with a toothpick and balance two crossed swizzle sticks on each Toothpick and secure them with an olive. Add a Spoon, straws and serve.

CHI CHI

45 mL vodka
20 mL coconut cream
20 mL Malibu
15 mL (1/2 oz) lime cordial
15 mL (1/2 oz) lemon cordial
1 slice pineapple
60 mL (1 oz) pineapple juice
1 dash cream

Method
Blend until smooth and pour into a champagne saucer and serve.

CHICAGO

40 mL brandy
1 dash Angostura bitters
1 tsp Cointreau
2 ice cubes
Sparkling white wine

Method
Place ingredients in a champagne saucer, top with white wine and serve.

CHIQUITA

45ml Smirnoff Vodka
10ml Banana Liqueur
10ml lime juice
half a sliced banana
pinch of sugar

Method
Blend with ice and pour. Garnish with banana slices.

CHOC MINT

30 mL (1 oz) crème de cacao
50 mL cream
15 mL (1/2 oz) white crème de menthe

Method
Shake and strain into a champagne saucer and serve.

CHOCBERRY

30 mL (1 oz) Afrikoko
60 mL (1 oz) cream
15 mL (1/2 oz) Framboise
5 strawberries

Method
Blend until smooth, pour into a champagne saucer and serve.

CHOCOLATE BABY

45 mL crème de cacao
Coca-Cola

Method
Half fill a 10 oz highball glass with ice, add crème de cacao. Top with Coca-Cola and serve with straws. Shake and strain into a 3 oz cocktail glass and serve.

CHOCOLATE CHIP MINT

30ml White Creme de Cacao
30ml Green Creme de Menthe
2 scoops vanilla ice cream
15ml lemon juice
2 chocolate chips
top up with lemonade

Method
Blend with ice and strain then top up with lemonade. Serve with chocolate chip cookies on a side plate.

CHOCOLATE CHIP SHOOTER

15 mL (1/2 oz) Vandermint
15 Bailey's Irish cream
15 mL (1/2 oz) crème de menthe

Method
Layer in a shot glass and serve.

CHOCOLATE NOUGAT SHOOTER

10 mL Frangelico
10 mL yellow Chartreuse
10 mL Bailey's Irish cream

Method
Layer in a shot glass and serve.

CHOCOLATE SOLDIER

25 mL brandy
1 dash orange bitters
20 mL dry vermouth
2 ice cubes
10 mL crème de cacao

Method
Blend and pour into a champagne
saucer and serve.

CHOCOLATE STINGER

30 mL (1 oz) crème do cacao
30 mL (1 oz) crème de menthe

Method
Shake and strain into a 3 oz
cocktail glass and serve.

CHOW CHE HUA

30 mL (1 oz) Midori
1 peeled Kiwi fruit
30 mL (1 oz) Cointreau
garnish:
1 pineapple wedge
90 mL pineapple juice

Method
Blend until smooth, pour into a
colada glass. Garnish with
pineapple wedge and serve.

CHURCHES

30 mL (1 oz) Scotch whiskey
15 mL (1/2 oz) Drambuie
15 mL (1/2 oz) sweet vermouth
1 dash Angostura bitters

Method
Shake and strain over ice in a 3 oz
cocktail glass and serve.

CIDER CUP

75 mL sweet apple cider
1/4 tsp sugar
15 mL (1/2 oz) brandy
15 mL (1/2 oz) pineapple juice
15 mL (1/2 oz) sweet sherry
15 mL (1/2 oz) lemon juice
soda water
garnish:
nutmeg
crushed ice

Method
Place all ingredients except nutmeg
and soda into a 10 oz highball glass
and stir until sugar is dissolved. Top
with soda, sprinkle with nutmeg.
Serve with straws.

CLARET CUP

90 mL claret
1 tsp sugar
15 mL (1/2 oz) maraschino
crushed ice
soda water
garnish:
nutmeg

Method
Stir all ingredients except soda and
nutmeg in a brandy Balloon until
sugar is dissolved.
Top with soda, sprinkle with
nutmeg and serve.

CLARET FLIP

90 mL claret
1 egg yolk
2 tsp sugar syrup
2-3 ice cubes

Method
Shake and strain into a 5 oz
cocktail glass and serve.

CLIFF HANGER

40 mL vodka
15 mL (1/2 oz) Peter Herring
15 mL (1/2 oz) Galleon Liverno
lemonade

Method
Place 2 ice cubes in a 5 oz cocktail
glass, Pour vodka and Peter Herring
over top. Top with lemonade, float
Galleon Liverno and serve.

CLOVER CLUB

45 mL gin
1 egg white
4 dashes grenadine
cracked ice
juice 1/2 lemon

Method
Shake and strain into a champagne
saucer and serve.

CLUB FORREST

15 mL (1/2 oz) port wine
1 egg yolk
15 mL (1/2 oz) Chartreuse
5 mL sugar syrup
5 mL white curaçao
garnish:
nutmeg

Method
Shake and strain into a 3 oz
cocktail glass, sprinkle with nutmeg
and serve.

COATHANGER
SHOOTER

15 mL (1/2 oz) Cointreau
7 mL grenadine
15 mL (1/2 oz) tequila
1 Drop milk

Method
Layer in a shot glass and serve.

C

COFFEE

30 mL (1 oz) brandy
1 tsp sugar
30 mL (1 oz) port wine
cracked ice
1 dash curaçao
garnish:
nutmeg
1 egg yolk

Method
Shake and strain into a 5 oz
cocktail glass, sprinkle with nutmeg
and serve.

COFFEE BOMB

15 mL (1/2 oz) Cointreau
15 mL (1/2 oz) Bailey's Irish cream
hot coffee
cream (float)

Method
Fill a Goblet with hot coffee and
add other ingredients.
Add sugar if desired, float cream
and serve.

COINTREAU CAIPIRINHA

30ml Cointreau
1/4 fresh lime or lemon
crushed ice

Method
Cut lime into pieces and place in a
175ml Prism Rocks Glass. Extract
juice by using the Cointreau Pestle,
fill glass with crushed ice and add
Cointreau and mini pestle. Stir.

COINTREAU MUPPET SHOOTER

30 mL (1 oz) Cointreau
30 mL (1 oz) Tonic water

Method
Layer on a shot glass and serve.

COLD DUCK

90 mL chilled Moselle
1/2 tsp sugar
30 mL (1 oz) Sparkling white wine
1 tbsp hot water
garnish: lemon peel

Method
Dissolve sugar in hot water in a
shaker, add other ingredients.
Shake and strain into a 5 oz
cocktail glass, garnish with lemon
peel and serve.

COLORADO

20 mL cherry brandy
20 mL cream
20 mL kirsch
2-3 ice cubes

Method
Shake and strain into a 3 oz
cocktail glass and serve.

COLUMBIA SKIN

1/2 lemon, thinly peeled
30ml Ballantine's Scotch Whisky
1 cup of boiling water

Method
Pour in order into a 300ml Beer
Mug. Garnish with a slice of lemon.

COLUMBUS

20 mL rum
20 mL lemon juice
20 mL apricot brandy
2-3 ice cubes

Method
Shake and strain into 3 oz cocktail
glass and serve.

COMFORT AND BOURBON

45 mL Southern Comfort
45 mL cold water
45 mL bourbon
cracked ice

Method
Half fill an Old Fashioned glass
with cracked ice. Add ingredients,
garnish with a twist of lemon and
serve.

COMFORT BABY

45 mL Southern Comfort
1 Cube sugar
45 mL fresh milk
2 ice cubes
nutmeg

Method
Place sugar cube in an Old
Fashioned glass and add liquid
ingredients. Stir gently until sugar
is dissolved, sprinkle with nutmeg
and serve.

COMFORTABLE SCREW

30 mL (1 oz) vodka
orange juice
15 mL (1/2 oz) Southern Comfort
ice

Method
In a 10 oz highball glass, Half fill
glass with ice and build vodka and
Southern Comfort. Top
with orange juice and serve.

COMMODORE

30 mL (1 oz) bourbon
30 mL (1 oz) lemon juice
30 mL (1 oz) crème de cacao
crushed ice

Method
Shake and strain into champagne
glass and serve.

COMMONWEALTH

30ml Canadian Club Whisky
15ml Vandermint Liqueur
15ml lemon juice

Method
Shake over ice and strain. Garnish
with a slice of lemon.

CONCORD

30 mL (1 oz) gin
10 mL dry vermouth
15 mL (1/2 oz) orange curaçao

Method
Shake and strain into a 3 oz
cocktail glass and serve.

CONSTELLATION

45 mL dark rum
1 dash Angostura bitters
45 mL Italian vermouth
1 dash lime juice
45 mL green ginger wine
cracked ice

Method
Shake and strain into 5 oz cocktail
glass and serve.

CONTESSA

20 mL brandy
20 mL orange juice
20 mL Cointreau
20 mL fresh cream
20 mL Galliano Liverno
1 maraschino cherry

Method
Shake and strain into a 5 w.
champagne glass. Slit cherry and
place on lip of glass and serve.

COOL CUCUMBER

30 mL (1 oz) Benedictine
15 mL (1/2 oz) lemon juice
chilled champagne
garnish:
1 long strip cucumber

Method
Pour Benedictine and lemon juice
into a champagne flute. Top with
champagne, add Cucumber and serve.

COOPERSTOWN

25 mL gin
garnish:
1 sprig mint
15 mL (1/2 oz) dry vermouth
crushed ice
15 mL (1/2 oz) Bianco vermouth

Method
Place ingredients in mixing glass
and stir, strain into a 3 oz cocktail
glass, garnish with sprig of mint
and serve.

COPACABANA

25 mL apricot brandy
15 mL (1/2 oz) lemon juice
15 mL (1/2 oz) brandy
garnish:
1 slice orange
15 mL (1/2 oz) Cointreau
crushed ice

Method
Shake and strain into a 3 oz
cocktail glass, garnish with orange
slice and serve over ice.

COPENHAGEN SPECIAL

30ml Aquavit
30ml Arrack
15ml lemon juice

Method
Shake over ice and strain. Garnish
with a slice of lemon.

CORONATION

15 mL (1/2 oz) gin
15 mL (1/2 oz) French vermouth
15 mL (1/2 oz) Dubonnet

Method
Stir ingredients in a mixing glass,
strain into a 3 oz cocktail glass
and serve.

CORPSE REVIVER

30 mL (1 oz) brandy
30 mL (1 oz) white rum
30 mL (1 oz) Fernet Branca

Method
Shake and strain into a 3 oz
cocktail glass and serve.

CORPSE REVIVER NO. 2.

30 mL (1 oz) brandy
15 mL (1/2 oz) sweet vermouth
30 mL (1 oz) Fernet Branca

Method
Shake and strain into a 3 oz
cocktail glass and serve.

CORUBA CARIBBEAN

30 mL (1 oz) Coruba rum
90 mL orange juice
15 mL (1/2 oz) Malibu
30 mL (1 oz) cream
1 dash blue curaçao
1 pineapple wedge
lemonade

Method
Shake rum, Malibu, cream and
orange juice and strain into a 10 oz
highball glass. Add blue curaçao
and garnish with the pineapple
wedge. Add straws and serve.

C

COUNTRY

30 mL (1 oz) Scotch whiskey
15 mL (1/2 oz) lime juice
15 mL (1/2 oz) cream
crushed ice

Method
Shake and strain into a 3 oz
cocktail glass and serve.

COVENANT'S RING SHOOTER

10 mL parfait amour
10 mL advocaat
10 mL crème de menthe
sambuca (float)

Method
Layer in order in a 4 oz shot glass.
Float sambuca and serve.

COWBOY

40 mL bourbon
30 mL (1 oz) cream
4 ice cubes

Method
Shake ingredients and strain
into a wine glass over crushed ice
and serve.

CROCODILE COOLER

30 mL (1 oz) Midori
60 mL (1 oz) sweet and sour
30 mL (1 oz) lemon vodka
lemonade
15 mL (1/2 oz) Cointreau

Method
Build over ice in a 10 oz highball
glass, add straws and serve.

CRUSTA AMOUR

50 mL tawny port
1 tbsp sugar (glass rim)
5 mL Cointreau
2 dashes lime juice
2 dashes peach bitters
crushed ice
15 mL (1/2 oz) lemon juice
garnish:
1 spiral lemon peel
5 mL maraschino

Method
sugar rim an champagne glass.
Shake remaining ingredients and
strain into glass. Garnish with
lemon peel and serve.

CRUSTA BRANDY

90 mL brandy
1 dash Angostura bitters
3 dashes maraschino
garnish:
1 maraschino cherry

Method
Shake and strain into a champagne
saucer. Garnish with cherry and
serve.

CRUSTA DAWN

40 mL white rum
15 mL (1/2 oz) lemon juice
1 tbsp apricot brandy
15 mL (1/2 oz) orange juice
1 dash grenadine
spiral orange peel
1 tbsp castor sugar
2-3 ice cubes

Method
sugar Rim a champagne saucer and place remaining ingredients in a shaker. Shake and strain into the glass and serve

CRUSTA VODKA

40 mL vodka
15 mL (1/2 oz) orange juice
15 mL (1/2 oz) sweet vermouth
50 mL pineapple juice
15 mL (1/2 oz) brandy
1 tbsp castor sugar
1 dash Angostura bitters
2-3 ice cubes
1 dash orange bitters
garnish:
1 spiral orange peel

Method
sugar Rim a champagne saucer. Shake remaining ingredients and strain into the glass. Garnish with spiral of orange peel and serve.

CUBE LIBRE

30 mL (1 oz) white rum
juice 1/2 lemon
Coca-Cola
ice

Method
Pour ingredients over ice in a 10 oz highball glass, add straws and serve.

CURRENT RUM

60 mL (1 oz) rum
soda water
15 mL (1/2 oz) blackcurrant juice
ice

Method
Stir rum and juice together in a 5 oz cocktail glass with one ice cube, top with soda water and serve.

CYBER PUNCH

30 mL (1 oz) vodka
30 mL (1 oz) lemon juice
30 mL (1 oz) gin
1 tsp sugar
30 mL (1 oz) Bacardi rum
1 dash grenadine
30 mL (1 oz) triple sec
180 mL beer

Method
Pour ingredients into a 12 oz Hurricane glass. Serve with straws.

C

CYCLONE

90 mL vodka
10 mL Pernod
30 mL (1 oz) dry vermouth
garnish:
1 twist lemon peel

Method
Half fill a mixing glass with cracked ice and add ingredients. Stir and strain into a 5 oz cocktail glass, garnish with lemon peel and serve.

CYCLONE TRACY

30 mL (1 oz) Tia Maria
30 mL (1 oz) Scotch whiskey
30 mL (1 oz) Kahlúa
milk
30 mL (1 oz) Bailey's Irish cream
crushed ice

Method
Shake ingredients except milk and strain into an 8 oz highball glass. Top with milk and serve with straws.

CZAR'S DELIGHT

1 tbsp vodka
75 mL cream
1 tbsp mint liqueur
garnish:
frosted mint leaves
150 mL milk
2 ice cubes

Method
Shake ingredients except mint leaves and pour into a rocks glass, garnish with mint leaves and serve.

D.J. SPECIAL

30 mL (1 oz) brandy
30 mL (1 oz) Benedictine
30 mL Cointreau
Coca-Cola

Method
Shake ingredients except Coca-Cola and pour over ice in a brandy Balloon. Top with Coca-Cola and serve with straws.

D'ARTAGNAN

90 mL Americano vermouth
garnish:
1 maraschino cherry
30 mL (1 oz) orange curaçao
cracked ice

Method
Shake and strain into a 5 oz cocktail glass, garnish with cherry and serve.

DAIQUIRI

American

30 mL (1 oz) white rum
1 tsp sugar
1 tsp Cointreau
garnish:
1 slice lime
15 mL (1/2 oz) lime juice
1 maraschino cherry

Method
Shake and strain over crushed ice in a 5 oz cocktail glass.

Banana

30 mL (1 oz) white rum
30 mL (1 oz) orange juice
30 mL (1 oz) dark rum
1/2 banana
2 tbsp banana liqueur
30 mL (1 oz) orange juice
3 tbsp cream
ice

Method
Blend and pour into a 10 oz highball glass. Garnish with orange and banana wheels. Add straws and serve.

Kings

45 mL Bacardi rum
15 mL (1/2 oz) lemon juice
15 mL (1/2 oz) parfait amour
1/4 tsp sugar
1 dash egg white

Method
Blend until smooth, pour into a champagne saucer and serve.

D

Kiwi fruit

30 mL (1 oz) Bacardi light rum
30 mL (1 oz) lemon juice
30 mL (1 oz) Cointreau
15 mL (1/2 oz) sugar syrup
30 mL (1 oz) Midori
1/2 kiwifruit

Method
Blend ingredients until smooth, pour
Into a champagne saucer and serve.

Lime

45 mL Bacardi rum
30 mL (1 oz) lime juice
20 mL Cointreau

Method
Shake and strain into a 3 oz
cocktail glass and serve.

Mango

45 mL Bacardi rum
20 mL lemon juice
30 mL (1 oz) Cointreau
15 mL (1/2 oz) sugar syrup
30 mL (1 oz) mango liqueur
1/2 mango

Method
Blend until smooth and pour into a
champagne glass and serve.

Midori

30 mL (1 oz) Midori
20 mL lemon juice
40 mL white rum

Method
Shake and strain into a 3 oz
cocktail glass and serve.

Original

90 mL white rum
1 tsp sugar
30 mL (1 oz) lemon or lime juice
fruit for garnish

Method
Shake and strain into a chilled
cocktail glass, garnish and serve.

Peach

45 mL Bacardi rum
20 mL lemon juice
30 mL (1 oz) Cointreau
15 mL (1/2 oz) sugar syrup
30 mL (1 oz) peach tree
1/2 peach

Method
Blend until smooth, pour into a
champagne glass and serve.

Rockmelon

45 mL Bacardi rum
20 mL lemon juice
30 mL (1 oz) Cointreau
15 mL (1/2 oz) sugar syrup
30 mL (1 oz) mango liqueur
1/3 Rockmelon

Method
Blend until smooth and pour into a
champagne glass and serve.

Strawberry

90 mL white rum
30 mL (1 oz) lemon juice
1 tsp strawberry liqueur
60 mL (1 oz) milk
10 strawberries
ice

Method
Blend until smooth, pour into a
colada glass, garnish with a
strawberry and serve.

DAIRY DREAM

15 mL (1/2 oz) Galliano Liverno
30 mL (1 oz) banana liqueur
20 mL vodka
60 mL (1 oz) cream

Method
Shake and strain into a 5 oz
cocktail glass and serve.

DAME PENNY

45 mL dry gin
1 dash egg white
30 mL (1 oz) dry vermouth
soda water
30 mL (1 oz) lemon juice
cracked ice
30 mL (1 oz) sugar syrup
garnish:
1/2 slice lemon

Method
Half fill shaker with cracked ice and
add ingredients except soda water.
Shake and strain into a 10 oz
highball glass. Garnish with
lemon slice, straws, swizzle sticks
and serve.

DANGEROUS VIOLETS

30 mL (1 oz) parfait amour
30 mL (1 oz) Bacardi rum
30 mL (1 oz) gin
lemonade

Method
Shake ingredients except lemonade
and pour over ice in a 10 oz
highball glass. Top with lemonade,
add straws and serve.

DAYDREAM ISLAND

60 mL (1 oz) dry gin
15 mL (1/2 oz) orange juice
15 mL (1/2 oz) blue curaçao
garnish:
1 maraschino cherry
30 mL (1 oz) Galliano Liverno
cracked ice
1/2 egg white

Method
Shake and strain into a 5 oz
cocktail glass, garnish with cherry
and serve.

DEAD BANANA

60 mL (1 oz) banana liqueur
milk
60 mL (1 oz) grenadine

Method
Shake banana liqueur, grenadine
and strain into a 10 oz highball
glass, top with milk and serve
with straws.

DEAN'S DELIGHT

30 mL (1 oz) tequila
30 mL (1 oz) Benedictine
30 mL (1 oz) crème de menthe
crushed ice
15 mL (1/2 oz) brandy
soda water (OPTIONAL)

Method
Shake and strain into an Old
Fashioned glass over crushed ice.
Add soda water if Desired.

D

DEATH BY CHOCOLATE

30 mL (1 oz) Bailey's Irish cream
30 mL (1 oz) crème de cacao
30 mL (1 oz) Kahlúa
90 mL Thickened cream
30 mL (1 oz) Tia Maria
garnish:
grated chocolate

Method
Shake and strain into a champagne
saucer, garnish with grated
chocolate and serve.

DEATH BY CHOCOLATE NO. 2

30 mL (1 oz) Bailey's Irish cream
30 mL (1 oz) crème de cacao
30 mL (1 oz) Kahlúa
90 mL Thickened cream
30 mL (1 oz) Afrikoko
garnish:
grated chocolate

Method
Shake and strain into a champagne
saucer, garnish with grated
chocolate and serve.

DEATH BY CHOCOLATE NO. 3

30 mL (1 oz) Bailey's Irish cream
30 mL (1 oz) Kahlúa
30 mL (1 oz) crème de cacao
90 mL Thicken cream
30 mL (1 oz) Cadbury's chocolate
liqueur
garnish:
grated chocolate

Method
Shake and strain into a champagne
saucer, garnish with grated
chocolate and serve.

DEATH IN THE AFTERNOON

15 mL (1/2 oz) Pernod
1 sugar Cube
champagne

Method
Place the sugar Cube in a 6 oz tulip
glass and add Pernod, top with
champagne and serve.

DEEP THROAT SHOOTER

20 mL Kahlúa
Thickened cream
20 mL Grand Marnier

Method
Layer in a shot glass and serve.

DEPTH CHARGE

340 mL beer
30 mL (1 oz) Cointreau

Method
Pour beer into a 375 mL glass, fill a 1 oz shot glass with Cointreau. Drop shot glass into beer in front of Customer.

DE RIGUEUR

30ml Scotch Whisky
10ml grapefruit juice
10ml honey

Method
Shake over ice and pour. Garnish with a swizzle stick.

DESERT COOLER

60 mL (1 oz) Southern Comfort
75 mL pineapple juice
15 mL (1/2 oz) bourbon
75 mL grapefruit juice
cracked ice

Method
Half fill a 10 oz glass with cracked ice, shake remaining ingredients and strain over ice and serve.

DESERT ISLAND

30 mL (1 oz) Bacardi light rum
60 mL (1 oz) pineapple juice
45 mL Midori
cream

Method
Shake all ingredients except cream and strain into a 5 oz champagne saucer, top with cream and serve.

DESERT ROSE

30 mL (1 oz) Midori
60 mL (1 oz) pineapple juice
30 mL (1 oz) Bailey's Irish cream
60 g rockmelon
15 mL (1/2 oz) Glayva
garnish:
pineapple wedge

Method
Blend and pour into a colada glass, garnish with pineapple wedge and serve with straws.

DESERT STORM

15 mL (1/2 oz) mango liqueur
60 mL (1 oz) pineapple juice
15 mL (1/2 oz) Bacardi rum
1 dash Tabasco Sauce
15 mL (1/2 oz) gin

Method
Shake and strain into a 4 ?/. cocktail glass and serve.

D

DESHLER

30 mL (1 oz) Canadian whiskey

1 dash Angostura bitters

15 mL (1/2 oz) Dubonnet

garnish:

1 strip lemon peel

1 dash Cointreau

1 strip orange peel

Method
Shake and strain into a 3 oz cocktail glass, garnish with lemon and orange peel and serve.

DESPINA

90 mL sweet vermouth

garnish:

1 twist orange peel

30 mL (1 oz) Galliano Liverno

Method
Shake and strain into a 5 oz cocktail glass, garnish with orange peel and serve.

DEVIL

45 mL brandy

45 mL crème de Menthe

Method
Shake and strain into a 3 oz cocktail glass and serve.

DEVIL'S HANDBRAKE SHOOTER

15 mL (1/2 oz) banana liqueur

15 mL (1/2 oz) cherry brandy

15 mL (1/2 oz) mango liqueur

Method
Layer in order in a shot glass and serve.

DIPLOMAT

45 mL vodka

90 mL pineapple juice

45 mL Midori

5 mL lemon juice

Method
Shake and strain into a 8 oz highball glass and serve with straws.

DIRTY MOTHER

30 mL (1 oz) tequila

milk

30 mL (1 oz) Tia Maria

Method
Shake and strain over ice in a 10 oz highball glass, top with milk and serve.

DIZZY BLOND

60 mL (1 oz) advocaat
lemonade
30 mL (1 oz) Pernod
garnish:
1 maraschino cherry

Method
Half fill a 10 oz highball glass with
cracked ice and add advocaat and
Pernod. Top with lemonade,
garnish with cherry and serve.

DOCTOR DANGEROUS

45 mL brandy
60 mL (1 oz) milk
45 mL Bailey's Irish cream

Method
Shake and strain into an Old
Fashioned glass and serve.

DIZZY DAME

30 mL (1 oz) brandy
30 mL (1 oz) cream
15 mL (1/2 oz) Kahlúa
1/2 scoop ice
15 mL (1/2 oz) cherry brandy

Method
Blend and pour into a flute glass
and serve.

DOG'S SPECIAL

30 mL (1 oz) Midori
30 mL (1 oz) pineapple juice
30 mL (1 oz) vodka
15 mL (1/2 oz) cream

Method
Float ingredients in order in a 4 oz
cocktail glass and serve.

DIZZY WHISTLE

15ml Frangelico
10ml pineapple juice
10ml Green Creme de Menthe
10ml cream

Method
Layer pineapple juice onto
Frangelico then shake Green Creme
de Menthe with cream and layer.

DOLOMINT

30ml Gilbey's Gin
30ml Galliano
25ml lime juice
top up with soda
fresh mint leaves

Method
Pour over ice and top up with soda.
Coat rim of glass with sprig of mint
and add 2 fresh mint leaves.

D

DOROTHY LAMOUR

30 mL (1 oz) Bacardi rum
3 slices mango
30 mL (1 oz) banana liqueur
1 scoop ice
15 mL (1/2 oz) lemon juice

Method
Blend and pour into a flute glass
and serve.

DOUBLE JEOPARDY

45 mL Frangelico
1 scoop vanilla ice cream
45 mL Opal Nera
milk

Method
Blend all ingredients except milk,
pour into a 10 oz highball glass.
Top with milk and serve with straws
and a Parfait Spoon.

DOUBLE BLAZER

*30 mL (1 oz) white crème de
menthe*
30 mL (1 oz) Southern Comfort

Method
Pour crème de menthe into a white
wine glass. Slowly add Southern
Comfort and ignite. Serve and
extinguish flame in front of
Customer.

DRAGON'S FIRE
SHOOTER

15 mL (1/2 oz) cherry advocaat
15 mL (1/2 oz) Galleon Liverno
15 mL (1/2 oz) orange curaçao
15 mL (1/2 oz) Southern Comfort
15 mL (1/2 oz) blue curaçao
15 mL (1/2 oz) advocaat

Method
Layer in order in a shot glass and
serve.

DOUBLE DATE

15ml Midori
15ml White Creme de Menthe
15ml DOM Benedictine

Method
Layer in order.

DRAMBUIE HIGH

30 mL (1 oz) Drambuie
20 mL coconut cream
30 mL (1 oz) Golden rum
30 mL (1 oz) pineapple juice
30 mL (1 oz) cream
1/2 banana
1 scoop crushed ice

Method
Blend until smooth, pour into a 10
oz highball glass. Garnish with
pineapple leaves and serve.

DUBONNET

60 mL (1 oz) Dubonnet
garnish:
1 twist lemon
60 mL (1 oz) gin

Method
Stir ingredients in a 3 oz cocktail
glass, garnish with lemon and serve.

DUNK

30 mL (1 oz) dry vermouth
5 mL curaçao
30 mL (1 oz) gin
garnish:
1 maraschino cherry
15 mL (1/2 oz) Galliano Liverno

Method
Stir and strain into a 3 oz cocktail
glass, garnish with cherry and
serve.

DUCHESS

45 mL dry vermouth
45 mL Pernod
45 mL sweet vermouth
garnish:
1 strip orange peel

Method
Stir and strain into a 5 oz cocktail
glass, garnish with orange peel
and serve.

DYEVTCHKA

30ml Smirnoff Vodka
30ml Cointreau
20ml fresh lime juice
20ml fresh lemon juice
15ml pineapple juice

Method
Shake with ice and pour. Garnish
with a pineapple wedge & cherry.
Comments: Open up to the
hidden secrets of the Eastern block
of Europe.

DUKE OF MARLBOROUGH

30ml Sherry
30ml Cinzano Rosso Vermouth
30ml lime juice
2 dashes raspberry cordial

Method
Shake and pour over ice.
Garnish with a red cherry and
a swizzle stick.

Banana Daiquiri

Death in the Afternoon

Depth Charge

Double Jeopardy

Fruit Tingle

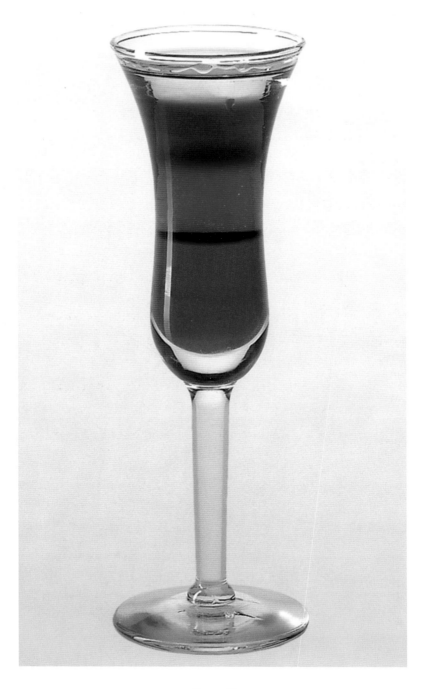

Face off

D

EL BURRO

15 mL (1/2 oz) Kahlúa
30 mL (1 oz) cream
15 mL (1/2 oz) rum
1/2 banana
30 mL (1 oz) coconut cream

Method
Blend ingredients with a Scoop and ice. Pour into a 9 oz cocktail glass. Garnish with a banana slice, mint leaves and serve.

ELDORADO

30 mL (1 oz) white rum
30 mL (1 oz) advocaat
30 mL (1 oz) crème de cacao
garnish:
1 tsp grated coconut

Method
Shake and strain into 4 oz cocktail glass and serve.

EL DIABLO

30ml Jose Cuervo Tequila
15ml Creme de Cassis
10ml lime juice
top up with ginger ale

Method
Build over ice and top up with ginger ale. Garnish with puréed lime.

ELECTRIC BANANA SHOOTER

15 mL (1/2 oz) banana liqueur
15 mL (1/2 oz) tequila
15 mL (1/2 oz) lime juice

Method
Layer in order in a shot glass and serve.

ELECTRIC BLUE

15 mL (1/2 oz) vodka
30 mL (1 oz) dry vermouth
15 mL (1/2 oz) blue curaçao
lemonade

Method
Pour vodka, vermouth and curaçao over ice in a 10 oz highball glass. Top with lemonade and serve.

EL REVOLTO SHOOTER

15 mL (1/2 oz) crème de menthe
15 mL (1/2 oz) Cointreau
15 mL (1/2 oz) Bailey's Irish cream

Method
Layer in order in a shot glass and serve.

EDITOR'S CURSE

30 mL (1 oz) Scotch whiskey
30 mL (1 oz) orange juice
30 mL (1 oz) Van der Hum

Method
Stir in 4 oz cocktail glass and serve.

EDWARD VIII

45 mL Canadian whiskey
2 tbsp water
1 dash Pernod
garnish:
1 strip orange peel
2 tbsp Italian vermouth
cracked ice

Method
Stir and strain into and Old
Fashioned glass and serve.

EGG SOUR

30 mL (1 oz) brandy
juice 1/4 lemon
30 mL (1 oz) white curaçao
1 tbsp castor sugar
1 egg
cracked ice

Method
Shake and strain into sour glass
and serve.

EGGNOG

30 mL (1 oz) brandy
1 egg
1 tbsp sugar
ice
milk
garnish:
nutmeg

Method
Shake brandy, egg and sugar with
ice and strain into an Old
Fashioned glass. Fill with milk,
sprinkle with nutmeg and serve.

EH-BOMB SHOOTER

10 mL crème de menthe
10 mL ouzo
10 mL Bailey's Irish cream
15 mL (1/2 oz) tequila

Method
Layer in order in a shot glass and
serve.

E

EARLY SUMMER

30 mL (1 oz) gin
30 mL (1 oz) orange juice
30 mL (1 oz) apricot brandy
garnish:
1 slice apple
30 mL (1 oz) Calvados
cracked ice

Method
Shake and strain into a 5 oz
cocktail glass, garnish with apple
slice and serve.

EARTHQUAKE

30 mL (1 oz) rye whiskey
30 mL (1 oz) gin 30 mL (1 oz)
Pernod
cracked ice

Method
Half fill shaker with ice and add
ingredients. Shake and strain into a
5 oz cocktail glass and serve.

EAST INDIA

40 mL white rum
1 tbsp pineapple juice
1 tbsp Cointreau
garnish:
1 maraschino cherry
1 dash Angostura bitters
cracked ice

Method
Shake ingredients and strain into a
3 oz cocktail glass. Garnish with
cherry and serve.

EAST WIND

25 mL vodka
2-3 dashes white rum
15 mL (1/2 oz) dry vermouth
cracked ice
15 mL (1/2 oz) sweet vermouth

Method
Shake and strain into a 3 oz
cocktail glass and serve.

EDGEMOORE

30 mL (1 oz) white rum
90 mL pineapple juice
30 mL (1 oz) dark rum
soda water
30 mL (1 oz) Irish mint
garnish:
2 maraschino Cherries

Method
Shake all ingredients except soda.
Pour into a 10 oz highball glass,
top with soda, garnish with
Cherries and serve.

ELECTRIC LEMONADE

30 mL (1 oz) triple sec
30 mL (1 oz) vodka
30 mL (1 oz) tequila
30 mL (1 oz) gin
30 mL (1 oz) white rum
lemonade

Method
Shake all ingredients except
lemonade and strain into a 10 oz
highball glass. Top with lemonade
and serve.

ELEPHANT WALK

30 mL (1 oz) gin
1 dash Angostura bitters
15 mL (1/2 oz) tequila
garnish:
1/2 orange slice
1 dash grenadine
1/2 lemon slice
15 mL (1/2 oz) orange juice
1 Stick Cucumber

Method
Fill an Old Fashioned glass with
cracked ice, add ingredients and
garnish with fruit and cucumber.
Add swizzle stick and serve.

EMERALD QUEEN

60 mL (1 oz) vodka
10 mL blue curaçao
40 mL dry vermouth
garnish:
1 maraschino cherry
20 mL Galliano Liverno
cracked ice

Method
Half fill mixing glass with cracked
ice, add ingredients and stir. Strain
into 5 oz champagne glass, garnish
with cherry and serve.

EMPIRE

25 mL gin
garnish:
2 maraschino Cherries
15 mL (1/2 oz) Calvados
cracked ice
15 mL (1/2 oz) apricot brandy

Method
Shake and strain into 3 oz cocktail
glass, garnish with Cherries and
serve.

E

ESME'S PERIL

190 mL Bacardi rum
60 mL (1 oz) lemon juice
30 mL (1 oz) dark rum
30 mL (1 oz) orange juice
2 tbsp banana liqueur
3 tbsp cream
1/2 banana
2 tsp sugar
4 strawberries
ice

Method
Blend all ingredients until smooth,
pour into a Tankard and serve.

EVERGREEN

15 mL (1/2 oz) dry vermouth
15 mL (1/2 oz) Midori
30 mL (1 oz) dry gin
7 mL blue curaçao

Method
Shake ingredients and strain into a
3 oz cocktail glass. Garnish with a
cherry and serve.

ETON BLAZER

25 mL gin
15 mL (1/2 oz) lemon juice
25 mL kirsch
soda water
2 tsp sugar syrup
garnish:
2 maraschino Cherries

Method
Place ingredients except soda and
Cherries in a 10 oz highball glass,
top with soda, garnish with cherries
and serve.

EXXON VALDESE SHOOTER

30 mL (1 oz) sambuca
30 mL (1 oz) Opal Nera

Method
Layer in shot glass an serve.

FACE-OFF SHOOTER

10 mL grenadine

10 mL parfait amour

15 mL (1/2 oz) crème de menthe

10 mL sambuca

Method
Layer in order in a shot glass and serve.

FALLEN ANGEL

30 mL (1 oz) gin

juice 1/2 lemon

2 dash crème de menthe

cracked ice

1 dash Angostura bitters

Method
Shake and strain into a 3 oz cocktail glass and serve.

FAIR LADY

60 mL (1 oz) gin

270 mL grapefruit juice

1 dash Cointreau

Powdered sugar

1 egg white

ice

Method
Rim two 5 oz cocktail glass with egg white and sugar. Shake remaining ingredients and strain into glasses and serve.

FERNET-BRANCA

45 mL Fernet Branca

45 mL Pernod

Method
Mix with ice in an Old Fashioned glass and serve.

FIGHTING BOB

60 mL (1 oz) gin

1 dash Angostura bitters

15 mL (1/2 oz) cherry brandy

1 tsp lemon juice

15 mL (1/2 oz) Chartreuse

soda water

Method
Shake ingredients except soda. pour into highball glass. Top with soda water and serve.

FALCON'S DELIGHT SHOOTER

30 mL (1 oz) sambuca

30 mL (1 oz) tequila

30 mL (1 oz) crème de cacao

Method
Layer in shot glass and serve.

E

FIRE AND ICE

20 mL tequila
10 mL crème de menthe

Method
Layer in shot glass and serve.

FIREMAN'S SOUR

80 mL white rum
garnish:
6 small lemon triangles
1 tsp grenadine
3 maraschino Cherries
15 mL (1/2 oz) lemon juice
3 ice cubes
soda water

Method
Shake ice, rum, lemon juice and
grenadine. Strain into a Tumble
glass and add lemon triangles. Top
with soda and serve.

FJORD

30ml Milne Brandy
10ml Aquavit
10ml orange juice
10ml lime juice
5ml Grenadine

Method
Shake over ice and strain then
add Grenadine. Garnish with an
orange slice.

FIZZ

Bacardi

60 mL (1 oz) Bacardi rum
soda water
60 mL (1 oz) lemon juice
cracked ice

Method
Shake all ingredients except soda
water and strain over ice in a 10 oz
highball glass. Top with soda water,
add straws and serve.

Banana

30 mL (1 oz) banana liqueur
1/2 banana
30 mL (1 oz) lemon juice
soda water
15 mL (1/2 oz) sugar syrup
ice
1 egg white

Method
Blend all ingredients except soda
water, pour into a 10 oz highball
glass. Top with soda water, add
straws and serve.

FLAME THROWER SHOOTER

20 mL crème de cacao
25 mL B & B

Method
Layer in shot glass and serve.

FLAMING DIAMOND SHOOTER

10 mL strawberry liqueur
10 mL Grand Marnier
10 mL vodka

Method
Layer in shot glass and serve.

FLAMING ORGY SHOOTER

10 mL grenadine
15 mL (1/2 oz) brandy
10 mL crème de menthe
10 mL tequila

Method
Layer in order in a shot glass and serve.

FLAMING SAMBUCA

30ml Romana Sambuca
3 coffee beans

Method
Pour Romana Sambuca, float coffee beans and light. Shoot after flame extinguished.

FLIRT WITH DIRT

30 mL (1 oz) Kahlúa
30 mL (1 oz) Malibu
15 mL (1/2 oz) Vandermint
1 float cream

Method
Shake Kahlúa, Vandermint and Malibu and strain into a 3 oz cocktail glass. Float cream and serve.

FLOWER

30 mL (1 oz) tequila
15 mL (1/2 oz) mango liqueur
15 mL (1/2 oz) white curaçao
75 mL orange juice

Method
Blend for two seconds, pour into a highball glass over ice and serve.

FLORIDA

30 mL (1 oz) Bacardi rum
soda water
1 tbsp crème de menthe
cracked ice
1 tbsp lime juice
1 sprig mint
1 tbsp pineapple juice

Method
Shake all ingredients except soda water, Strain over ice in a 10 oz highball glass. Top with soda water, garnish with mint, straws and serve.

FLUFFY DUCK

30 mL (1 oz) advocaat
15 mL (1/2 oz) gin
Galleon Liverno
lemonade

Method
Mix advocaat in a 10 oz highball glass with ice. Top with lemonade and float Galleon Liverno on top and serve.

F

FLUFFY DUCK (INTERNATIONAL)
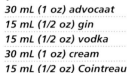

30 mL (1 oz) advocaat
15 mL (1/2 oz) gin
15 mL (1/2 oz) vodka
30 mL (1 oz) cream
15 mL (1/2 oz) Cointreau
lemonade

Method
Place all ingredients except lemonade
in a 10 oz highball glass and stir.
Top with lemonade and serve.

FLUFFY DUCK NO. 2

15 mL (1/2 oz) vodka
15 mL (1/2 oz) orange curaçao
30 mL (1 oz) advocaat
30 mL (1 oz) cream
lemonade

Method
Mix all ingredients except
lemonade in a 10 oz highball glass.
Top with lemonade and serve.

FLUFFY DUCK NO. 3

30 mL (1 oz) gin
30 mL (1 oz) orange juice
30 mL (1 oz) advocaat
soda water
15 mL (1/2 oz) Cointreau
ice

Method
Place all ingredients except soda in
a 10 oz highball glass and stir. Top
with soda and serve.

FLYING CARPET

30 mL (1 oz) vodka
15 mL (1/2 oz) banana liqueur
15 mL (1/2 oz) advocaat
30 mL (1 oz) cream

Method
Shake and strain into a 3 oz
cocktail glass and serve.

FLYING DUTCHMAN

10ml Cointreau
30ml Gilbey's Gin

Method
Coat glass with Cointreau then
pour Gilbey's Gin over ice. Garnish
with a lemon twist.

FLYING HIGH

30 mL (1 oz) Bailey's Irish cream
15 mL (1/2 oz) Drambuie
30 mL (1 oz) Cointreau
ice

Method
Shake and strain into a 3 oz
cocktail glass and serve.

FOG CUTTER

15ml Coruba Rum
10ml Milne Brandy
15ml Orgeat
25ml lemon juice
150ml orange juice

Method
Shake over ice and pour. Garnish with a strawberry.

FOREIGN AFFAIR

15 mL (1/2 oz) Cointreau
30 mL (1 oz) Rubis
30 mL (1 oz) vodka
orange juice

Method
Shake and strain ingredients into a 10 oz highball glass. Top with orange juice and serve.

FORTY WINKS

1 teaspoon honey
15ml Peach Liqueur
15ml Orange Curacao
4-5 drops Grenadine

Method
Pour Peach Liqueur onto honey, layer Orange Curacao, then drop Grenadine.

FORWARD PASS

30 mL (1 oz) vodka
30 mL (1 oz) Cointreau
30 mL (1 oz) dry vermouth
30 mL (1 oz) pure lemon juice

Method
Shake ingredients and strain into a 5 oz cocktail glass and serve.

FOURTH OF JULY

30 mL (1 oz) bourbon
orange juice
30 mL (1 oz) Kahlúa
cream
Galleon Liverno

Method
Place bourbon and Kahlúa in a 10 oz highball glass. Fill to 2.5 cm (1/2 inch) from top with orange juice and add cream. Float Galleon Liverno on top and serve.

401 SHOOTER

10 mL Kahlúa
5 mL Bailey's Irish cream
10 mL banana liqueur
5 mL Jack Daniel's

Method
Layer in order in a shot glass and serve.

F

FRAISE ANNÉE

30 mL (1 oz) strawberry liqueur
45 mL cream
30 mL (1 oz) white cream de cacao
garnish:
4 strawberries
15 mL (1/2 oz) brandy

Method
Blend ingredients and pour into a colada glass. Garnish with a strawberry and serve.

FRANGELICO LUAU

45ml Frangelico
200ml pineapple juice
dash of Grenadine

Method
Blend with ice and pour. Garnish with a pineapple slice and leaves.

FRAPPÉ

Byrrh

60 mL (1 oz) Byrrh
garnish:
1 twist lemon
cracked ice

Method
Fill 3 oz cocktail glass with ice and pour Byrrh over ice. Garnish with lemon and serve.

Crème de menthe

60 mL (1 oz) crème de menthe
garnish:
1 twist lemon
cracked ice

Method
Fill 3 oz cocktail glass with ice and pour crème de menthe over ice. Garnish with lemon and serve.

Grand Marnier

60 mL (1 oz) Grand Marnier
garnish:
grated chocolate
cracked ice

Method
Fill 3 oz cocktail glass with cracked ice and pour Grand Marnier over top. Garnish with grated chocolate and serve.

Midori & Cointreau

15 mL (1/2 oz) Midori
crushed ice
15 mL (1/2 oz) Cointreau

Method
Fill a 5 oz cocktail glass with crushed ice. Build ingredients over ice, garnish with cherry, 2 Short straws and serve.

Southern peach

30 mL (1 oz) strawberry liqueur
crushed ice
30 mL (1 oz) Southern Comfort

Method
Build ingredients over crushed ice in a 140 mL cocktail glass and serve.

FREDDY FUDPUCKER

60 mL (1 oz) tequila
garnish:
1 slice orange
Galliano
1 maraschino cherry
orange juice
ice

Method
Fill a 10 oz highball glass with ice, add tequila and fill 1/2 inch from top with orange juice. Float Galleon Liverno, garnish with orange slice and cherry and serve.

FRENCH

30 mL (1 oz) gin
1 tsp grenadine
20 mL Pernod
ice

Method
Shake and strain into 3 oz cocktail glass and serve.

FRENCH 69

15 mL (1/2 oz) gin
5 mL lemon juice
10 mL Pernod
5 mL sugar syrup
champagne

Method
Pour ingredients into champagne glass, top with champagne and serve.

FRENCH 75

45 mL gin
juice 1/2 lemon
90 mL champagne
1 tsp Powered sugar
cracked ice
garnish:
1 twist lemon peel

Method
Combine gin, sugar, lemon juice and ice in a mixing glass. Strain into a 10 oz highball glass and fill with champagne. Garnish with lemon peel and serve.

FRENCH 95

45 mL bourbon
juice 1/2 lemon
90 mL champagne
1 tsp Powdered sugar
cracked ice
garnish:
1 twist lemon peel

Method
Combine bourbon, sugar, lemon juice and ice in a mixing glass. Strain into a 10 oz highball glass and fill with champagne. Garnish with lemon peel and serve.

FRENCH CONNECTION

45 mL brandy
20 mL amaretto

Method
Shake and strain into an Old Fashioned glass and serve.

F

FRENCH FANTASY

30 mL (1 oz) vodka
30 mL (1 oz) crème de Grand Marnier
15 mL (1/2 oz) Tia Maria
30 mL (1 oz) orange juice
30 mL (1 oz) pineapple juice
garnish:
1 slice banana

Method
Blend and pour into a 5 oz cocktail glass, garnish with a slice of banana and a maraschino cherry and serve.

FRENCH GREENERY

30 mL (1 oz) Pernod
3 ice cubes
30 mL (1 oz) crème de menthe
garnish:
1 sprig mint

Method
Pour ingredients over ice in a Old Fashioned glass. Garnish with the sprig of mint and serve.

FRENCH KISS

30 mL (1 oz) gin
garnish:
1 maraschino cherry
30 mL (1 oz) dry vermouth
crushed ice
30 mL (1 oz) Dubonnet

Method
Stir in mixing glass. Pour into a 5 oz cocktail glass and serve.

FRENCH SAFARI

30 mL (1 oz) Rubis
15 mL (1/2 oz) Afrikoko
15 mL (1/2 oz) Cointreau
30 mL (1 oz) cream

Method
Shake and strain into a 3 oz cocktail glass and serve.

FRISCO SOUR

60ml Ballantine's Scotch Whisky
10ml lemon juice
10ml lime juice
10ml Grenadine
top up with soda

Method
Shake with ice and pour then top up with soda. Garnish with a lime slice.

FROTH AND BUBBLE

60 mL (1 oz) vodka
15 mL (1/2 oz) orange juice
15 mL (1/2 oz) blue curaçao
1/2 egg white
15 mL (1/2 oz) Galleon Liverno
garnish:
1 maraschino cherry

Method
Shake and strain into a 5 oz cocktail glass, garnish with cherry and serve.

FROZEN AQUAVIT

45ml Aquavit
10ml Kirsch
10ml lime juice
10ml sugar syrup
10ml egg white

Method
Blend over ice and pour. Garnish with one cocktail onion.

FROZEN LEANGO

30 mL (1 oz) gin
60 mL (1 oz) orange juice
30 mL (1 oz) banana liqueur
2 scoops ice
30 mL (1 oz) mango liqueur

Method
Blend and pour into a 12 oz tulip glass and serve with straws.

FROZEN MUDSLIDE

30ml Smirnoff Vodka
20ml Baileys Irish Cream
20ml Kahlúa
top up with milk
whipped cream
hundreds and thousands,
confectionary balls
thickened chocolate

Method
Blend with ice, pour into glass. Top up with milk then add whipped cream in a swirling motion. With a teaspoon slide the thickened chocolate (or Ice Magic), thereby creating a Mud Slide. Place strawberry on side of glass with hundreds and thousands.

FRUIT CUP

10ml Mango Liqueur
10ml passionfruit pulp
10ml guava juice

Method
Layer passionfruit pulp onto Mango Liqueur, then pour in order.

FRUIT PASSION

30 mL (1 oz) vodka
15 mL (1/2 oz) passionfruit pulp
30 mL (1 oz) rum
pineapple juice

Method
One third fill a 10 oz highball glass with cracked ice, add vodka, rum and passionfruit pulp. Stir and top with pineapple juice, garnish with a pineapple wedge, straws and serve.

F

FRUIT SALAD

I10ml Banana Liqueur
10ml Strawberry Liqueur
10ml Malibu

Method
Layer in order, then float vanilla
ice cream.

FRUIT SOUR

30 mL (1 oz) Scotch whiskey
garnish:
1 maraschino cherry
30 mL (1 oz) lemon juice
1 orange slice
30 mL (1 oz) fruit liqueur
cracked ice

Method
Shake and strain into a 5 oz
cocktail glass, garnish and serve.

FRUIT TINGLE

30 mL (1 oz) vodka
lemonade
15 mL (1/2 oz) parfait amour
1 dash grenadine
15 mL (1/2 oz) blue curaçao

Method
Build ingredients over ice in a
colada glass, top with lemonade,
add grenadine. Serve with straws.

FULL MOON

30 mL (1 oz) vodka
20 mL coconut cream
15 mL (1/2 oz) blue curaçao
cracked ice
20 mL cream
garnish:
Shaved chocolate

Method
Shake and strain into a 3 oz
cocktail glass, garnish with
chocolate and serve.

G.R.B.

30 mL (1 oz) Galleon Liverno

30 mL (1 oz) Bacardi rum

10 mL grenadine

garnish:

1 mint leaf

Method
Build over ice in a 3 oz cocktail
glass, garnish with mint leaf
floating on top and serve.

GALLIANO HOT SHOT

15 mL (1/2 oz) Galleon Liverno

5 mL cream (float)

25 mL hot black coffee

Method
Top Galliano with black coffee in
a 3 oz shot glass. Float cream
and serve.

GARDEN CITY

60 mL (1 oz) brandy

30 mL (1 oz) orange juice

30 mL (1 oz) sweet vermouth

garnish:

1 maraschino cherry

15 mL (1/2 oz) Pernod

ice

Method
Shake and strain into a 5 oz
cocktail glass, garnish with
cherry and serve.

GARIBALDI

45 mL Campari

ice

orange juice

Method
Half fill a 10 oz highball glass with
ice and build Campari. Top with
orange juice, add straws and serve.

GASLIGHT

30 mL (1 oz) Metaxa brandy

1 dash Galleon Liverno

15 mL (1/2 oz) apricot brandy

Method
Shake and strain into a 3 oz
cocktail glass and serve.

GEISHA

I30ml Jim Beam Bourbon

30ml Gekkeikan Sake

10ml lemon juice

10ml sugar syrup

Method
Shake over ice and strain. Garnish
with a red cherry.

G

GEISHA DELIGHT

30 mL (1 oz) Midori
5 mL coconut rum
15 mL (1/2 oz) Galliano
60 mL (1 oz) pineapple juice
15 mL (1/2 oz) Cointreau
garnish:
1 pineapple wedge

Method
Blend and pour into a 10 oz colada glass, garnish with pineapple wedge and serve.

GEORGIA PEACH

30ml Bacardi
30ml Peach Liqueur
90ml cranberry juice

Method
Build over ice and pour. Garnish with a peach slice.

GERMAN CHOCOLATE CAKE

30ml Kahlúa
30ml Malibu
30ml chocolate syrup
2 chopped pecan nuts
2 scoops vanilla ice cream

Method
Blend without ice and pour over crushed ice. Garnish with shredded pecans.

GET GOING

45 mL gin
30 mL (1 oz) Cola Tonic
30 mL (1 oz) lemon juice
1 dash sugar syrup
1 dash grenadine
lemonade

Method
Half fill a 10 oz highball glass with cracked ice. Add ingredients, top with lemonade, add straws and serve.

GHETTO BLASTER SHOOTER

10 mL Kahlúa
10 mL rye whiskey
25 mL tequila

Method
Layer in a shot glass and serve.

GIBSON DRY

20 mL gin
garnish:
1 Pickled Onion
20 mL French vermouth
cracked ice

Method
Stir ingredients and strain into a 3 oz cocktail glass. Garnish with Onion and serve.

GIBSON SWEET

20 mL gin
garnish:
1 Pickled Onion
20 mL sweet vermouth
cracked ice

Method
Stir ingredients and strain into a
3 oz cocktail glass. Garnish with
Onion and serve.

GIGOLO'S DELIGHT

30 mL (1 oz) gin
garnish:
2 strips orange peel
60 mL (1 oz) sweet vermouth

1 maraschino cherry
2 tbsp orange juice
cracked ice

Method
Shake and strain over ice in a rocks
glass. Garnish with orange peel,
cherry and serve.

GILROY

15 mL (1/2 oz) cherry brandy
10 mL lemon juice
15 mL (1/2 oz) gin
1 dash orange bitters
10 mL sweet vermouth
cracked ice

Method
Shake and strain into a 3 oz
cocktail glass and serve.

GIMLET

20 mL gin
garnish:
1 twist lemon
10 mL lime juice
cracked ice

Method
Shake and strain into a 3 oz
cocktail glass, garnish with twist of
lemon and serve.

GIN

45 mL gin
1 dash egg white
15 mL (1/2 oz) sugar syrup
soda water
15 mL (1/2 oz) lemon juice
cracked ice

Method
Half fill a 10 oz highball glass with
cracked ice, add gin, sugar syrup,
lemon juice and egg white. Top
with soda, add straws and serve.

GIN AND IT

30 mL (1 oz) sweet vermouth
ice
45 mL gin

Method
Shake and strain into a 5 oz
cocktail glass and serve.

G

GIN AND SIN

60 mL (1 oz) gin
soda water
30 mL (1 oz) lime juice
cracked ice

Method
Shake ingredients except soda water and strain into an Old Fashioned glass. Top with soda water and serve.

GIN COOLER

60 mL (1 oz) gin
ginger beer
60 mL (1 oz) lemon juice
cracked ice
1/2 tbsp sugar

Method
Shake ingredients except ginger beer and strain into a 10 oz highball glass. Top with ginger beer, add straws and serve.

GIN FIX

30 mL (1 oz) gin
30 mL (1 oz) lemon juice
30 mL (1 oz) Galleon Liverno
30 mL (1 oz) cold water
30 mL (1 oz) grenadine
Shaved ice

Method
Fill a 10 oz highball glass with Shaved ice, add ingredients and stir. Garnish with fruit and serve.

GIN SLING

60 mL (1 oz) gin
soda water
1 dash grenadine
cracked ice
30 mL (1 oz) lemon juice
garnish:
1 lemon slice

Method
Pour ingredients over ice in a 5 oz cocktail glass. Garnish with lemon slice and serve.

GIN SQUASH

30 mL (1 oz) gin
lemonade or soda water
15 mL (1/2 oz) lemon cordial
ice

Method
Half fill a 10 oz highball glass with ice. Add gin and almost top with lemonade or soda. Finally add cordial and stir. Serve with straws.

GIN TROPICAL

30 mL (1 oz) gin
soda water
30 mL (1 oz) passionfruit
1 maraschino cherry
15 mL (1/2 oz) blue curaçao
1 slice orange

Method
Shake ingredients except soda water, orange slice and cherry. Strain into a 10 oz highball glass, garnish with orange and cherry and serve.

GIN TWIST

30 mL (1 oz) gin
1 dash orange bitters
30 mL (1 oz) Dubonnet
garnish:
1 slice orange
10 mL Pernod
cracked ice

Method
Shake and strain into a 5 oz cocktail glass. Garnish with slice of orange and serve.

GIN WALL BANGER

30 mL (1 oz) gin
garnish:
1/2 slice orange
15 mL (1/2 oz) Galleon Liverno
cracked ice
180 mL orange juice

Method
Half fill a 10 oz highball glass with ice. Add ingredients and stir. Garnish with orange slice and serve.

GINGER SIN

30 mL (1 oz) gin
30 mL (1 oz) lime juice
ginger beer
cracked ice

Method
Stir ingredients and strain into a 10 oz highball glass. Top with ginger beer and serve.

GIRL TALK

45 mL While rum
1 dash Angostura bitters
15 mL (1/2 oz) sweet vermouth
15 mL (1/2 oz) orange juice
15 mL (1/2 oz) dry vermouth
garnish:
1 maraschino cherry
cracked ice

Method
Half fill mixing glass with cracked ice. Add ingredients and stir. Strain into a 5 oz cocktail glass. Garnish with cherry and serve.

GLOBE GLADNESS

30 mL (1 oz) Grand Marnier
1 dash Galleon Liverno
15 mL (1/2 oz) Schnapps
lemonade
15 mL (1/2 oz) Tia Maria

Method
Shake Grand Marnier, Tia Maria and Schnapps. Strain into a 10 oz highball glass. Top with lemonade. Float Galleon Liverno and serve.

GLASGOW

30ml Ballantine's Scotch Whisky
10ml lemon juice
5ml Cinzano Dry Vermouth
5ml almond extract

Method
Shake over ice and pour then add cubed ice. Garnish with shredded almonds and a dried flower.

G

GODDAUGHTER

30 mL (1 oz) sambuca
30 mL (1 oz) cream
30 mL (1 oz) amaretto
5 mL grenadine

Method
Shake ingredients and strain into a champagne saucer. Garnish with Flake chocolate, strawberry and a sprig of mint.

GODFATHER

45 mL Scotch whiskey
20 mL Galleon amaretto
ice

Method
Build into a 5 oz Old Fashioned glass filled with ice and serve.

GODMOTHER

45 mL vodka
ice
20 mL Galleon amaretto

Method
Build into a 5 oz Old Fashioned glass filled with ice and serve.

GOLD PASSION

30 mL (1 oz) Bacardi rum
chilled pineapple juice
30 mL (1 oz) vodka
30 mL (1 oz) passionfruit

Method
Pour ingredients over ice in a large Tumbler glass and top with pineapple juice. Garnish with a slice of pineapple, pineapple leaves, cherry and serve.

GOLDEN

60 mL (1 oz) Bacardi rum
1 egg yolk
1 tsp sugar
soda water
60 mL (1 oz) lemon juice
cracked ice

Method
Shake ingredients except soda water and strain over ice in a 10 oz highball glass. Top with soda water, add straws and serve.

GOLDEN CADILLAC NO. 1

30 mL (1 oz) Galleon Liverno
30 mL (1 oz) cream
30 mL (1 oz) white crème de menthe
cracked ice

Method
Shake and strain into a 3 oz cocktail glass and serve.

GOLDEN CADILLAC NO. 2

30 mL (1 oz) Galleon Liverno
30 mL (1 oz) cream
30 mL (1 oz) white crème de cacao
ice

Method
Shake and strain into a 5 oz cocktail glass and serve.

GOLDEN DRAGON

30 mL (1 oz) Galleon Liverno
15 mL (1/2 oz) white curaçao
20 mL cream
1 dash egg white

Method
Shake and strain into a 3 oz
cocktail and serve.

GOLDEN DREAM NO. 1

20 mL Galleon
15 mL (1/2 oz) orange juice
15 mL (1/2 oz) Cointreau
15 mL (1/2 oz) cream

Method
Shake and strain into a 3 oz
cocktail glass and serve.

GOLDEN DREAM NO. 2

30 mL (1 oz) brandy
15 mL (1/2 oz) lemon juice
30 mL (1 oz) Grand Marnier
60 mL (1 oz) orange juice

Method
Shake and strain into 5 oz cocktail
glass and serve.

GOLDEN DREAM NO. 3

15 mL (1/2 oz) Galliano Liverno
60 mL (1 oz) cream
15 mL (1/2 oz) Cointreau
ice
15 mL (1/2 oz) orange juice
garnish:
frosted strawberry
60 mL (1 oz) cream
chocolate Flakes

Method
Shake and strain into a 6 oz
tulip glass, garnish with frosted
strawberry, chocolate flakes
and serve.

GOLDEN FLEECE

30 mL (1 oz) advocaat
60 mL (1 oz) milk
20 mL Galleon Liverno
30 mL (1 oz) cream

Method
Shake and strain into a champagne
saucer and serve.

GOLDEN LOVER

30 mL (1 oz) Midori
75 mL milk
20 mL Galleon Liverno
30 mL (1 oz) cream

Method
Blend and pour into a 10 oz
highball glass and serve.

G

GOLDEN NEST

30 mL (1 oz) Galleon Liverno
45 mL orange juice
30 mL (1 oz) rum
garnish:
1 slice orange

Method
Shake and strain into a 5 oz
cocktail glass, garnish with orange
slice and serve.

GOLDEN ORCHID

30 mL (1 oz) Scotch whiskey
15 mL (1/2 oz) maraschino
30 mL (1 oz) advocaat
ice

Method
Shake and strain into a 5 oz
cocktail glass and serve.

GOLDEN SHOT

30 mL (1 oz) Scotch whiskey
90 mL orange juice
1 egg yolk
ice

Method
Blend and pour into a rocks glass
and serve.

GOLDEN SLIPPER

30ml Yellow Chartreuse
10ml Apricot Brandy
1 egg yolk

Method
Shake over ice and strain.

GONE TROPPO

45 mL peach liqueur
3 strawberries
35 mL banana liqueur
1 scoop ice
30 mL (1 oz) pineapple juice
garnish:
pineapple wedge
2 pineapple leaves

Method
Blend ingredients except pineapple
juice and pour into a 6 oz tulip
glass. Float pineapple juice on top.
Garnish with a pineapple wedge,
cherry and two pineapple leaves
and serve.

GOOD MORNING

20 mL rum
1 egg white
20 mL port
15 mL (1/2 oz) lemon juice
1 tsp sugar
3 ice cubes

Method
Shake and strain into a small
Tumbler glass and serve.

GORGEOUS GRACE

30 mL (1 oz) brandy
1 slice orange
15 mL (1/2 oz) Cointreau
cracked ice
champagne

Method
Stir all ingredients except
champagne. Strain into a
champagne saucer and top with
champagne. Garnish with orange
slice and serve.

GRAND BAILEY'S SHOOTER

20 mL Bailey's Irish cream
10 mL Grand Marnier

Method
Layer in a shot glass and serve.

GRAND SLAM SHOOTER

10 mL banana liqueur
10 mL Grand Marnier
10 mL Bailey's Irish cream

Method
Layer in order in a shot glass and
serve.

GRASSHOPPER

45 mL crème de menthe
60 mL (1 oz) cream
30 mL (1 oz) crème de cacao
cracked ice

Method
Shake and strain into a champagne
saucer and serve.

GRAVE DIGGER

40 mL dry vermouth
1 dash Angostura bitters
20 mL brandy
40 mL orange juice
20 mL Cointreau

Method
Shake and strain into a 5 oz
cocktail glass and serve.

GREAT WHITE NORTH SHOOTER

15 mL (1/2 oz) Kahlúa
15 mL (1/2 oz) ouzo
15 mL (1/2 oz) Bailey's Irish cream

Method
Layer in order in a shot glass and
serve.

G

GREEDY

45 mL Midori
2 scoops crushed ice
30 mL (1 oz) Framboise
1 tsp raspberry syrup
5 mL grenadine
30 mL (1 oz) lime juice

Method
Blend Midori, lime juice and one
scoop of ice until frozen and place
in a champagne saucer. Blend other
ingredients until semi frozen, add
to other mixture and serve.

GREEK BUCK

30ml Milne Brandy
10ml lemon juice
top up with ginger ale
10ml Aphrodite Ouzo

Method
Shake Brandy with lemon juice and
top up with ginger ale then float
Aphrodite Ouzo. Garnish with a
lemon slice.

GREEK GOD

15ml Aphrodite Ouzo
15ml Pernod

Method
Pour in order then shoot.

GREEN

15 mL (1/2 oz) crème de menthe
25 mL lemon juice
50 mL gin
1 egg white
10 mL sugar syrup
cracked ice
soda water

Method
Shake all ingredients except soda
water and strain over ice in a 10 oz
highball glass. Top with soda water,
add straws and serve.

GREEN BACK

30ml Beefeater Gin
10ml lime juice
10ml Green Creme de Menthe

Method
Stir over ice and pour. Garnish with
a lime slice (optional).

GREEN DEVIL

3 tbsp vodka
2 tbsp crushed ice
1 1/2 tbsp crème de menthe
garnish:
1 strip lemon peel
juice 1/2 lemon

Method
Mix and strain into a 3 oz cocktail
glass, garnish with lemon peel and
serve.

GREEN DRAGON

40 mL Midori
8 mL lemon juice
15 mL (1/2 oz) Galleon Liverno
30 mL (1 oz) cream

Method
Place Midori in a champagne saucer, shake Galleon Liverno and cream. Strain over Midori and serve.

GREEN EYES

30 mL (1 oz) Midori
15 coconut milk
30 mL (1 oz) Gold rum
15 mL (1/2 oz) lime juice
45 mL pineapple juice

Method
Blend ingredients and pour into a 10 oz colada glass. Garnish with pineapple wedge, straws and serve.

GREEN DRAGON NO. 2

45 mL vodka
cracked ice
45 mL crème de menthe

Method
Shake and strain into a small Goblet glass and serve.

GREEN HAT

30 mL (1 oz) gin
soda water
30 mL (1 oz) crème de menthe
cracked ice

Method
Half fill a large Tumbler glass with cracked ice, add gin and crème de menthe. Top with soda water, add straws and serve.

GREEN DRAGON NO. 3

30 mL (1 oz) light rum
30 mL (1 oz) vodka
30 mL (1 oz) Midori
lemonade

Method
Shake all ingredients except lemonade, strain over ice into a Goblet glass. Garnish with Watermelon wedge, cherry and serve.

GREEN LAND

30 mL (1 oz) Midori
Tonic water
30 mL (1 oz) white wine

Method
Build ingredients in a 10 ?/. highball glass over ice and serve.

G

GREEN PARADISE

45 mL Midori
15 mL (1/2 oz) orange juice
20 mL Cointreau
15 mL (1/2 oz) pineapple juice
10 mL lemon juice
1 scoop crushed ice
grenadine

Method
Blend all ingredients except
grenadine until frozen. Place a tbsp
grenadine in the bottom of a 5 oz
cocktail glass. Pour in frozen
ingredients and serve.

GREEN SEA

30 mL (1 oz) vodka
20 mL crème de menthe
20 mL dry vermouth
cracked ice

Method
Shake and strain into a small
Goblet glass and serve.

GREEN SILKS

30 mL (1 oz) Midori
60 mL (1 oz) cream
15 mL (1/2 oz) Grand Marnier
60 g Rockmelon
30 mL (1 oz) pineapple juice

Method
Blend with ice and pour into a 10
oz colada glass. Garnish with
pineapple leaves, straws and serve.

GREEN SLAMMER

45 mL vodka
30 mL (1 oz) Midori
15 mL (1/2 oz) Galleon Liverno
30 mL (1 oz) lemon juice

Method
Shake and strain into an Old
Fashioned glass and serve.

GREEN SOLDIERS

30 mL (1 oz) lemon juice
1 egg white
15 mL (1/2 oz) lemon juice
cracked ice

Method
Shake and strain into a 3 oz
cocktail glass, garnish with a lemon
wheel and serve.

GREEN WITH ENVY

30 mL (1 oz) ouzo
120 mL pineapple juice
15 mL (1/2 oz) blue curaçao
garnish:
1 maraschino cherry

Method
Shake and strain into a 10 oz
highball glass, garnish with cherry,
straws and serve.

GREENHORN

60 mL (1 oz) crème de menthe
soda water
20 mL lemon juice
cracked ice

Method
Shake all ingredients except soda
water over ice into a 10 oz highball
glass. Top with soda water, add
straws and serve.

GREENPEACE SORBET

30 mL (1 oz) Cointreau
1 kiwifruit (peeled)
60 mL (1 oz) Riesling
2 scoops crushed ice

Method
Blend until smooth and pour into a
5 oz cocktail glass and serve.

GRINGO

30 mL (1 oz) tequila
30 mL (1 oz) vodka
30 mL (1 oz) Midori
10 mL lemon juice

Method
Shake and strain into a 5 oz
cocktail glass and serve.

GYPSY

30 mL (1 oz) vodka
1 dash Angostura bitters
15 mL (1/2 oz) Benedictine
cracked ice
garnish: 1 strip lemon peel

Method
Shake and strain into a 3 oz
cocktail glass, garnish with lemon
peel and serve.

GYPSY KING

7ml lime cordial
10ml Parfait Amour
10ml Green Creme de Menthe
10ml Yellow Chartreuse

Method
Pour in order, then layer Yellow
Chartreuse.

Frappé

Fluffy Duck

Fluffy Duck No.2

Grasshopper

G.R.B.

Green with Envy

G

HAIR OF THE DOG

60 mL (1 oz) Scotch whiskey
30 mL (1 oz) honey
60 mL (1 oz) cream
ice

Method
Fill an Old Fashioned glass with ice, shake other ingredients and strain over ice and serve.

HAIRLESS DUCK

30 mL (1 oz) advocaat
15 mL (1/2 oz) Bacardi rum
30 mL (1 oz) vodka
orange juice

Method
Shake advocaat, vodka and rum together and strain over ice in a 10 oz highball glass. Top with orange juice, add straws and serve.

HALF NELSON

10ml Green Creme de Menthe
10ml Strawberry Liqueur
10ml Grand Marnier

Method
Layer in order then shoot.

HALO

30 mL (1 oz) sambuca
lemonade
30 mL (1 oz) gin

Method
Place sambuca and gin in a 5 oz Tumbler. Slowly top with lemonade and serve.

HARBOUR LIGHTS

15 mL (1/2 oz) Kahlúa
15 mL (1/2 oz) green Chartreuse
15 mL (1/2 oz) sambuca

Method
Layer in order in a 45 mL cordial glass, add a Straw and serve.

HARBOUR MIST

30 mL (1 oz) banana liqueur
15 mL (1/2 oz) blue curaçao
20 mL Grand Marnier
30 mL (1 oz) cream

Method
Shake and strain into a 5 oz cocktail glass and serve.

HARD ON

30 mL (1 oz) Bailey's Irish cream
30 mL (1 oz) Kahlúa
30 mL (1 oz) banana liqueur

Method
Float ingredients in a 3 oz cocktail glass and serve.

HARD ON (TROPICAL)

30 mL (1 oz) Kahlúa
30 mL (1 oz) mango liqueur
30 mL (1 oz) Bailey's Irish cream

Method
Layer ingredients in a 3 oz cocktail glass and serve.

HARD ON (BLACK)

30 mL (1 oz) Opal Nera
30 mL (1 oz) banana liqueur
30 mL (1 oz) Bailey's Irish cream

Method
Layer ingredients in a 3 oz cocktail glass and serve.

HARLEQUIN

30 mL (1 oz) cognac
ice
15 mL (1/2 oz) Grand Marnier

Method
frost a 5 oz cocktail glass with harlequin frosting. coffee and sugar. Stir and strain liquid ingredients into glass and serve.

HARD ON (BLOODY)

30 mL (1 oz) Kahlúa
30 mL (1 oz) strawberry liqueur
30 mL (1 oz) Bailey's Irish cream

Method
Layer ingredients in a 3 oz cocktail glass and serve.

HARVEY COWPUNCHER

45 mL Galleon Liverno
cracked ice
120 mL milk

Method
Half fill a 10 oz highball glass with cracked ice. Pour Galleon Liverno over ice and top with milk.

H

HARVEY WALLBANGER

30 mL (1 oz) vodka
garnish:
1 maraschino cherry
30 mL (1 oz) Galleon Liverno
1 slice orange
orange juice

Method
Place Galleon Liverno and vodka over ice in a 10 oz highball glass. Top with orange juice, garnish with cherry, orange slice , straws and serve.

HARVEY WALLBANGER NO. 2

40 mL vodka
2 tsp Galleon Liverno
60 mL (1 oz) orange juice
ice

Method
Build vodka and orange juice over ice in a 6 oz Old Fashioned glass. Float Galleon Liverno over top and serve.

HARVEY WALLBANGER NO. 3

30 mL (1 oz) vodka
orange juice
15 mL (1/2 oz) Galleon Liverno
ice

Method
Three-quarters fill a 10 oz highball glass with ice. Pour in vodka and top with orange juice and stir. Float Galliano Liverno on top, add straws and serve.

HAVANA CLUB

40 mL Bacardi rum
garnish:
1 maraschino cherry
20 mL sweet vermouth
cracked ice

Method
Shake and strain into a 3 oz cocktail glass and serve.

HAWAIIAN HONEYMOON

45 mL Bacardi rum
1 dash grenadine
60 mL (1 oz) orange juice
garnish:
1 maraschino cherry
30 mL (1 oz) pineapple juice
1 pineapple wedge
1 dash lemon juice
1 orange slice
Pernod (float)

Method
Mix liquid ingredients except Pernod. Pour into a 5 oz cocktail glass. Float Pernod, garnish with fruit and serve.

HAWAIIAN PUNCH

20ml Southern Comfort
20ml Amaretto di Galliano
15ml Smirnoff Vodka
40ml pineapple juice
40ml orange juice
20ml lime juice
20ml Grenadine

Method
Shake over ice and pour then add
Grenadine. Garnish with lime
squeeze, lemon squeeze, orange
slice and a red cherry.

HAZY CUBAN

30 mL (1 oz) Bacardi rum
30 mL (1 oz) coconut cream
30 mL (1 oz) milk
60 mL (1 oz) pineapple juice
garnish: 1 slice pineapple

Method
Blend and pour into an Old
Fashioned glass and serve.

HEAD STUD

30 mL (1 oz) Galleon Liverno
30 mL (1 oz) Afrikoko
60 mL (1 oz) cream

Method
Layer in a 5 oz cocktail glass
and serve.

HEARTBREAKER

30 mL (1 oz) strawberry liqueur
60 mL (1 oz) cream
15 mL (1/2 oz) Tia Maria
4 strawberries
15 mL (1/2 oz) Cointreau

Method
Blend until smooth and pour into a
8 oz colada glass and serve.

HEAVENLY CLOUD

45 mL Kahlúa
60 mL (1 oz) cream
45 mL Rubis
1/2 banana
4 strawberries

Method
Blend until smooth, pour into a
champagne saucer and serve.

HELEN'S HANGOVER

30 mL (1 oz) advocaat
pineapple juice
30 mL (1 oz) Galleon Liverno

Method
Pour advocaat and Galleon Liverno
over ice in a 10 oz highball glass.
Top with orange juice, add straws
and serve.

H

HELL RAISER SHOOTER

30 mL (1 oz) Midori
30 mL (1 oz) strawberry liqueur
30 mL (1 oz) sambuca

Method
Layer in a 3 oz shot glass and serve.

HEMMINGWAY

40 mL Cointreau
40 mL grapefruit juice
40 mL Bacardi rum
cracked ice
Sparkling white wine

Method
Shake all ingredients except white wine, strain into a 5 oz champagne saucer. Top with white wine and serve.

HIGHBALL BACARDI

30 mL (1 oz) Bacardi rum
soda water
30 mL (1 oz) Cointreau
3 ice cubes
1 tsp lemon juice

Method
Shake ingredients except soda water. Pour into a 10 oz highball glass and top with soda water. Serve with straws.

Bourbon

60 mL (1 oz) bourbon
soda water
2 dashes Angostura bitters
ice
1 dash lemon juice

Method
Place ingredients except soda water in a 10 oz highball glass, stir rapidly and top with soda water and serve.

Brandy

30 mL (1 oz) brandy
2 dash Angostura bitters
1 tsp sugar syrup
soda water
1 tsp lemon juice
3 ice cubes

Method
Shake ingredients except soda water, pour into a 10 oz highball glass, top with soda water and serve.

Crystal

20 mL sweet vermouth
soda water
1 tsp sugar syrup
1 spiral orange juice
20 mL Bianco vermouth
2 ice cubes

Method
Place all ingredients in a 10 oz highball glass and stir. Top with soda water and serve.

Ginger

30 mL (1 oz) Scotch whiskey
dry ginger ale
1 strip lemon peel
ice

Method
Place ingredients in a 10 oz highball glass and stir. Top with dry ginger ale and serve.

Island

15 mL (1/2 oz) brandy
1 dash orange bitters
15 mL (1/2 oz) sweet vermouth
soda water
2 ice cubes

Method
Place ingredients in a 10 oz highball glass, top with soda and serve.

Saki

90 mL saki
soda water
1/4 lemon, squeezed
garnish:
1 slice lemon
1 tsp castor sugar
ice

Method
Stir ingredients except soda water and lemon slice. Pour into a 10 oz highball glass, top with soda water, garnish with lemon slice and serve.

Whiskey

30 mL (1 oz) rye whiskey
dry ginger ale
3 drops Angostura bitters
ice

Method
Half fill a 10 oz highball glass with ice. Add whiskey and Angostura bitters, top with ginger ale and serve.

HIGHLAND FLING

30 mL (1 oz) Scotch whiskey
30 mL (1 oz) orange juice
30 mL (1 oz) Kahlúa
30 mL (1 oz) cream

Method
Blend until smooth, pour over ice in a 10 oz highball glass. Add straws and serve.

HITLER'S GRENADE

15 mL (1/2 oz) crème de cacao
15 mL (1/2 oz) vodka
15 mL (1/2 oz) advocaat
15 mL (1/2 oz) B & B
15 mL (1/2 oz) tequila
15 mL (1/2 oz) sambuca
15 mL (1/2 oz) gin
Coca-Cola

Method
Shake ingredients except Coca-Cola. Pour over ice in a 10 oz highball glass. Top with Coca-Cola, add straws and serve.

H

HOLLYWOOD NIGHTS

30 mL (1 oz) vodka

soda water

15 mL (1/2 oz) peach liqueur

Midori (float)

30 mL (1 oz) pineapple juice

Method

Three-quarters fill a 10 oz highball glass with ice, add vodka, peach liqueur and pineapple juice. Top with soda water, float Midori, add straws and serve.

HOME MAID

15 mL (1/2 oz) Bailey's Irish cream

30 mL (1 oz) cream

30 mL (1 oz) banana liqueur

90 mL milk

Method

Shake and strain into a champagne saucer and serve.

HONEY BEE

30 mL (1 oz) brandy

15 mL (1/2 oz) honey

15 mL (1/2 oz) Galliano Liverno

60 mL (1 oz) cream

15 mL (1/2 oz) grenadine

cracked ice

Method

Shake and strain into a 5 oz cocktail glass and serve.

HONEY FLOW

30 mL (1 oz) white rum

45 mL cream

15 mL (1/2 oz) Galliano Liverno

garnish:

1 maraschino cherry

15 mL (1/2 oz) honey

cracked ice

Method

Shake and strain into a champagne saucer, garnish with cherry and serve.

HONEYED NUTS

30 mL (1 oz) Frangelico

30 mL (1 oz) honey

15 mL (1/2 oz) Kahlúa

120 mL cream

15 mL (1/2 oz) advocaat

ice

Method

Blend ingredients and pour into a brandy Balloon rimmed with crushed Hazelnuts and honey and serve.

HONEY TEA

1 orange spice tea bag

30ml Drambuie

top up with hot water

Method

Pour in order then top up with hot water. Garnish with a lemon twist.

HONEYMOON

30 mL (1 oz) Benedictine
1/2 orange, squeezed
30 mL (1 oz) Calvados
cracked ice

Method
Shake and strain into a 3 oz
cocktail glass and serve.

HONEYMOON PARADISE

30 mL (1 oz) blue curaçao
25 mL lemon juice
15 mL (1/2 oz) Cointreau
1 scoop ice cream
champagne

Method
Blend all ingredients except
champagne until frozen. Pour into
a champagne saucer, top with
champagne and serve.

HORANGI

45 mL vodka
30 mL (1 oz) passionfruit juice
30 mL (1 oz) advocaat
cracked ice

Method
Shake and strain into a champagne
saucer and serve.

HORNY BULL SHOOTER

10 mL vodka
10 mL tequila
10 mL rum

Method
Layer in a shot glass and serve.

HORSE GUARDS

20 mL rum
1 egg yolk
20 mL Cointreau
garnish:
1 spiral lemon peel
Sparkling white wine
3 ice cubes

Method
Shake ingredients except wine and
lemon peel. Strain into Tumbler
glass, top with wine and garnish
with lemon peel and serve.

HORSE'S NECK

30 mL (1 oz) brandy
ginger ale
4 drops Angostura bitters
ice

Method
Hang a lemon spiral in a 10 oz
highball glass. Fill the glass with ice
and build brandy and bitters. Top
with ginger ale and serve.

HOT BUTTERED RUM

30 mL (1 oz) dark rum

1 tsp sugar

1 tbsp Butter

boiling water

1 pinch nutmeg

Method
Mix ingredients in a mixing glass.
Strain into a 10 oz highball glass
and top with tomato juice serve
with straws.

HOT DANISH CIDER

180ml apple cider, heated

15ml Orgeat

Method
Build. Garnish with a cinnamon
stick.

HOT MILK PUNCH

30ml Bacardi

30ml Milne Brandy

sugar to taste

top up with hot milk

Method
Build and top up with hot milk.
Garnish with sprinkle of cinnamon
stick.

HOT TODDIES

45 mL any Spirit

garnish:

slice lemon

1 tsp sugar

sprinkle cinnamon

2 cloves

boiling water

Method
Mix ingredients in a 10 oz Tankard,
fill with boiling water poured over
a spoon. Garnish with lemon and
cinnamon and serve.

HURRICANE

30 mL (1 oz) Bacardi rum

30 mL (1 oz) passoa

15 mL (1/2 oz) lemon cordial

45 mL lemon juice

45 mL sugar syrup

15 mL (1/2 oz) Bacardi Gold(float)

Method
Shake ingredients and pour into a
Hurricane glass. Garnish with slice
of orange and a cherry, float
Bacardi Gold and serve.

HURRICANE GREG SHOOTER

20 mL Opal Nera
20 mL cherry advocaat 20 mL blue curaçao
20 mL advocaat

Method
Layer in Test tube or shot glass and serve.

HUSH HONEY

30 mL (1 oz) gin
30 mL (1 oz) fresh cream
15 mL (1/2 oz) Galliano Liverno
15 mL (1/2 oz) honey
garnish: 1 maraschino cherry
ice

Method
Shake and strain into a champagne glass. Place cherry on lip of glass and serve.

I LOVE YOU

30 mL (1 oz) Kahlúa
30 mL (1 oz) Galliano Liverno
30 mL (1 oz) Bailey's Irish cream

Method
Float ingredients in a 3 oz cocktail glass and serve.

ICE KACHANG

30ml Smirnoff Vodka
15ml Peach Liqueur
30ml cranberry juice
30ml orange juice
top up with lemonade
diced fruit pieces

Method
Mix ingredients and pour over crushed ice. Serve with two straws and a long spoon.
Comments: Known as a dessert delight from the old Portuguese trading port of Malacca, East Malaysia, this cocktail will add another dimension to how you can consume alcohol.

ICE WINGS

75 mL vodka
ice
30 mL (1 oz) white crème de menthe

Method
Shake and strain into a 3 oz cocktail glass and serve.

ICHIGO

30 mL (1 oz) strawberry liqueur
20 mL pineapple juice
15 mL (1/2 oz) Galliano Liverno
20 mL orange juice

Method
Shake and strain into a cocktail glass and serve.

H

ILLUSION

45 mL vodka
90 mL lemon juice
15 mL (1/2 oz) Cointreau
splash lime cordial

Method
Shake and strain into a 5 oz
cocktail glass and serve.

INDEPENDENCE

30 mL (1 oz) bourbon
1 tbsp lemon juice
1 tbsp brandy
1 sprig mint
60 mL (1 oz) orange juice

Method
Shake ingredients and strain into a
4 oz cocktail glass, garnish with
sprig of mint and serve.

INDEPENDENCE DAY PUNCH

30ml Jim Beam Bourbon
100ml pineapple juice
20ml lime juice
15ml lime juice
top up with soda

Method
Stir over ice and pour then top up
with soda. Garnish with a
pineapple slice and American
'Independence Day' Flag.

INDO SHINER

1 teaspoon of sugar
120ml pineapple juice
30ml lemon juice
15ml lime juice
1 dash Angostura Bitters
5ml blue vegetable colouring

Method
Blend over ice and pour. Garnish
with a lemon and lime slice.

INKAHLÚARABLE

10ml Kahlúa
10ml Cointreau
10ml Grand Marnier

Method
Layer in order then shoot.

INK STREET

30 mL (1 oz) Scotch whiskey
30 mL (1 oz) lemon juice
30 mL (1 oz) orange juice
cracked ice

Method
Shake and strain into a champagne
glass, garnish with a twist of
orange peel and serve.

INSPIRATION

45 mL Frangelico
60 mL (1 oz) pineapple juice
15 mL (1/2 oz) banana liqueur
30 mL (1 oz) cream

Method
Shake and strain into a 150 mL
cocktail glass. Garnish with a
strawberry and mint leaf on rim
and serve.

INTERNATIONAL

20 mL brandy
garnish:
1 lemon wedge
20 mL green Chartreuse
3 ice cubes
15 mL (1/2 oz) pineapple juice

Method
Shake and strain into a 3 oz
cocktail glass and serve.

INTIMATE

20 mL vodka
garnish:
1 black olive
20 mL apricot brandy
1 twist lemon peel
20 mL dry vermouth
ice
2 dashes orange bitters

Method
Mix liquid ingredients and strain
into a 3 oz cocktail glass. Garnish
with olive, lemon peel and serve.

IRISH BANANA

30 mL (1 oz) Bailey's Irish cream
50 mL cream
30 mL (1 oz) banana liqueur
1/2 banana
15 mL (1/2 oz) advocaat
ice

Method
Blend until smooth, pour into a
5 oz champagne saucer and serve.

IRISH CHEER

30 mL (1 oz) Midori
30 mL (1 oz) lime juice
45 mL dry gin
garnish:
1 maraschino cherry

Method
Shake and strain into a 5 oz
cocktail glass, garnish with cherry
and serve.

IRISH COFFEE

30 mL (1 oz) Irish whiskey
sugar (to taste)
hot coffee
cream (lightly wrapped)

Method
Mix whiskey and sugar in an Irish
coffee Mug. Pour in hot coffee,
top with cream and serve.

IRISH EYES

45 mL Irish whiskey
60 mL (1 oz) fresh cream
60 mL (1 oz) crème de menthe
garnish:
1 maraschino cherry

Method
Shake and strain into a 5 oz champagne glass. Garnish with cherry and serve.

IRISH FLAG

15 mL (1/2 oz) crème de menthe
15 mL (1/2 oz) brandy
15 mL (1/2 oz) Bailey's Irish cream

Method
Layer in order in a 2 oz port glass and serve.

IRISH MONKEY SHOOTER

20 mL banana liqueur
25 mL Bailey's Irish cream

Method
Layer in a shot glass and serve.

IRON LADY

15 mL (1/2 oz) Malibu
45 mL cream
20 mL Rubis
5 mL vanilla Essence
15 mL (1/2 oz) white crème de cacao
1 Scoop ice cream

Method
Blend until smooth, pour into a 4 oz cocktail glass serve.

ISLAND COOLER

15 mL (1/2 oz) vodka
2 scoops crushed ice
30 mL (1 oz) orange juice
2 drops grenadine
30 mL (1 oz) Midori
1/4 kiwifruit
8 mL lemon juice

Method
Blend vodka, orange juice and ice until frozen and place in a 5 oz champagne saucer, add grenadine. Blend Midori, kiwifruit and lemon juice and add to glass, serve.

ISLAND OF CAPRI

30 mL (1 oz) Bailey's Irish cream
30 mL (1 oz) cream
30 mL (1 oz) Galleon Liverno

Method
Float ingredients in a 3 oz cocktail glass and serve.

ITALIAN STALLION

30 mL (1 oz) Galleon Liverno
50 mL cream
30 mL (1 oz) sambuca

Method
Shake and strain into a champagne saucer and serve.

J.F. KENNEDY

30 mL (1 oz) red crème de menthe
light beer
30 mL (1 oz) vodka

Method
Place crème de menthe and vodka
in a Middy glass and stir. Top with
light beer and serve.

JACK IN THE BOX

60 mL (1 oz) brandy
1 dash Angostura bitters
60 mL (1 oz) pineapple juice
ice

Method
Shake an strain into a 5 oz cocktail
glass and serve.

JACK ROSE

45 mL brandy
1/2 lemon, squeezed
1 tsp grenadine

Method
Shake and strain into a 3 oz
cocktail glass and serve.

JANE'S TOUCH SHOOTER

10 mL Kahlúa
10 mL Bailey's Irish cream
10 mL Frangelico

Method
Layer in order in a shot glass
and serve.

JAPANESE EGGNOG

45 mL Cointreau
90 mL milk
45 mL Midori
1 dash egg white

Method
Shake and strain into an Old
Fashioned glass and serve.

JAPANESE SLIPPER

30 mL (1 oz) Cointreau
30 mL (1 oz) Midori
30 mL (1 oz) Margimix

Method
Float ingredients in a 3 oz cocktail
glass and serve.

JAPANESE SLIPPER NO. 2

30 mL (1 oz) Midori
30 mL (1 oz) lemon juice
30 mL (1 oz) Cointreau
ice

Method
Shake and strain into a 3 oz
cocktail glass and serve.

JAPANESE SUNRISE

30 mL (1 oz) Midori
30 mL (1 oz) lemon juice
10 mL Galleon Liverno
garnish:
3-4 strawberries
10 mL orange curaçao

Method
Blend and pour into a 5 oz cocktail
glass, garnish with a slice of
rockmelon, 1/2 strawberry and serve.

J

JAPANESE TRAFFIC LIGHTS

30 mL (1 oz) Midori
30 mL (1 oz) Rubis
30 mL (1 oz) banana liqueur

Method
Float ingredients in a 3 oz cocktail glass and serve.

JAW BREAKER

30 mL (1 oz) Kahlúa
30 mL (1 oz) sambuca
30 mL (1 oz) banana liqueur

Method
Float ingredients over ice in a 4 oz cocktail glass and serve.

JEALOUS JUNE

30 mL (1 oz) Midori
15 mL (1/2 oz) Cointreau
20 mL white rum
90 mL pineapple juice

Method
Shake and strain into a highball glass and serve.

JELLYBEAN

30 mL (1 oz) ouzo
lemonade
15 mL (1/2 oz) raspberry cordial
ice

Method
Place ouzo and cordial in a 5 oz cocktail glass with ice and stir. Top with lemonade and serve.

JELLYBEAN (GARBO'S)

45 mL ouzo
1 dash grenadine
15 mL (1/2 oz) gin
lemonade
15 mL (1/2 oz) vodka
ice

Method
Place ice in a 10 oz highball glass, add ingredients. Top with lemonade and serve.

JELLYBEAN NO. 2

30 mL (1 oz) vodka
1 splash grenadine
30 mL (1 oz) Pernod
lemonade

Method
Pour ingredients over ice in a 10 oz highball glass, top with lemonade and serve.

JELLYFISH SHOOTER

30 mL (1 oz) Bailey's Irish cream
15 mL (1/2 oz) amaretto
30 mL (1 oz) vodka
1 dash grenadine

Method
Layer amaretto, vodka and Bailey's in a Test Tube or shot glass, add grenadine and serve.

JEUNE HOMME

30 mL (1 oz) dry vermouth

15 mL (1/2 oz) Benedictine

15 mL (1/2 oz) gin

1 dash Angostura bitters

15 mL (1/2 oz) Cointreau

3 ice Cubes

Method
Shake ingredients and strain into
a 3 oz cocktail glass and serve.

JOGGERS

30 mL (1 oz) Benedictine

1 spiral lemon peel

45 mL cognac

soda water

15 mL (1/2 oz) lemon juice

Method
Half fill a 10 oz highball glass with
ice, drop in lemon peel and add
lemon juice. Top with soda water
and serve with straws.

JOHN COLLINS

30 mL (1 oz) gin

1 tsp sugar

1 lemon, squeezed

1 slice lemon

1 dash Angostura bitters

ice

soda water

Method
Place all ingredients except soda
water and lemon in a 10 oz
highball glass and stir until sugar
is dissolved. Add soda water,
garnish with lemon slice and straws
and serve.

JUNGER STERN

30 mL (1 oz) Midori

4 pineapple pieces

15 mL (1/2 oz) banana liqueur

pulp 1/2 passionfruit

3 pureed strawberries

Scoop crushed ice

Method
Pour pureed strawberries down the
side of a 10 oz highball glass. Blend
other ingredients and carefully add
to the glass. Garnish with a cherry
and pineapple leaves and serve.

JUNGLE JUICE

45 mL white rum

30 mL (1 oz) pineapple juice

45 mL Drambuie

30 mL (1 oz) cream

45 mL coconut cream

1/2 banana

Method
Blend until smooth, place in a
champagne glass and serve.

J

K.G.B.

30 mL (1 oz) Bailey's Irish cream
30 mL (1 oz) Kahlúa
30 mL (1 oz) Grand Marnier

Method
Layer in a 3 oz cocktail glass and
serve.

KAHLÚA CREAM

30 mL (1 oz) vodka
15 mL (1/2 oz) cream
15 mL (1/2 oz) Kahlúa
ice

Method
Shake and strain into a 3 oz
cocktail glass and serve.

KAHLÚA JAFFA

15 mL (1/2 oz) Kahlúa
15 mL (1/2 oz) orange juice
15 mL (1/2 oz) Scotch whiskey
30 mL (1 oz) cream

Method
Shake and strain into a champagne
saucer, top with mixture of cream
and Grand Marnier and serve.

KAKURI

30 mL (1 oz) Pimm's no. 1 cup
5 mL lemon juice
15 mL (1/2 oz) mango liqueur
ice
15 mL (1/2 oz) Bianco vermouth

Method
Shake and strain into a 3 oz
cocktail glass and serve.

KAMIKAZE

30 mL (1 oz) vodka
15 mL (1/2 oz) lemon juice
30 mL (1 oz) tequila
1 slice lime juice

Method
Mix ingredients and strain into a
champagne saucer. Garnish with
slice of lime and serve.

KANGAROO

60 mL (1 oz) brandy
1 egg
30 mL (1 oz) Galliano Liverno
ice

Method
Shake and strain into a champagne
saucer and serve.

KATANGA

45 mL vodka
garnish:
1 sprig mint
30 mL (1 oz) apricot brandy
ice
2 tsp lime juice

Method
Shake and strain into a 3 oz
cocktail glass, garnish with mint
and serve.

KEEP GOING

30 mL (1 oz) white rum
15 mL (1/2 oz) grapefruit juice
15 mL (1/2 oz) anisette liqueur
lemonade
30 mL (1 oz) Cola Tonic
1/2 slice lemon
15 mL (1/2 oz) lime juice
cracked ice

Method
Half fill a 10 oz highball glass with
cracked ice, shake ingredients and
strain into glass. Garnish with slice
of lemon, straws and serve.

KELLY'S COMFORT

30 mL (1 oz) Southern Comfort
15 mL (1/2 oz) sugar syrup
30 mL (1 oz) Bailey's Irish cream
4 strawberries (1 FOR GARNISH)
60 mL (1 oz) milk
crushed ice

Method
Blend until smooth, pour into a
10 oz highball glass, garnish with
strawberry, straws and serve.

KEY WEST COOLER

15ml Smirnoff Vodka
15ml Peach Liqueur
15ml Midori
15ml Malibu
100ml cranberry juice
100ml orange juice

Method
Stir over ice and pour. Garnish with
an orange slice.

KICK IN THE BALLS

30 mL (1 oz) rum
30 mL (1 oz) orange juice
30 mL (1 oz) Midori
30 mL (1 oz) cream
15 mL (1/2 oz) coconut cream
garnish:
2 melon Balls

Method
Shake and strain into a champagne
saucer, garnish with melon Balls
marinated in rum and serve.

KIM'S KLANGER

30 mL (1 oz) gin
1/4 lemon, squeezed
1 dash Coca-Cola
ice

Method
Mix and strain into a 3 oz cocktail
glass and serve.

K

KING ALFONSO

30 mL (1 oz) Kahlúa
ice
whipped cream

Method
Fill a 6 oz cocktail glass with
cracked ice, build Kahlúa over ice.
Top with whipped cream and serve.

KINGS CROSS NUT

60 mL (1 oz) brandy
garnish:
nutmeg
30 mL (1 oz) Tia Maria
3 ice cubes
1 coconut

Method
Remove the top from the coconut
and remove milk. Place half the milk,
brandy and Tia Maria in a shaker.
Shake, pour into coconut, dust with
nutmeg and serve with straws.

KIR

15 mL (1/2 oz) crème de cassis
dry white wine

Method
Place crème de cassis in a flute glass,
top with white wine and serve.

KIR IMPERIAL

15 mL (1/2 oz) crème de Framboise
chilled champagne

Method
Place crème de Framboise in a flute
glass, top with champagne and serve.

KIR ROYALE

15 mL (1/2 oz) crème de Cassis
Sparkling white wine

Method
Place crème de cassis in a flute glass,
top with Sparkling wine and serve.

KISS MY ASTEROID

30 mL (1 oz) Midori
pineapple juice
30 mL (1 oz) blue curaçao
crushed ice
15 mL (1/2 oz) Cointreau

Method
Build Midori, Cointreau and
pineapple juice in a 13 oz
Hurricane glass. Add blue curaçao
to one large scoop crushed ice and
float it on top of the pineapple
juice, add straws and serve.

KIWI

30 mL (1 oz) Bacardi rum
1 dash sugar
30 mL (1 oz) Midori
ice
15 mL (1/2 oz) Cointreau
1 kiwifruit
45 mL lemon juice

Method
Blend and pour into a 10 oz
highball glass, add straws
and serve.

KLONDYKE

40 mL Calvados
garnish:
1 olive
15 mL (1/2 oz) dry vermouth

1 strip lemon peel
1 dash Angostura bitters
ice

Method
Mix ingredients and strain into a 3 oz cocktail glass. Garnish with olive, lemon peel and serve.

KNEE BREAKER

30 mL (1 oz) Cointreau
15 mL (1/2 oz) Peter Heering
30 mL (1 oz) parfait amour
1 dash Frangelico

Method
Shake and strain into a 3 oz cocktail glass and serve.

KNOCKOUT

30 mL (1 oz) Scotch whiskey
1 egg yolk
2 tsp sugar syrup
cracked ice
Sparkling white wine

Method
Shake all ingredients except wine and strain into a flute glass. Top with wine and serve.

KOTUKA (THE FLYER)

30 mL (1 oz) vodka
1 dash lime juice
15 mL (1/2 oz) Benedictine
garnish:
1 maraschino cherry
3 drops grenadine
cracked ice

Method
Shake and strain into a 5 oz cocktail glass, garnish with cherry and serve.

KRAZY KAT SHOOTER

30 mL (1 oz) Malibu
30 mL (1 oz) Kahlúa
30 mL (1 oz) banana liqueur

Method
Layer in a shot glass and serve.

KU KLUX KLANGER

30 mL (1 oz) white rum
30 mL (1 oz) vodka
30 mL (1 oz) Southern Comfort
lemonade

Method
Pour ingredients over crushed ice in a 5 oz cocktail glass and serve

L

L.I.I.T

15 mL (1/2 oz) gin
15 mL (1/2 oz) Bacardi rum
15 mL (1/2 oz) vodka
15 mL (1/2 oz) tequila
15 mL (1/2 oz) Margimix
Coca-Cola (top up)

Method
Place ingredients into a 10 oz
highball glass with two ice cubes.

LADY BROWN

40 mL gin
20 mL orange juice
20 mL Grand Marnier
garnish:
2 orange Segments
15 mL (1/2 oz) lemon juice
cracked ice

Method
Shake and strain into a 5 oz
cocktail glass. Garnish with orange
Segments and serve.

LADY IN RED

30 mL (1 oz) vodka
10 mL lemon juice
30 mL (1 oz) Rubis
1 dash egg white
10 mL grenadine
4 strawberries

Method
Blend and pour into a champagne
saucer and serve.

LADY KILLER SHOOTER

15 mL (1/2 oz) Kahlúa
5 mL Frangelico
10 mL Midori

Method
Layer in a shot glass and serve.

LADY LEON

30 mL (1 oz) gin
30 mL (1 oz) Galleon Liverno
30 mL (1 oz) dry vermouth
garnish:
1 twist lemon peel
30 mL (1 oz) orange curaçao
cracked ice

Method
Shake and strain into a champagne
saucer, garnish with lemon peel
and serve.

LADY LION

20 mL Kahlúa
15 mL (1/2 oz) brandy
20 mL Bailey's Irish cream
60 mL (1 oz) cream

Method
Shake and strain into a champagne
saucer and serve.

LADY LOO

60 mL (1 oz) vodka

30 mL (1 oz) Galleon Liverno

30 mL (1 oz) sweet vermouth

garnish:

1 maraschino cherry

30 mL (1 oz) dry vermouth

cracked ice

Method

Shake and strain into a champagne saucer, garnish with cherry and serve.

LADY LOVE

30 mL (1 oz) vodka

30 mL (1 oz) Galleon Liverno

30 mL (1 oz) dry vermouth

garnish:

1 twist orange peel

30 mL (1 oz) orange curaçao

cracked ice

Method

Shake and strain into a champagne glass, garnish with orange peel and serve.

LADY LYNNE

45 mL gin

10 mL lime juice

30 mL (1 oz) parfait amour

ice

1 dash egg white

garnish:

1 strawberry

Method

Shake and strain into a 3 oz cocktail glass. Garnish with strawberry and serve.

LADY M

45 mL Frangelico

2 scoops vanilla ice cream

45 mL Midori

garnish:

grated chocolate

Method

Blend for twenty seconds and pour into a 10 oz Hurricane glass. Garnish with a sprinkle of grated chocolate and serve.

LADY'S PLEASURE

60 mL (1 oz) vodka

1 dash egg white

30 mL (1 oz) Galliano Liverno

cracked ice

Method

Shake and strain into a champagne glass and serve.

LADY THROAT KILLER

20ml Kahlúa

15ml Midori

10ml Frangelico

Method

Layer in order then shoot. Comments: This superb mixture offers an exquisite after-taste.

LAMBORGHINI

30 mL (1 oz) Kahlúa
15 mL (1/2 oz) cream
30 mL (1 oz) sambuca
nutmeg

Method
Layer the Kahlúa and sambuca in a 3 oz Martini glass and ignite with a match. Sprinkle a small amount of nutmeg over flame to produce sparks. After a few seconds, spoon the cream over the top.

LAMBORGHINI (INTERNATIONAL)

15 mL (1/2 oz) Galliano Liverno
30 mL (1 oz) Kahlúa
20 mL sambuca
15 mL (1/2 oz) cream

Method
Float ingredients in a port glass and serve.

LAMBORGHINI NO. 2

20 mL Kahlúa
20 mL sambuca
20 mL Cointreau
20 mL cream

Method
Layer Kahlúa, Cointreau and sambuca in a 5 oz cocktail glass and ignite with a match. Pour cream over the top to extinguish the flame.

LAMBORGHINI NO. 3

15 mL (1/2 oz) Galliano Liverno
30 mL (1 oz) Kahlúa 15 mL (1/2 oz) green Chartreuse
15 mL (1/2 oz) cream

Method
Float ingredients in a port glass and serve.

LAMBORGHINI NO. 4

30 mL (1 oz) sambuca
30 mL (1 oz) Bailey's Irish cream
15 mL (1/2 oz) cream

Method
Layer sambuca and Bailey's in a port glass, ignite with a match. Sprinkle a small amount of nutmeg over the flame to produce sparks. Pour cream over the top and serve.

LANDSLIDER SHOOTER

10 mL amaretto
10 mL Grand Mariner
10 mL Bailey's Irish cream

Method
Layer in order in a shot glass and serve.

LASER BEAM SHOOTER

25 mL Galliano Liverno
20 mL tequila

Method
Layer in shot glass and serve.

LAST EMPEROR

30 mL (1 oz) Canadian whiskey
30 mL (1 oz) Bianco vermouth
15 mL (1/2 oz) Grand Mariner
30 mL (1 oz) orange juice
1 dash Angostura bitters
garnish:
1 strip orange peel

Method
Place ingredients in a 5 oz
cocktail glass. Add strip of orange
peel and serve.

LAST STRAW

30 mL (1 oz) Bailey's Irish cream
30 mL (1 oz) Cointreau
15 mL (1/2 oz) Rubis
30 mL (1 oz) cream
6 strawberries (2 FOR GARNISH)

Method
Shake ingredients except
strawberries and strain into a 5 oz
cocktail glass. Garnish with
strawberries and serve.

LE PARIS

15 mL (1/2 oz) Cointreau
8 mL Campari
40 mL Bacardi rum
20 mL lemon juice
30 mL (1 oz) Rubis
5 strawberries

Method
Blend until smooth and pour into a
champagne saucer and serve.

LEATHER AND LACE SHOOTER

10 mL Kahlúa
10 mL Bailey's Irish cream
10 mL vodka

Method
Layer in order in a shot glass
and serve.

LENA

60 mL (1 oz) bourbon
15 mL (1/2 oz) Campari
30 mL (1 oz) sweet vermouth
15 mL (1/2 oz) Galleon Liverno
15 mL (1/2 oz) dry vermouth
garnish:
1 maraschino cherry

Method
Stir ingredients and strain into a
5 oz cocktail glass. Garnish with
cherry and serve.

L

LEONARDO DE MANGO

30 mL (1 oz) Midori
70 mL apple juice
15 mL (1/2 oz) Bailey's Irish cream
30 g mango
30 mL (1 oz) mango liqueur

Method
Blend and Pour into a colada glass
and serve.

LEPRECHAUN DANCER

60 mL (1 oz) Irish whiskey
soda water
60 mL (1 oz) lemon juice
garnish:
lemon peel
dry ginger ale
ice

Method
Place whiskey, lemon juice and ice
in a 10 oz highball glass. Top with
equal parts of soda water and dry
ginger ale. Place lemon peel in top
of glass and serve with straws.

LICK SIP SUCK

30ml Jose Cuervo Tequila
lemon in quarters or slices
salt

Method
Pour Tequila into glass. On the flat
piece of skin between the base of
your thumb and index finger, place
a pinch of salt. Place a quarter of
the lemon by you on the bar. Lick
the salt off your hand, shoot the
Tequila and then suck the lemon in
quick succession.

LIEUTENANT

15 mL (1/2 oz) apricot brandy
1 tsp sugar
30 mL (1 oz) bourbon
15 mL (1/2 oz) grapefruit juice
3 ice Cubes
garnish:
1 maraschino cherry

Method
Shake and strain into a 3 oz
cocktail glass. Garnish with cherry
and serve.

LEVIATHAN

60 mL (1 oz) brandy
30 mL (1 oz) orange juice
30 mL (1 oz) sweet vermouth
ice

Method
Shake and strain into a 3 oz
cocktail glass and serve.

LIGHT FINGERS

60 mL (1 oz) white rum
cracked ice
30 mL (1 oz) parfait amour
1 dash grenadine (add last)
30 mL (1 oz) anisette liqueur

Method
Pour ingredients over half a mixing
glass of cracked ice. Stir gently and
strain into a 5 oz cocktail glass.
Add dash grenadine and serve.

LIME SPIDER

45ml lime milk shake syrup
1 tablespoon of sugar
1 small scoop vanilla ice cream
top up with lemonade

Method
Pour over ice and top up with
lemonade. Garnish with a banana
slice and whipped cream. Serve
with spoons and straws.

LIGHTHOUSE SHOOTER

15 mL (1/2 oz) Kahlúa
15 mL (1/2 oz) tequila
15 mL (1/2 oz) Grand Marnier

Method
Layer in order in a shot glass
and serve.

LIGHTS OF HAVANA

60ml soda water
40ml Malibu
25ml Midori
60ml orange juice
60ml pineapple juice

Method
Shake over ice and pour. Garnish
with a straw and a lime wheel.

LION D'OR

30 mL (1 oz) gin
cracked ice
60 mL (1 oz) Grand Marnier
garnish:
1 strip orange peel
30 mL (1 oz) orange juice

Method
Shake and strain into a 5 oz
cocktail glass, garnish with orange
peel and serve.

LONDON FOG

10ml White Creme de Menthe
5ml Anisette
2 dashes of Angostura Bitters

Method
Stir over ice and strain. Garnish
with a mint sprig.

L

LONE STAR SHOOTER

15 mL (1/2 oz) cherry brandy
5 mL Bacardi rum
l0 mL parfait amour

Method
Layer in order in a shot glass and
serve.

LONG BAY BREAKOUT SHOOTER

15 mL (1/2 oz) strawberry liqueur
10 mL Opal Nera
l0 mL Midori
10 mL gin

Method
Layer ingredients in a 2 oz shot
glass and serve.

LONG GREEN

40 mL Midori
soda water
20 mL lemon juice
garnish:
1 lemon wheel
soda water
1 maraschino cherry

Method
Build ingredients over ice in a 10 oz
highball glass. Garnish with lemon
wheel, cherry and serve.

LONG ISLAND ICED TEA

15 mL (1/2 oz) tequila
15 mL (1/2 oz) Cointreau
15 mL (1/2 oz) Bacardi rum
30 mL (1 oz) lemon juice
15 mL (1/2 oz) vodka
Coca-Cola (top up)
15 mL (1/2 oz) gin
cracked ice

Method
Pour ingredients over ice in a 10 oz
highball glass. Top with Cocoa Cola
and serve with straws

LONG NECK

45 mL vodka
1 dash grenadine (LAST)
30 mL (1 oz) Midori
1 scoop crushed ice
30 mL (1 oz) lemon juice

Method
Blend until frozen, place in an Old
Fashioned glass. Add grenadine
and serve.

LONG SLOE COMFORTABLE SCREW UP AGAINST THE WALL

30 mL (1 oz) vodka
orange juice (top up)
15 mL (1/2 oz) Southern Comfort
ice
15 mL (1/2 oz) sloe gin
garnish:
1 orange wheel
15 mL (1/2 oz) Galliano Liverno

Method
Build ingredients over ice in a 10 oz highball glass. Top with orange juice, garnish with orange wheel, straws and serve.

LOUISIANA LULLABY

30ml Coruba Rum
10ml Dubonnet
5ml Grand Marnier

Method
Shake over ice and strain. Garnish with a twist of lemon.

LOVE BITE

I10ml Cherry Brandy
10ml Parfait Amour
10ml cream

Method
Layer in order.

LOVE DORI

30 mL (1 oz) Midori
60 mL (1 oz) cream
20 mL vodka
nutmeg GARNISH)
15 mL (1/2 oz) Galliano Liverno (float)

Method
Shake Midori, vodka and cream, strain into a champagne saucer. Float Galliano Liverno, sprinkle with nutmeg and serve.

LOVE POTION NUMBER 9

60 mL (1 oz) Bacardi rum
1/2 egg white
30 mL (1 oz) Cointreau
garnish:
1 maraschino cherry
15 mL (1/2 oz) lemon juice
cracked ice

Method
Shake and strain into a champagne saucer, garnish with cherry and serve.

LOVER

60 mL (1 oz) Scotch whiskey
cracked ice
30 mL (1 oz) Campari
garnish:
1 twist orange peel
30 mL (1 oz) Bianco vermouth

Method
Shake and strain into a champagne saucer, garnish with orange peel and serve.

Harvey Wallbanger

Kir

Lady M

Lamborgini

Long Island Ice Tea

Jellybean

L

LOVING EYES

30 mL (1 oz) Bailey's Irish cream
60 mL (1 oz) cream
30 mL (1 oz) Cointreau
garnish:
nutmeg
15 mL (1/2 oz) Galliano Liverno
(float)

Method
Shake and strain into a champagne
saucer, Ignite and sprinkle with
nutmeg. Serve while flaming.

LOW FLYER

20 mL Kahlúa
1/2 banana
20 mL Malibu
30 mL (1 oz) cream
20 mL banana liqueur

Method
Blend until smooth and pour into a
champagne saucer and serve.

LUCKY DIP

60 mL (1 oz) vodka
1/2 egg white
30 mL (1 oz) crème de banana
cracked ice
30 mL (1 oz) lemon Squash

Method
Shake and strain into a champagne
saucer and serve.

LUCY'S LAMENT

30 mL (1 oz) brandy
30 mL (1 oz) cream
30 mL (1 oz) Tia Maria
cracked ice
15 mL (1/2 oz) Cointreau
3 maraschino Cherries GARNISH)

Method
Shake and strain into a flute glass,
drop Cherries in and serve.

LUPY'S LUNCHTIME PICK-ME-UP

45 mL brandy
150 mL chilled milk
15 mL (1/2 oz) white curaçao
1 egg

Method
Blend and pour into a 10 oz
highball glass and serve with
straws.

LYNCHBURG LEMONADE

20ml Jack Daniel's
20ml Cointreau
20ml fresh lime juice
top up with lemonade or soda

Method
Pour in order then top up with
lemonade or soda. Garnish with
twisted lemon rind.

M

MACAULEY

30 mL (1 oz) brandy
1 orange wedge
60 mL (1 oz) curaçao
cracked ice
30 mL (1 oz) dry vermouth

Method
Shake and strain into a 10 oz
highball glass over ice and serve.

MACHINE GUN KELLY

45 mL Scotch whiskey
1 dash orange bitters
30 mL (1 oz) sweet vermouth
cracked ice
30 mL (1 oz) dry vermouth
garnish:
1 twist lemon peel

Method
Shake and strain into a champagne
saucer, garnish with lemon peel
and serve.

MACLEAY STREET

30 mL (1 oz) bourbon
1 dash grenadine
15 mL (1/2 oz) Galliano Liverno
orange juice (top up)

Method
Shake and strain into a 10 oz
highball glass, top with orange
juice, stir and serve.

MADAM BUTTERFLY

30 mL (1 oz) passoa
30 mL (1 oz) cream
15 mL (1/2 oz) Midori
15 mL (1/2 oz) Midori
*15 mL (1/2 oz) white crème de
cacao*
30 mL (1 oz) pineapple juice

Method
Shake passoa, 15 mL (1/2 oz)
Midori, white crème de cacao,
pineapple juice and pour into a
margarita glass. Shake cream and
15 mL (1/2 oz) Midori, layer over
top and serve.

MADRAS

30ml Smirnoff Vodka
80ml cranberry juice
30ml orange juice

Method
Build over ice then top up float
orange juice. Garnish with an
orange slice.

MAGNOLIA BLOSSOM

30 mL (1 oz) bourbon
2 tsp cream
2 tsp lemon juice
cracked ice
2 dashes grenadine

Method
Shake and strain into a 3 oz
cocktail glass and serve.

M

MAI TAI

20 mL dark rum

20 mL lime juice

20 mL white rum

crushed ice

20 mL Cointreau

garnish:

1 pineapple wedge

10 mL orange syrup

2 maraschino Cherries

10 mL grenadine

Method
Fill a 10 oz highball glass with crushed ice and build ingredients. Garnish with pineapple wedge, Cherries, straws and serve.

MAI TAI NO. 2

15 mL (1/2 oz) white rum

15 mL (1/2 oz) pineapple juice

15 mL (1/2 oz) Golden rum

15 mL (1/2 oz) orange juice

15 mL (1/2 oz) tequila

5 mL grenadine

15 mL (1/2 oz) triple sec

cracked ice

15 mL (1/2 oz) apricot brandy

garnish:

1 pineapple wedge

15 mL (1/2 oz) lemon juice

2 maraschino Cherries

Method
Blend all ingredients except grenadine and pour into a brandy Balloon. Add grenadine, garnish with pineapple wedge, Cherries, straws and serve.

MAIDEN'S BLUSH

60 mL (1 oz) gin

ice

30 mL (1 oz) grenadine

Method
Shake and strain into a 3 oz cocktail glass and serve.

MAIDEN'S BLUSH NO. 2

60 mL (1 oz) vodka

30 mL (1 oz) lemon juice

15 mL (1/2 oz) Galliano Liverno

garnish:

1 maraschino cherry

1/2 eggwhite

cracked ice

30 mL (1 oz) grenadine

Method
Shake and strain into a 5 oz cocktail glass and serve.

MALIBU MAGIC

30 mL (1 oz) Malibu

5 strawberries

30 mL (1 oz) strawberry liqueur

60 mL (1 oz) cream

30 mL (1 oz) orange juice

garnish:

1 twist orange peel

Method
Blend and pour into a 10 oz Hurricane glass, garnish with 1 strawberry, orange peel, straws and serve.

MALIBU STING

25 mL Malibu
30 mL (1 oz) lemonade
25 mL gin
garnish:
1 strawberry, slit
25 mL blue curaçao
crushed ice
60 mL (1 oz) pineapple juice

Method
Shake all ingredients except lemonade and pour into a flute glass. Add lemonade, garnish with strawberry on lip of glass and serve.

MAMA ROSA

30ml Romana Sambuca
30ml Cherry Advocaat
top up with soda water

Method
Build over ice then top up with soda. Garnish with a maraschino cherry and pineapple leaves.

MANDARIN SLING

20ml Kahlúa
20ml Dark Creme de Cacao
10ml chocolate syrup
2 scoops orange sherbert
1/2 a mandarin

Method
Blend without ice. Garnish with a mandarin or orange slice.

MANGO

60 mL (1 oz) mango liqueur
1 dash sugar syrup
15 mL (1/2 oz) lemon juice
soda water
30 g mango

Method
Blend ail ingredients except soda water and pour into a 10 oz highball glass. Top with soda water, add straws and serve.

MANGO COLADA

30 mL (1 oz) white rum
30 mL (1 oz) cream
30 mL (1 oz) coconut cream
2 slices mango
30 mL (1 oz) mango liqueur
1 scoop crushed ice
90 mL pineapple juice

Method
Blend and pour into a 13 oz tulip glass and serve.

MANGO DELICIOUS

30 mL (1 oz) Bacardi rum
80 mL pineapple juice
30 mL (1 oz) mango liqueur
1/2 mango
30 mL (1 oz) coconut cream
1 small scoop crushed ice
30 mL (1 oz) cream

Method
Blend and pour into a white wine glass and serve.

M

MANGO LANTIS

30 mL (1 oz) mango liqueur
1 dash grenadine (LAST)
45 mL orange juice
1 scoop crushed ice
5 mL lemon juice

Method
Blend until frozen and scoop into a 5 oz cocktail glass. Add grenadine and serve.

MANGO TANGO

20 mL mango liqueur
30 mL (1 oz) orange juice
15 mL (1/2 oz) rum
30 mL (1 oz) cream
15 mL (1/2 oz) white crème de cacao

Method
Shake and strain into a 5 oz cocktail glass and serve.

MANGOTISM

30 mL (1 oz) mango liqueur
60 mL (1 oz) cream
25 mL Frangelico
20 mL advocaat

Method
Blend and pour into a 10 oz highball glass, add straws and serve.

MANHATTAN BRANDY

90 mL brandy
cracked ice
30 mL (1 oz) sweet vermouth
garnish:
1 maraschino cherry
1 dash Angostura bitters

Method
Place ingredients in a mixing glass and stir gently. Strain into a 5 oz cocktail glass, garnish with cherry and serve.

MANHATTAN DRY

45 mL rye whiskey
1 dash Angostura bitters
20 mL dry vermouth
cracked ice

Method
Stir gently in a mixing glass and strain into a 3 oz cocktail glass and serve.

MANHATTAN SWEET

45 mL rye whiskey
20 mL sweet vermouth
cracked ice

Method
Stir gently in a mixing glass and strain into a 3 oz cocktail glass and serve.

MAPLES

45 mL gin
60 mL (1 oz) pineapple juice
20 mL white crème de cacao
cracked ice
1 dash cream

Method
Shake and strain into an Old
Fashioned glass and serve.

MARCONI

30 mL (1 oz) sweet vermouth
cracked ice
60 mL (1 oz) Pernod

Method
Shake and strain into a 3 oz
cocktail glass and serve.

MARDI GRAS

20 mL Cointreau
30 mL (1 oz) banana liqueur
20 mL Tia Maria
cracked ice

Method
Shake and strain into a 3 oz
cocktail glass and serve.

MARGARET'S MADNESS SHOOTER

20 mL Tia Maria
20 mL cherry advocaat
20 mL blue curaçao
20 mL advocaat

Method
Layer in shot glass and serve.

MARGARITA

45 mL tequila
1 dash egg white
30 mL (1 oz) Cointreau
1 slice lime
30 mL (1 oz) lime juice
cracked ice

Method
Rim the lip of a margarita glass
with salt. Shake liquid ingredients
and strain into glass. Garnish with
slice of lime and serve.

MARTIN LUTHER KING

30 mL (1 oz) vodka
Coca-Cola
30 mL (1 oz) gin
cracked ice

Method
Shake all ingredients except Coca-
Cola. Strain into a 10 oz highball
glass over ice. Top with Cocoa Cola
and serve.

M

MARTINI (DRY)

60 mL (1 oz) dry gin
ice
30 mL (1 oz) dry vermouth
garnish:
1 green olive

Method
Shake or stir and strain into a 5 oz cocktail glass and serve with olive in glass.

MARTINI (EXTRA DRY)

120 mL dry gin
ice
1 dash dry vermouth
garnish:
1 green olive

Method
Shake or stir and strain into a 5 oz cocktail glass and serve.

MARTINI (SWEET)

60 mL (1 oz) gin
garnish:
1 maraschino cherry
30 mL (1 oz) sweet vermouth
ice

Method
Mix and strain into a 3 oz cocktail glass with cherry and serve.

MARY QUEEN OF SCOTS

30 mL (1 oz) Scotch whiskey
garnish:
1 maraschino cherry
15 mL (1/2 oz) Drambuie
1 tbsp castor sugar
15 mL (1/2 oz) green Chartreuse
3 ice cubes
15 mL (1/2 oz) lemon juice

Method
Dip the rim of a 3 oz cocktail glass in lemon juice then in sugar. Shake Scotch whiskey, Drambuie and Chartreuse with ice and strain into rimmed glass. Garnish with cherry and serve.

MEDITERRANEAN

60ml water
60ml plain yoghurt
10ml dried mint
pinch of salt

Method
Blend with ice. Garnish with mint leaves.

MELON BALL

30 mL (1 oz) Midori
30 mL (1 oz) strawberry liqueur
30 mL (1 oz) banana liqueur
1 strawberry

Method
Float liquid ingredients in a 3 oz cocktail glass, place strawberry on lip of glass and serve.

MELON ROCK

60 mL (1 oz) Midori
60 g honeydew melon
30 mL (1 oz) lemon juice
garnish:
1 slice honeydew melon
10 mL sugar syrup

Method
Blend and pour into a colada
glass, garnish with melon and
straws and serve.

MELON TREE

30 mL (1 oz) Midori
120 mL milk
30 mL (1 oz) peach tree
1 dash cream
20 mL Galliano Liverno
1 scoop ice cream

Method
Blend and pour into a 10 oz
highball glass and serve with
straws.

MÉNAGE À TROIS

30ml Pernod
30ml Malibu
60ml pineapple juice
15ml coconut cream
1 scoop orange sherbert
1 scoop vanilla ice cream

Method
Blend with ice. Garnish with
a plastic swizzle stick with three
straws.

MERRY WIDOW

60 mL (1 oz) cherry brandy
garnish:
1 maraschino cherry
60 mL (1 oz) maraschino liqueur
cracked ice

Method
Shake and strain into a 5 oz
cocktail glass, garnish with cherry
on lip of glass and serve.

METROPOLIS

30 mL (1 oz) Midori
30 mL (1 oz) Bailey's Irish cream

Method
Fill an Old Fashioned glass
with cracked ice, build ingredients
and serve.

MEXICAN BERRY SHOOTER

10 mL Kahlúa
l0 mL tequila
10 mL strawberry liqueur

Method
Layer in order in a shot glass
and serve.

M

MEXICAN FLAG SHOOTER

15 mL (1/2 oz) grenadine
15 mL (1/2 oz) tequila
15 mL (1/2 oz) crème de menthe

Method
Layer in order in a shot glass
and serve.

MEXICAN PUMPER SHOOTER

15 mL (1/2 oz) grenadine
15 mL (1/2 oz) tequila
15 mL (1/2 oz) Kahlúa

Method
Layer in order in a shot glass and
serve.

MEXICAN MADNESS

30 mL (1 oz) tequila
1/2 banana
30 mL (1 oz) Bailey's Irish cream
60 mL (1 oz) pineapple juice
15 mL (1/2 oz) Malibu
crushed ice

Method
Blend until smooth and pour into a
Fancy glass and serve.

MEXICAN RUNNER

30ml Jose Cuervo Tequila
15ml Tia Maria
15ml Grand Marnier
15ml Blackberry Liqueur
30ml lemon juice
half a banana
2 strawberries

Method
Blend over ice and pour. Garnish
with a strawberry with umbrella
parasol.

MEXICAN MANGO

30 mL (1 oz) tequila
15 mL (1/2 oz) white curaçao
30 mL (1 oz) mango liqueur
60 mL (1 oz) orange juice

Method
Blend with ice and pour into a
colada glass. Add straws and serve.

MIAMI ADVICE

30 mL (1 oz) Malibu
garnish:
1 slice banana
30 mL (1 oz) banana liqueur
cream

Method
Layer in a 3 oz cocktail glass,
place banana slice on lip of glass
and serve.

MICHAELANGELO

90g zucchini
90ml tomato juice
1 thinly sliced onion
1 dash Italian seasoning

Method
Blend with ice then pour. Garnish with a zucchini slice.

MIDNIGHT ROSE

30 mL (1 oz) advocaat
cream
15 mL (1/2 oz) strawberry liqueur
1/2 strawberry (GARNISH»
15 mL (1/2 oz) kirsch
cracked ice

Method
Shake and strain into 5 oz cocktail glass, garnish with strawberry and serve.

MIDNIGHT SAX

30ml Midori
30ml Southern Comfort
30ml orange and mango fruit juices
top up with ginger ale

Method
Pour over ice and stir, then top up with ginger ale. Garnish with slices of oranges in the glass and orange rind on the side.

MIDNIGHT SLIDE

30ml Opal Nero
7ml lemon juice

Method
Pour Opal Nero, then float lemon juice.

MIDORI ALEXANDER

30 mL (1 oz) Midori
cracked ice
30 mL (1 oz) white curaçao
garnish:
nutmeg
60 mL (1 oz) cream

Method
Shake and strain into a 5 oz cocktail glass, sprinkle with nutmeg and serve.

MIDORI AND MILK

60 mL (1 oz) Midori
90 mL milk

Method
Half fill a 10 oz highball glass with ice. Pour ingredients into glass and serve with straws.

M

MIDORI AVALANCHE

30 mL (1 oz) blue curaçao
60 mL (1 oz) pineapple juice
30 mL (1 oz) Midori
garnish:
1 pineapple wedge
15 mL (1/2 oz) triple sec

Method
Pour curaçao into a 10 oz Hurricane glass. Blend remaining ingredients with ice and add to glass, garnish with pineapple wedge. straws and serve.

MIDORI COLADA

30 mL (1 oz) Midori
90 mL pineapple juice
30 mL (1 oz) white rum
1 slice pineapple
30 mL (1 oz) coconut cream
1 scoop crushed ice
30 mL (1 oz) cream
garnish:
1 pineapple wedge

Method
Blend until smooth and pour into a 10 oz tulip glass, garnish with pineapple wedge, straws and serve.

MIDORI COOLER

30 mL (1 oz) Midori
60 mL (1 oz) soda water

Method
Pour Midori over ice an a 10 oz highball glass, top with soda water. Add straws and serve.

MIDORI MARGARITA

30 mL (1 oz) Midori
20 mL Cointreau
30 mL (1 oz) tequila
5 mL sugar syrup
30 mL (1 oz) lemon juice

Method
Shake and strain into a Salt Rimmed margarita glass and serve.

MIDORI MELTDOWN

45 mL Midori
Angostura bitters
15 mL (1/2 oz) lime juice
soda water

Method
Blend ingredients except soda and pour into a sugar rimmed Hurricane glass. Top with soda and add a dash of Angostura bitters and serve.

MIDORI MIST

30 mL (1 oz) Midori
champagne

Method
Build ingredients into a flute glass and serve.

MIDORI SOUR

30 mL (1 oz) Midori
60 mL (1 oz) lemon juice
1 tsp sugar

Method
Blend and strain into a 3 oz cocktail
glass and serve.

MIDORI SPLICE

45 mL Midori
15 mL (1/2 oz) cream (float)
30 mL (1 oz) Malibu
cracked ice
120 mL pineapple juice

Method
Build ingredients in a 9 oz brandy
Balloon, float cream and serve.

MIKADO

60 mL (1 oz) Midori
1 slice pineapple
15 mL (1/2 oz) vodka
60 mL (1 oz) pineapple juice
15 mL (1/2 oz) banana liqueur
crushed ice

Method
Blend until smooth and pour into
a 10 oz highball glass and .serve
with straws.

MILES OF SMILES SHOOTER

15 mL (1/2 oz) crème de menthe
15 mL (1/2 oz) rye whiskey
15 mL (1/2 oz) amaretto

Method
Layer in order in a shot glass
and serve.

MIMOSA

chilled champagne
chilled orange juice

Method
Half fill a champagne flute with
orange juice, top with champagne
and serve.

MINT JULEP

60 mL (1 oz) bourbon
1 tbsp water
1 tbsp Chopped mint
crushed ice
1 tsp sugar
garnish:
mint leaves

Method
Muddle sugar, mint and water in
a 5 oz cocktail glass. Half fill glass
with crushed ice and add bourbon.
Garnish with mint leaves and serve.

M

Bourbon

60 mL (1 oz) bourbon
garnish:
1 slice lemon
1 dash dark rum

mint leaves
1/2 tsp sugar
cracked ice

Method
Muddle bourbon, sugar and mint leaves in a 10 oz highball glass. Half fill a 10 oz highball glass with ice and add rum. Garnish with mint leaves. lemon slice and serve with straws.

Mod's

80 mL bourbon
2 tsp sugar
2 tsp white crème de menthe
garnish:
1 sprig mint
2 pieces pineapple
Finely crushed ice

Method
Muddle mint and sugar in a 10 oz highball glass. Half fill glass with crushed ice, add bourbon and pineapple Pieces. Float crème de menthe and serve with straws.

MISS AILEEN

30 mL (1 oz) advocaat
30 mL (1 oz) Galliano Liverno
30 mL (1 oz) Vandermint
ice

Method
Shake and strain into a 3 oz cocktail glass and serve.

MISS ANDREA

20 mL crème de menthe
15 mL (1/2 oz) Midori
15 mL (1/2 oz) parfait amour
soda water

Method
Shake ingredients except soda water. Strain into a 10 oz highball glass. Top with soda water and float Galliano Liverno and serve.

MISSION IMPOSSIBLE

30 mL (1 oz) Cointreau
30 mL (1 oz) Midori
30 mL (1 oz) strawberry liqueur
30 mL (1 oz) banana liqueur

Method
Layer in a 4 oz cocktail glass and serve.

MISSISSIPPI MUD

30 mL (1 oz) Kahlúa
Coca-Cola
30 mL (1 oz) Southern Comfort
garnish:
sprinkle grated chocolate
1 small scoop ice cream
cracked ice

Method
Place Kahlúa, Southern Comfort
and ice cream in a 10 oz highball
glass. Top with Coca-Cola.
Sprinkle grated chocolate over the
top. Add two straws and serve.

MOCHA MINT

20ml Kahlúa
20ml White Creme de Menthe
20ml White Creme de Cacao

Method
Shake with ice and strain. Garnish
with peppermint chocolate flakes.

MODEL "T" SHOOTER

15 mL (1/2 oz) tequila
15 mL (1/2 oz) Tia Maria
15 mL (1/2 oz) banana liqueur

Method
Layer in order in a shot glass and
serve.

MOLFETTA MADNESS

30 mL (1 oz) sambuca
20 mL cream
30 ms Mandarin liqueur
garnish:
1 slice orange
30 mL (1 oz) orange juice
cracked ice

Method
Shake and strain into a 4 oz
cocktail glass. Garnish with orange
slice and serve.

MONK'S MADNESS

20 mL strawberry liqueur
60 mL (1 oz) cream
30 mL (1 oz) crème de cacao
cracked ice
50 mL Benedictine
garnish:
shaved chocolate

Method
Shake and strain into a 5 oz
cocktail glass frosted with shaved
chocolate.

MONKEY GLAND

60 mL (1 oz) dry gin
30 mL (1 oz) orange juice
15 mL (1/2 oz) Pernod
cracked ice
15 mL (1/2 oz) grenadine

Method
Shake and strain into a 5 oz
cocktail glass and serve.

MONKEY'S HABITS

60 mL (1 oz) vodka
30 mL (1 oz) lemon juice
15 mL (1/2 oz) Pernod
cracked ice
15 mL (1/2 oz) grenadine

Method
Shake and strain into a champagne
glass and serve.

MONKEY'S PUNCH SHOOTER

10 mL Kahlua
15 mL (1/2 oz) Bailey's Irish cream
15 mL (1/2 oz) crème de menthe

Method
Layer in order in a shot glass and
serve.

MONKEY'S TAIL

30 mL (1 oz) Cointreau
30 mL (1 oz) lemon vodka
20 mL apricot nectar
30 mL (1 oz) cream

Method
Shake and strain into a 5 oz
cocktail glass and serve.

MONTE CARLO

30ml Canadian Club Rye Whisky
10ml Benedictine
2 dashes of Angostura Bitters

Method
Shake with ice and strain.

MONTMARTRE

10ml Cointreau
30ml Gilbey's Gin
10ml Cinzano Sweet Vermouth

Method.
Coat glass with Cointreau then
pour Gilbey's Gin and Cinzano
Sweet Vermouth over ice. Garnish
with a red cherry.

MOOMBA

30 mL (1 oz) Bacardi rum
1 dash grenadine
30 mL (1 oz) Grand Marnier
cracked ice
15 mL (1/2 oz) orange juice
garnish:
1 twist orange peel
10 mL lemon juice

Method
Shake and strain into a 5 oz
cocktail glass, garnish with orange
peel and serve.

MOON BEAM

30 mL (1 oz) Midori
30 mL (1 oz) cream
20 mL vodka
20 mL orange juice
15 mL (1/2 oz) Grand Marnier
garnish:
1 slice kiwifruit

Method
Shake and strain into 5 oz cocktail glass, garnish with kiwifruit and serve.

MOON CRATER

30 mL (1 oz) vodka
garnish:
nutmeg
30 mL (1 oz) advocaat

1 maraschino cherry
orange soda
cracked ice
fresh cream (float)

Method
Place vodka and advocaat in a 10 oz highball glass, top with orange soda. Float cream, dust with nutmeg and garnish with cherry and serve.

MOON'S ECLIPSE

30 mL (1 oz) Campari
30 mL (1 oz) fresh cream
30 mL (1 oz) Drambuie
garnish:
nutmeg
30 mL (1 oz) Amsterdam

1 maraschino cherry
30 mL (1 oz) orange juice

Method
Shake and strain into a champagne saucer, sprinkle with nutmeg. Garnish with cherry and serve.

MORNING GLORY

30ml J&B Scotch Whisky
30ml Milne Brandy
5ml Pernod
5ml White Curacao
dashes Angostura Bitters
top up with soda

Method
Shake with ice and pour then top up with soda. Garnish with an orange twist.

MORNING STAR

30 mL (1 oz) Bacardi rum

lemonade (top up)

20 mL Galliano Liverno

cracked ice

45 mL advocaat

Method
Shake and strain into a 10 oz highball glass, top with lemonade. Add straws and serve.

MOROCCAN COCKTAIL

30ml Gilbey's Gin

30ml Cointreau

5ml Orange Curacao

Method
Shake with ice and strain. Garnish with a lemon wheel.

MOSCOW MULE

60 mL (1 oz) vodka

cracked ice

30 mL (1 oz) lemon juice

garnish:

1 sprig mint

ginger beer (top up)

Method
Shake and strain into a 10 oz highball glass, top with ginger beer. Garnish with sprig of mint, straws and serve.

MOULIN ROUGE

30 mL (1 oz) gin

Sparkling white wine (top up)

20 mL apricot brandy

garnish:

1 orange slice

20 mL lemon juice

cracked ice

1 tsp grenadine

Method
Shake and strain into a champagne saucer, top with Sparkling white wine. Garnish with orange slice and serve.

MOUNT COOK SUNSET

45 mL vodka

15 mL (1/2 oz) lemon juice

15 mL (1/2 oz) maraschino liqueur

15 mL (1/2 oz) orange juice

1 dash grenadine

cracked ice

Method
Shake and strain into a champagne saucer and serve.

MOUNT FUJI

I30ml Gilbey's Gin

15ml lemon juice

10ml heavy cream

1 egg white

Method
Shake with ice and strain. Garnish with a red cherry.

MOUNT TEMPLE

30 mL (1 oz) Kahlúa
30 mL (1 oz) coconut liqueur
30 mL (1 oz) tequila

Method
Build over ice in a 3 oz cocktail glass and serve.

MOUNTAIN

45 mL Scotch whiskey
30 mL (1 oz) Galleon Liverno
30 mL (1 oz) green ginger wine
45 mL pineapple juice

Method
Shake and strain into a champagne saucer and serve.

MUCHO MARGARITA

30 mL (1 oz) tequila
30 mL (1 oz) Cointreau
30 mL (1 oz) Margimix

Method
Shake and strain into a Salt rimmed 3 oz cocktail glass and serve.

MULE'S HIND LEG

15 mL (1/2 oz) Calvados
15 mL (1/2 oz) Benedictine
15 mL (1/2 oz) apricot liqueur
10 mL Maple syrup
15 mL (1/2 oz) gin
cracked ice

Method
Place ingredients in a mixing glass and stir gently. Strain into a 3 oz cocktail glass and serve.

MYRA

15 mL (1/2 oz) vodka
30 mL (1 oz) dry red wine
15 mL (1/2 oz) sweet vermouth
cracked ice

Method
Place ingredients in a mixing glass and stir gently. Strain into a 3 oz cocktail glass and serve.

N

NAPOLEON

45 mL gin

1 dash white curaçao

1 dash Fernet Branca

cracked ice

Method

Stir and strain into a 3 oz cocktail glass and serve.

NAPOLEON SEDUCTION

15 mL (1/2 oz) mango liqueur

30 mL (1 oz) cream

30 mL (1 oz) Mandarin Napoleon

20 g mango

15 mL (1/2 oz) Sabra

garnish:

1 maraschino cherry

Method

Blend until smooth and pour into a colada glass, garnish with cherry and serve.

NATASHA

15 mL (1/2 oz) Pear brandy

1 dash orange bitters

15 mL (1/2 oz) apricot brandy

garnish:

1 maraschino cherry

15 mL (1/2 oz) sweet vermouth

cracked ice

Method

Shake and strain into a 3 oz cocktail glass, garnish with cherry and serve.

NAUGHTY NUPTIAL

30 mL (1 oz) Tia Maria

1/2 banana

15 mL (1/2 oz) Jamaican rum

cracked ice

60 mL (1 oz) orange juice

garnish:

1 pineapple wedge

60 mL (1 oz) pineapple juice

Method

Blend until smooth and pour into a champagne saucer, garnish with pineapple wedge and serve.

NEGRONI

30 mL (1 oz) gin

soda water

15 mL (1/2 oz) Campari

garnish:

1 twist lemon peel

30 mL (1 oz) sweet vermouth

cracked ice

Method

Stir gin, Campari, vermouth and ice in a mixing glass and strain into a 6 oz Old Fashioned glass. Add a splash of soda water, garnish with lemon peel and serve.

NEGRONI NO. 2

30 mL (1 oz) Campari
4 ice cubes
30 mL (1 oz) sweet vermouth
1 dash Angostura bitters
30 mL (1 oz) gin
garnish:
1 slice orange

Method
Place ice cubes in a 5 oz cocktail glass and add ingredients. Garnish with orange slice and serve.

NEUTRON BOMB SHOOTER

15 mL (1/2 oz) Kahlúa
I5 mL tequila
15 mL (1/2 oz) Bundaberg rum

Method
Layer in order in a shot glass and serve.

NEW ICED TEA

30 mL (1 oz) vodka
30 mL (1 oz) grapefruit juice
30 mL (1 oz) Cointreau
Coca-Cola
30 mL (1 oz) tequila
cracked ice
30 mL (1 oz) white rum
garnish:
1 sprig mint

Method
Fill a 10 oz highball glass with ice and add ingredients. Garnish with mint and Serve with straws.

NEW ORLEANS

60 mL (1 oz) gin
2 dashes orange flower water
30 mL (1 oz) lemon juice
1 dash vanilla Essence
1 tsp sugar
cracked ice
30 mL (1 oz) cream
soda water
1 egg white

Method
Shake al! ingredients except soda water and strain over ice in a 10 oz highball glass. Top with soda water, add straws and serve.

NEW YORK

60 mL (1 oz) Canadian whiskey
garnish:
1 twist orange peel
4 dashes grenadine
cracked ice

Method
Shake and strain into a 3 oz cocktail glass, garnish with orange peel and serve.

NEW YORKER

15 mL (1/2 oz) gin
1 dash Cointreau
45 mL French vermouth
cracked ice
15 mL (1/2 oz) sweet sherry

Method
Stir and strain into a 3 oz cocktail glass and serve.

N

NICKEL FEVER

1 tsp Southern Comfort
2 tbsp cream
1 tsp Galliano Liverno
2 tbsp orange juice
10 mL blue curaçao
cracked ice

Method
Shake and strain into a 3 oz
cocktail glass and serve.

19 DUKE DRIVE SHOOTER

15 mL (1/2 oz) Vandermint
15 mL (1/2 oz) banana liqueur
15 mL (1/2 oz) cherry brandy

Method
Layer in order in a shot glass and
serve.

NIGHT OF PASSION

60 mL (1 oz) gin
1 tbsp lemon juice
30 mL (1 oz) Cointreau
60 mL (1 oz) passionfruit juice
60 mL (1 oz) peach nectar
cracked ice

Method
Shake and strain into a rocks glass
and serve.

NOAH'S ARK

10ml Blue Curacao
10ml cream
10ml lemonade

Method
Shake Blue Curacao with cream,
then layer lemonade. Optionally,
place half a lychee nut in glass
before pouring.

NORMAN CONQUEST

60 mL (1 oz) Calvados
1 tsp grenadine
2 tbsp lemon juice
cracked ice

Method
Shake and strain into a 3 oz
cocktail glass and serve.

NIGHT STAR

45 mL vodka
20 mL goldwasser
45 mL dry vermouth
10 mL blue curaçao

Method
Stir and strain into a 5 oz cocktail
glass and serve.

NUDE BOMB SHOOTER

10 mL Kahlúa

10 mL banana liqueur

10 mL amaretto

Method
Layer in order in a shot glass and serve.

NUTTY IRISHMAN

30ml Frangelico

30ml Baileys Irish Cream

15ml fresh lime juice

top up with fresh milk

Method
Build over ice. Garnish with sprinkled nutmeg or chocolate flakes.

NUTTY BUDDY SHOOTER

15 mL (1/2 oz) Kahlúa

15 mL (1/2 oz) Frangelico

15 mL (1/2 oz) crème de menthe

Method
Layer in order in a shot glass and serve.

O

OCEANIC

45 mL Scotch whiskey
garnish:
1 spiral orange peel
15 mL (1/2 oz) Bianco vermouth
cracked ice
30 mL (1 oz) Kahlúa

Method
Mix in a mixing glass and strain into a champagne glass. Garnish with a spiral of orange peel and serve.

OFF THE LEASH

90 mL brandy
cracked ice
30 mL (1 oz) sweet vermouth
garnish:
1 maraschino cherry

Method
Mix in a mixing glass and strain into a champagne glass. Garnish with a maraschino cherry and serve.

OLD FASHIONED APPETISER

1 cube of ice
20ml Jim Beam Bourbon
20ml Dubonnet
5ml Cointreau
5ml Pernod
1 dash Angostura Bitters

Method
Build over ice. Garnish with lemon and orange peel.

OLD FASHIONED SCOTCH

30ml Ballantine's Scotch Whisky
dash Angostura Bitters
sugar cube
soda water

Method
Build over ice. Garnish with 1⁄2 slice of orange and lemon and a cherry. A swizzle stick may be used.

OIL FEVER

60 mL (1 oz) dark rum
cracked ice
60 mL (1 oz) Kahlúa
garnish:
1 spiral orange peel

OLD PAL

30 mL (1 oz) bourbon
garnish:
1 Piece lemon peel
15 mL (1/2 oz) dry vermouth
3 ice cubes
15 mL (1/2 oz) Campari

Method
Mix in a mixing glass and strain into a 3 oz cocktail glass. Garnish with lemon peel and serve.

OLD SAN FRANCISCO

30 mL (1 oz) kirsch

2 dashes grenadine

30 mL (1 oz) Knock

fresh cream

2 dashes lime cordial

1/2 tsp Instant coffee

Method

Mix kirsch, Kueck and grenadine with ice and strain into a 5 oz cocktail glass and add cordial. Mix coffee with cream and float on top and serve.

OPAL ROYALE

30 mL (1 oz) Opal Nera

30 mL (1 oz) cream

30 mL (1 oz) brandy

garnish:

1 maraschino cherry

15 mL (1/2 oz) white crème de menthe

Method

Shake and strain all ingredients except cream. Strain into a 5 oz cocktail glass and float cream. Garnish with cherry and serve.

OLÉ

45 mL tequila

5 mL blue curaçao

30 mL (1 oz) banana liqueur

cracked ice

Method

Stir tequila and banana liqueur and strain over ice in a 5 oz cocktail glass. Add blue curaçao and serve.

OPPENHEIM COCKTAIL

30ml Jim Beam Bourbon

20ml Grenadine

20ml Cinzano Rosso Vermouth

5ml Pernod

Method

Stir over ice and strain. Garnish with lemon and orange peel and a parasol.

OPAL MAGIC SHOOTER

30 mL (1 oz) Midori

30 mL (1 oz) Opal Nera

30 mL (1 oz) Cointreau

Method

Layer in a shot glass and serve.

ORANGE BLOSSOM

30 mL (1 oz) gin

cracked ice

60 mL (1 oz) orange juice

Method

Shake and strain into a 3 oz cocktail glass and serve.

O

ORANGE BOMB

45 mL Scotch whiskey

10 mL Pernod

30 mL (1 oz) orange juice

5 mL sugar syrup

soda water

cracked ice

Method
Shake all ingredients except soda water and strain into a 10 oz highball glass. Top with soda water and serve with straws.

ORANGE BUS

30 mL (1 oz) mango liqueur

30 mL (1 oz) banana liqueur

90 mL orange juice

cracked ice

Method
Shake and strain into an Old Fashioned glass and serve.

ORANGE NOG

1 egg

120ml milk

130ml orange juice

10ml sugar syrup

Method
Blend over ice and pour. Garnish with a sprinkle of ground nutmeg and twisted orange peel.

ORANGUTANG

30 mL (1 oz) Midori

90 mL orange juice

30 mL (1 oz) Mandarin Napoleon

garnish:

2 orange slices

90 mL pineapple juice

pineapple leaves

Method
Half fill a 10 oz highball glass with ice, add ingredients and garnish with orange slices, pineapple leaves. straws and serve.

ORGASM (MULTIPLE)

30 mL (1 oz) Bailey's Irish cream

30 mL (1 oz) Cointreau

30 mL (1 oz) Galleon Liverno

Method
Layer in order in a 3 ox cocktail glass and serve.

ORGASM (MULTIPLE NO. 2)

30 mL (1 oz) Bailey's Irish cream

30 mL (1 oz) cream

30 mL (1 oz) Cointreau

cracked ice

Method
Build in a 9 oz brandy Balloon and serve.

ORGASM (SCREAMING MULTIPLE)

30 mL (1 oz) Bailey's Irish cream
30 mL (1 oz) cream
30 mL (1 oz) Cointreau
cracked ice
15 mL (1/2 oz) Galliano Liverno

Method
Build in a 9 oz brandy Balloon
and serve.

ORGASM (SCREAMING)

30 mL (1 oz) Bailey's Irish cream
30 mL (1 oz) Cointreau
30 mL (1 oz) cherry brandy

Method
Layer in a 3 oz cocktail glass
and serve.

ORGASM SHOOTER

30 mL (1 oz) Bailey's Irish cream
cracked ice
30 mL (1 oz) Cointreau

Method
Layer in order in a shot glass
and serve.

ORGASM SHOOTER (SCREAMING NO. 2)

30 mL (1 oz) Bailey's Irish cream
30 mL (1 oz) Cointreau
30 mL (1 oz) Kahlúa

Method
Layer in order in a shot glass
and serve.

ORIENTAL BLOSSOM

30 mL (1 oz) banana liqueur
90 mL apple juice
30 mL (1 oz) Southern Comfort
30 mL (1 oz) cream
15 mL (1/2 oz) red curaçao
2 apple slices

Method
Shake and strain into a colada
glass, garnish with apple slices
and serve.

ORIENTAL PEARL

20 mL white rum
15 mL (1/2 oz) fresh cream
10 mL crème de cassis
cracked ice
15 mL (1/2 oz) Cola syrup

Method
Shake and strain into a champagne
glass and serve.

O

OUTER SPACE

45 mL vodka

10 mL lime juice.

45 mL Bacardi rum

garnish:

1 maraschino cherry

20 mL Galliano Liverno

Method
Shake and strain into a 5 oz
cocktail glass, garnish and serve.

PABLO

30 mL (1 oz) Bacardi rum

garnish:

1 slice pineapple

15 mL (1/2 oz) Cointreau

1 maraschino cherry

15 mL (1/2 oz) advocaat

cracked ice

Method
Shake and strain into a 5 oz
cocktail glass, garnish with
pineapple, cherry and serve.

OYSTER SHOOTER (HEARTSTARTER)

10ml Smirnoff Vodka

10ml tomato juice

5ml cocktail sauce

Worcestershire sauce to taste

Tabasco sauce to taste

1 fresh oyster

Method
Pour tomato juice onto the
Smirnoff Vodka, float the cocktail
sauce, dash sauces to taste and
drop in oyster. Shoot.

PADDY'S PERIL

60 mL (1 oz) Bailey's Irish cream

1 dash grenadine

30 mL (1 oz) vodka

crushed ice

coconut milk

Method
Shake and strain into a 5 oz
cocktail glass and serve.

PAGO PAGO

30ml Bacardi Gold Rum

10ml lime juice

10ml pineapple juice

5ml Green Chartreuse

5ml Cointreau

Method
Shake with ice and strain over 3
cube of ice. Garnish with a
pineapple wedge and a cherry.

PAINT BOX

30 mL (1 oz) cherry advocaat
30 mL (1 oz) advocaat
30 mL (1 oz) blue curaçao

Method
Layer in a 3 oz cocktail glass
and serve.

PALM SUNDAE

45 mL peach liqueur
3 strawberries
30 mL (1 oz) coconut liqueur
garnish:
1 orange wheel
15 mL (1/2 oz) banana liqueur
pineapple leaves
60 mL (1 oz) Tropical fruit juice
1 maraschino cherry

Method
Blend with ice and pour into a
10 oz Hurricane glass. Garnish and
serve with straws.

PALM TREE

15 mL (1/2 oz) Grand Marnier
15 mL (1/2 oz) mango liqueur
15 mL (1/2 oz) cognac
30 mL (1 oz) cream
15 mL (1/2 oz) Bacardi rum
garnish:
1 maraschino cherry
15 mL (1/2 oz) Malibu

pineapple leaves
15 mL (1/2 oz) peach liqueur

Method
Shake and strain into a 5 oz
margarita glass, garnish with
cherry, pineapple leaves and serve.

PALOMINO

20 mL Galliano Liverno
30 mL (1 oz) Kahlúa
45 mL cream

Method
Shake and strain into a 5 oz
cocktail glass and serve.

PANTY DROPPER SHOOTER

20 mL Frangelico
10 mL gin

Method
Layer in a shot glass and serve.

Madam Butterfly

Mai Tai

Margarita

Martini

Pretty Woman

Pina Colada

PAPAYA SLING

30ml Gilbey's Gin
15ml lime juice
20ml papaya juice or syrup
2 dashes of Angostura Bitters

Method
Shake with ice and pour then top up with soda. Garnish with lime juice.

PARADISE

45 mL Midori
1/2 kiwifruit
120 mL pineapple juice

Method
Blend until smooth, pour into an Old Fashioned glass and serve.

PARADISE NO. 2

30 mL (1 oz) gin
5 mL orange juice
15 mL (1/2 oz) apricot brandy
ice

Method
Shake and strain into a 3 ox cocktail glass and serve.

PARIS BY NIGHT

30 mL (1 oz) Pernod
lemonade (top up)
30 mL (1 oz) Strega
garnish:
1 slice orange
15 mL (1/2 oz) Amsterdam

1 maraschino cherry

Method
Place all ingredients except lemonade in a 10 oz highball glass, top with lemonade. Garnish with lemonade, add straws and serve.

PARIS PEACH

60 mL (1 oz) peach liqueur
10 mL Pernod

Method
Pour over ice in a 3 oz cocktail glass and serve.

PASSION OFF

30 mL (1 oz) vodka
45 mL fresh cream
15 mL (1/2 oz) Grand Marnier
garnish:
1 maraschino cherry
pulp 1 passionfruit

Method
Shake and pour into a champagne saucer, garnish with cherry and serve.

PASSIONATE SCENE

45 mL strawberry liqueur
1 tsp passionfruit pulp
60 mL (1 oz) orange juice
5 mL lemon juice

Method
Pour ingredients into 10 oz
highball glass, float passionfruit
pulp (DO NOT STIR) and serve.

PASSIONATE SCENE NO. 2

45 mL strawberry liqueur
1 tsp passionfruit pulp
60 mL (1 oz) orange juice
1 tsp passionfruit juice
60 mL (1 oz) lemonade
1 scoop crushed ice

Method
Pour all ingredients except
passionfruit fruit pulp, lemon juice
and lemonade into a 10 oz highball
glass. Add other ingredient except
passionfruit pulp and stir. Add
passionfruit pulp, add straws and
serve.

PAULA STAFFORD

30 mL (1 oz) gin
60 mL (1 oz) Cleopatra
60 Pimm's no. 1

Method
Shake and strain into a 5 oz
cocktail glass and serve.

PEACH ALMOND SHAKE

60ml Peach Liqueur
1 whole peeled peach
30ml Amaretto di Galliano
2 scoops of vanilla ice cream
top up with lemonade

Method
Blend with ice and pour then top
up with lemonade. Garnish with a
peach slice and shredded almonds
and a straw.

PEACH BOMB

45 mL peach liqueur
5 mL lemon juice
15 mL (1/2 oz) vodka

Method
Stir ingredients and pour over ice
in a 3 oz cocktail glass and serve.

PEACH EXPLOSION

45 mL peach liqueur
45 mL vodka

Method
Pour over ice in a 5 oz cocktail glass
and serve.

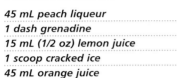

P

PEACH LANTIS

45 mL peach liqueur

1 dash grenadine

15 mL (1/2 oz) lemon juice

1 scoop cracked ice

45 mL orange juice

Method
Blend until frozen, scoop into a 10 oz highball glass and serve.

PEACH MARNIER

30 mL (1 oz) Grand Marnier

2 peaches (SKINNED AND SLICED)

30 mL (1 oz) white rum

crushed ice

20 mL sugar syrup

garnish:

pineapple slice

30 mL (1 oz) pineapple juice

Method
Blend with crushed ice until smooth, pour into a l0 oz highball glass. Garnish with a pineapple slice, straws and serve.

PEACH ME

30 mL (1 oz) Southern Comfort

30 mL (1 oz) cream

30 mL (1 oz) white crème de Calvados

1 dash grenadine

60 mL (1 oz) orange juice

2 peach halves

Method
Blend until smooth and pour into a 7 oz brandy Balloon and serve.

PEACH SURPRISE

30 peach liqueur

1 dash grenadine

15 mL (1/2 oz) Malibu

4 strawberries

Method
Blend until smooth and pour into a champagne saucer and serve.

PEACHY BUM

30 mL (1 oz) mango liqueur

30 mL (1 oz) cream

30 mL (1 oz) peach liqueur

30 mL (1 oz) orange juice

Method
Shake and strain into a 5 oz cocktail glass and serve.

PEARL HARBOUR

30 mL (1 oz) saki

lemonade

30 mL (1 oz) blue curaçao

cracked ice

Method
In a 7 oz brandy Balloon place 1 scoop of cracked ice. Pour in saki and curaçao, top with lemonade and serve with straws.

PENALTY SHOT SHOOTER

15 mL (1/2 oz) crème de menthe

15 mL (1/2 oz) vodka

15 mL (1/2 oz) Tia Maria

Method
Layer in order in a shot glass and serve.

PEPPERMINT

60 mL (1 oz) Vandermint
15 mL (1/2 oz) crème de menthe
30 mL (1 oz) fresh cream
garnish:
1 maraschino cherry
ginger beer
grated chocolate

Method
Shake all ingredients except ginger beer and strain over ice in a 10 oz highball glass. Top with ginger beer, garnish with cherry, chocolate, straws and serve.

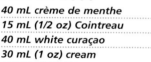

PEPPER 2000

40 mL crème de menthe
15 mL (1/2 oz) Cointreau
40 mL white curaçao
30 mL (1 oz) cream

Method
Shake crème de menthe and curaçao and strain into a 5 oz champagne saucer. Mix Cointreau and cream and float on top and serve.

PERFECT

45 mL dry gin
30 mL (1 oz) sweet vermouth
30 mL (1 oz) dry vermouth

Method
Stir and strain into a 3 oz cocktail glass and serve.

PERNOD POLYNESIAN

15 mL (1/2 oz) Pernod
30 mL (1 oz) cream
30 mL (1 oz) Southern Comfort
60 mL (1 oz) orange & mango juice
15 mL (1/2 oz) blue curaçao
2 ice cubes

Method
Place ice cubes in a 10 oz highball glass, pour liquid ingredients over ice and serve with straws.

PETER'S PRIDE

30 mL (1 oz) Galliano Liverno
60 mL (1 oz) pineapple juice
20 mL tequila
60 mL (1 oz) orange juice
30 mL (1 oz) Bacardi rum

Method
Shake and strain into a 10 oz highball glass and serve with straws.

PETITE FLEUR

60 mL (1 oz) Bacardi rum
cracked ice
30 mL (1 oz) Cointreau
garnish:
1 maraschino cherry
30 mL (1 oz) grapefruit juice

Method
Shake and strain into a 5 oz champagne glass, garnish with cherry and serve.

P

PHOTO FINISH

45 mL Bacardi rum
10 mL lime juice
45 mL apricot brandy
cracked ice
30 mL (1 oz) dry vermouth
garnish:
1 twist lemon peel

Method
Shake and strain into a 5 oz
cocktail glass, garnish with twist of
lemon peel and serve.

PIAFF

30 mL (1 oz) brandy
1 tbsp sugar
30 mL (1 oz) white curaçao
1 egg
15 mL (1/2 oz) lemon juice
cracked ice

Method
Shake and strain into a 5 oz
cocktail glass and serve.

PICADILLY PUNCH

30ml Courvoisier Cognac
10ml sugar
15ml lemon juice
1 clove
cinnamon stick
ground nutmeg

Method
Simmer all ingredients except for
Courvoisier Cognac. Pour Cognac
into ladle and ignite before
infusing the punch mix. Stir and
serve. Garnish with an orange slice
and a red cherry.

PICASSO

30ml Courvoisier Cognac
10ml Dubonnet
10ml lime juice
15ml sugar syrup

Method
Shake over ice and strain.
Garnish with an orange twist.

PICKLED BRAIN SHOOTER

30 mL (1 oz) Kahlúa
30 mL (1 oz) sweet vermouth
30 mL (1 oz) dry vermouth

Method
Layer in order in a shot glass and
serve.

PICK-ME-UP

30 mL (1 oz) cognac
30 mL (1 oz) sweet vermouth
30 mL (1 oz) dry vermouth

Method
Stir and strain into a 3 o/. cocktail
glass and serve.

PICK-ME-UP NO. 2

60 mL (1 oz) brandy
milk
1 dash Angostura bitters
soda water
1 tsp sugar

Method
In a 10 oz highball glass place
Angostura bitters, sugar and
brandy. Fill glass with milk and add
a dash of soda water and serve
with straws.

PIMM'S

45 mL Pimm's no. 1
garnish:
1 slice Cucumber
ginger ale

1 slice orange
3 ice cubes
1 maraschino cherry

Method
Place 3 ice cubes in a 10 oz highball
glass and pour Pimm's over and top
with ginger ale. Garnish with
Cucumber, orange slice, cherry,
straws and serve.

PIMM'S NO. 1 CUP

45 mL Pimm's no. 1
ice
lemonade
garnish:
1 lemon slice
ginger ale

Method
Build over ice using equal pans of
ginger ale and lemonade in a 10 oz
highball glass. Garnish with a slice
of lemon, straws and serve.

PIÑA COLADA

30 mL (1 oz) white rum
crushed ice
30 mL (1 oz) coconut milk
1 maraschino cherry
75 mL pineapple juice
garnish:
1 pineapple wedge
1 piece pineapple
1 maraschino cherry

Method
Blend until smooth and pour into a
large colada glass. Garnish with
pineapple wedge, cherry, straws
and serve.

PIÑA COLADA NO. 2

30 mL (1 oz) white rum
30 mL (1 oz) cream
30 mL (1 oz) coconut cream
pineapple Pieces
90 mL pineapple juice
garnish:
1 maraschino cherry

Method
Blend until smooth and pour into a
large colada glass. Garnish with
cherry, straws and serve.

PINCHGUT PERIL

30 mL (1 oz) Scotch whiskey

ice cubes

15 mL (1/2 oz) gin

Shaved ice

15 mL (1/2 oz) lime juice

1 pineapple wedge

pineapple Pieces

1 orange slice

1 dash grenadine

Method
Blend whiskey, gin, lime juice, grenadine and pineapple Pieces until smooth. Pour over Shaved ice into a 10 oz highball glass. Garnish with pineapple wedge, orange slice, straws and serve.

PINEAPPLE BOMBER

45 mL Southern Comfort

15 mL (1/2 oz) Galleon amaretto

90 mL pineapple juice

garnish:

1 pineapple wedge

Method
Shake and strain into a 5 oz cocktail glass, garnish with pineapple wedge and serve.

PINEAPPLE PLANTATION

30ml Amaretto di Galliano

30ml Southern Comfort

90ml pineapple juice

top up with lemonade

Method
Blend with ice and pour then top up with lemonade. Garnish with a pineapple wedge and a cherry.

PINK ANGEL

30 mL (1 oz) Bacardi rum

1 egg white

15 mL (1/2 oz) advocaat

30 mL (1 oz) fresh cream

15 mL (1/2 oz) cherry brandy

Method
Shake and strain into a 5 oz champagne glass and serve.

PINK CHEVROLET

30 mL (1 oz) strawberry

champagne

10 mL lemon juice

Method
Build ingredients in a flute glass and serve.

PINK ELEPHANT

30 mL (1 oz) vodka
30 mL (1 oz) fresh cream
30 mL (1 oz) Galliano Liverno
1 dash grenadine
30 mL (1 oz) almond liqueur
cracked ice
30 mL (1 oz) orange juice
garnish:
cinnamon

Method
Shake and strain into a 5 oz
champagne saucer, sprinkle with
nutmeg and serve.

PINK GIN

45 mL gin
30 mL (1 oz) water
3 dashes grenadine
2 ice cubes

Method
Place ice and Angostura bitters in a
Goblet glass and swirl. Discard
bitters and add ingredients and
serve.

PINK LADY

60 mL (1 oz) gin
4 dashes fresh cream
4 dashes grenadine
cracked ice
4 dashes brandy

Method
Shake and strain into 5 oz
champagne saucer and serve.

PINK LADY NO. 2

60 mL (1 oz) gin
cracked ice
4 dashes grenadine
1 dash egg white

Method
Shake and strain into a 5 oz
champagne glass and serve.

PINK MINTY

30 mL (1 oz) red crème de menthe
30 mL (1 oz) fresh cream
1 dash grenadine
cracked ice

Method
Shake and strain into a 3 oz
cocktail glass and serve.

PINK PANTHER

60 mL (1 oz) bourbon
45 mL coconut liqueur
90 mL vodka
15 mL (1/2 oz) grenadine
120 mL fresh cream
cracked ice

Method
Shake and Strain into a 12 oz
brandy Balloon and serve.

P

PINK POODLE

30 mL (1 oz) Campari
45 mL cream
30 mL (1 oz) gin
4 strawberries

Method
Blend until smooth, pour into a
5 oz cocktail saucer and serve.

PINK PUSSY

30 mL (1 oz) Campari
Bitter lemon Soft Drink
1 dash egg white
garnish:
1 slice lemon
15 mL (1/2 oz) peach brandy

Method
Shake all ingredients except Soft
Drink and strain into a 10 oz
highball glass. Top with Soft Drink,
garnish with slice of lemon, straws
and serve.

PINK SQUIRREL

30 mL (1 oz) amaretto
5 mL grenadine
30 mL (1 oz) white crème de cacao
50 mL cream

Method
Shake and strain into a 5 oz
champagne saucer and serve.

PINKY

60 mL (1 oz) brandy
15 mL (1/2 oz) grenadine
15 mL (1/2 oz) crème de banana
cracked ice
60 mL (1 oz) fresh cream

Method
Shake and strain into a champagne
saucer and serve.

PIPELINE SHOOTER

25 mL tequila
20 mL vodka

Method
Layer in a shot glass and serve.

PIRATES PLUNDER

30 mL (1 oz) Tia Maria
30 mL (1 oz) coconut cream
30 mL (1 oz) Bacardi rum
90 mL pineapple juice
20 mL Malibu
1 slice pineapple

Method
Blend until smooth and pour into
a 10 oz highball glass and serve
with straws.

PJ

30 mL (1 oz) vodka
1 dash egg white
30 mL (1 oz) Campari
garnish:
1 maraschino cherry
30 mL (1 oz) orange juice
cracked ice

Method
Shake and strain into a 5 oz
cocktail glass, garnish with cherry
and serve.

PLANTATION NIGHT

45 mL Kahlúa
4 strawberry liqueur
45 mL banana liqueur
1 banana
45 mL cream
1 scoop crushed ice

Method
Blend until smooth and pour into
a flute glass and serve.

PLANTER'S PUNCH

30ml Coruba Rum
30ml lemon or lime juice
60ml orange juice
5ml Grenadine

Method
Build over ice then add dash of
grenadine. Garnish with fruit slices.

PLAYGROUND

30 mL (1 oz) Bailey's Irish cream
30 mL (1 oz) Malibu
30 mL (1 oz) banana liqueur

Method
Layer in a 3 oz cocktail glass
and serve.

POLISH SIDECAR

Ingredients
Glass:
130ml Cocktail Glass
Mixers:
20ml Gilbey's Gin
20ml lemon juice
10ml Blackberry Liqueur

Method
Shake with ice and pour then float
blackberries. Garnish with
blackberries or raspberries.

POLYNESIA

30ml Bacardi
30ml Passionfruit Liqueur
10ml lime juice
half egg white

Method
Blend with ice and pour. Garnish
with passionfruit.

P

POPSICLE SHOOTER

15 mL (1/2 oz) Tia Maria

15 mL (1/2 oz) vodka

10 mL Bailey's Irish cream

Method
Layer in order in a shot glass
and serve.

PORT IN A STORM

45 mL port

1/3 strip orange peel

60 mL (1 oz) red wine

cracked ice

15 mL (1/2 oz) brandy

1 sprig mint

Method
Fill a large Goblet glass with ice.
Stir liquid ingredients and pour
over ice. Garnish with sprig of
mint and serve.

PORTO FLIP

45 mL port

1 egg yolk

10 mL cognac

cracked ice

10 mL sugar syrup

garnish:

nutmeg

Method
Shake and strain into a 5 oz
cocktail glass, sprinkle with
nutmeg and serve.

POTTS POINT SPECIAL

30 mL (1 oz) vodka

garnish:

1/4 slice pineapple

30 mL (1 oz) white curaçao

cracked ice

30 mL (1 oz) pineapple juice

Method
Shake and strain into a
champagne glass, garnish with
pineapple and serve.

POUSSE CAFÉ

15 mL (1/2 oz) brandy

15 mL (1/2 oz) grenadine

15 mL (1/2 oz) crème de Menthe

15 mL (1/2 oz) maraschino liqueur

15 mL (1/2 oz) Yvette liqueur

15 mL (1/2 oz) crème de cacao

Method
Layer in a 3 oz cocktail glass
and serve.

PRAIRIE FIRE SHOOTER

45 mL tequila

10 drops Tabasco Sauce

Method
Layer in order in a shot glass
and serve.

PRAIRIE OYSTER

30ml Milne Brandy
salt and pepper
Worcestershire sauce
Tabasco sauce
1 egg yolk

Method
Build, no ice.

PRETTY WOMAN

30 mL (1 oz) Midori
30 mL (1 oz) strawberry liqueur
30 mL (1 oz) Malibu
4 strawberries
1 Scoop crushed ice
crushed ice

Method
Blend Midori and Malibu with
1 scoop of crushed ice. Separately,
blend strawberry liqueur, fresh
strawberries and crushed ice. Pour the
first mixture into a 10 oz Hurricane
glass, followed by the second mixture.
Garnish with an Umbrella on
strawberry and serve with straws.

PRINCE OF WALES

15 mL (1/2 oz) Cointreau
1 dash Angostura bitters
15 mL (1/2 oz) brandy
garnish:
1/2 lemon slice
Sparkling white wine
cracked ice

Method
Shake ingredients except Sparkling
wine and strain into a 10 oz highball
glass. Top with wine, garnish with
lemon slice, straws and serve.

PURPLE SHELL

90 mL sloe gin
15 mL (1/2 oz) parfait amour
15 mL (1/2 oz) dry gin
45 mL fresh cream

Method
Shake and strain into a 5 oz
champagne glass and serve.

PURPLE WATERS

20 mL Bacardi rum
15 mL (1/2 oz) parfait amour
15 mL (1/2 oz) orange curaçao
15 mL (1/2 oz) yellow Chartreuse

Method
Layer in order in a 3 oz cocktail
glass and serve.

P.S. I LOVE YOU

30ml Amaretto di Galliano
30ml Kahlúa
30ml Baileys Irish Cream
5ml Grenadine

Method
Build over ice and stir. Garnish
with sprinkled nutmeg.

PUERTO RICAN PINK LADY

30ml Bacardi Gold Rum

10ml lemon juice

10ml Grenadine

half egg white

Method

Blend with ice and strain. Garnish with a strawberry splashed with Grenadine.

PUSSY FOOT

60ml orange juice

30ml lemon juice

30ml lime juice

5ml egg yolk

dash of Grenadine

Method

Shake over ice and pour. Garnish with an orange slice and red cherry.

PURPLE PEOPLE EATER

30ml Parfait Amour

30ml Gilbey's Gin

5ml lemon juice

Method

Shake over ice and strain. Garnish with a strawberry and pink parasol.

QUEBEC

130ml Canadian Club Whisky
10ml Cinzano Dry Vermouth
10ml Amer Picon
10ml Maraschino Liqueur

Method
Shake over ice and strain. Garnish with a cocktail onion.

QUEEN BEE

30 mL (1 oz) gin
1 dash Pernod
30 mL (1 oz) Cointreau
cracked ice

Method
Shake and strain into a 3 oz cocktail glass and serve.

QUEEN ELIZABETH

30 mL (1 oz) gin
15 mL (1/2 oz) lemon juice
15 mL (1/2 oz) Cointreau
garnish:
1 maraschino cherry
1 dash Pernod
crushed ice

Method
Shake and strain into a 3 oz cocktail glass, garnish with cherry and serve.

QUEEN'S PEG

30 mL (1 oz) gin
1 large ice cube
Sparkling white wine (top up)

Method
Place ice cube in a Goblet glass, add gin and top with wine before serving.

QUEENS

30 mL (1 oz) dry gin
30 mL (1 oz) pineapple juice
30 mL (1 oz) dry vermouth
garnish:
1 maraschino cherry
30 mL (1 oz) sweet vermouth

1 pineapple wedge

Method
Shake and strain into a 5 oz cocktail glass, garnish with cherry, pineapple wedge and serve.

QUICK FUCK SHOOTER

30 mL (1 oz) Midori
30 mL (1 oz) Kahlúa
30 mL (1 oz) Bailey's Irish cream

Method
Layer in order in a shot glass and serve.

QUICKSILVER SHOOTER

10 mL banana liqueur
10 mL vodka
10 mL tequila

Method
Layer in order in a shot glass and serve.

Q-R

R&R

30 mL (1 oz) Cointreau
30 mL (1 oz) Midori
30 mL (1 oz) tequila

Method
Layer in order in a 3 oz cocktail glass and serve.

RABBIT'S REVENGE

40 mL bourbon
Tonic water (top up)
3 dashes grenadine
garnish:
1 slice orange
30 mL (1 oz) pineapple juice
cracked ice

Method
Shake ingredients except Tonic water and strain into a Tumbler glass. Top with Tonic water, garnish with orange slice and serve with straws

RAFFLES' SINGAPORE SLING

30 mL (1 oz) gin
30 mL (1 oz) pineapple juice
30 mL (1 oz) cherry brandy
garnish:
1 orange wedge
15 mL (1/2 oz) triple sec

1 maraschino cherry
15 mL (1/2 oz) Benedictine

mint leaves
30 mL (1 oz) orange juice
cracked ice
30 mL (1 oz) lime juice

Method
Shake and strain into a 10 oz highball glass, garnish with orange wedge, cherry, mint leaves, swizzle stick, straws and serve.

RAGING BULL

30 mL (1 oz) Afrikoko
milk (top up)
30 mL (1 oz) Sabra
cracked ice

Method
Pour over ice in an Old Fashioned glass, top with milk and serve.

RAIDER SHOOTER

15 mL (1/2 oz) Bailey's Irish cream
15 mL (1/2 oz) Cointreau
15 mL (1/2 oz) Grand Marnier

Method
Layer in order in a shot glass and serve.

RAINBOW SHERBERT

15ml Midori
15ml Banana Liqueur
15ml Strawberry Liqueur
60ml orange juice
2 dashes Grenadine
2 scoops orange sherbert
blue vegetable dye

Method
Blend without ice. Garnish with assorted fruit and a dash of blue vegetable dye.

RAM

30 mL (1 oz) Malibu
45 mL orange juice
15 mL (1/2 oz) Galliano Liverno
whipped cream

Method
Shake ingredients except whipped cream and strain into a 5 oz champagne saucer. Float whipped cream and serve.

RAMONA

60 mL (1 oz) Bacardi rum
2 tsp castor sugar
30 mL (1 oz) Cointreau
cracked ice
60 mL (1 oz) lemon juice
garnish:
1 lemon slice
soda water

Method
Shake all ingredients except soda water and strain over ice in a 10 oz highball glass. Top with soda water, garnish with lemon slice. straws and serve.

Ramoz

60 mL (1 oz) gin
2 dashed orange flower water
30 mL (1 oz) lemon juice
2 egg Whites
30 mL (1 oz) lime juice
1 tsp sugar
30 mL (1 oz) heavy cream
cracked ice
soda water

Method
Shake and strain all ingredients except soda over ice in a 10 oz highball glass. Top with soda water, add straws and serve.

R

Ritz

30 mL (1 oz) brandy
chilled champagne
15 mL (1/2 oz) Cointreau
cracked ice
15 mL (1/2 oz) orange juice

Method
Shake ingredients except champagne. Strain into a 5 oz Epsom glass. Top with champagne and serve.

Silver

60 mL (1 oz) Bacardi rum
1 egg yolk
1 tsp sugar
soda water
60 mL (1 oz) lemon juice
cracked ice

Method
Shake all ingredients except soda water and strain over ice in a 10 oz highball glass. Top with soda water, add straws and serve.

Strawberry

30 mL (1 oz) strawberry liqueur
4 strawberries
30 mL (1 oz) lemon juice
soda water
15 mL (1/2 oz) sugar syrup
ice
1 egg white

Method
Blend all ingredients except soda water and pour into a 10 oz highball glass. Top with soda water, add straws and serve.

Vodka

30 mL (1 oz) vodka
1/2 tsp sugar
2 tsp lemon juice
garnish:
1/2 slice lime
1 egg white

1 strip lemon peel
soda water
cracked ice

Method
Shake all ingredients except soda water, strain over ice in a 10 oz highball glass. Top with soda water, garnish with lime slice. lemon peel, straws and serve.

RASPUTIN'S REVENGE

60 mL (1 oz) vodka
30 mL (1 oz) orange juice

Method
Shake and strain over ice in a rocks glass and serve.

RAY LONG

30 mL (1 oz) Bianco vermouth
1 tsp Pernod
20 mL brandy
cracked ice
1 dash Angostura bitters

Method
Mix ingredients and strain into a 3 oz cocktail glass and serve.

READY, SET, GO!

30 mL (1 oz) Midori
30 mL (1 oz) strawberry liqueur
30 mL (1 oz) banana liqueur

Method
Layer in a 3 oz cocktail glass and
serve.

RED CUCUMBER BOWL

150 mL red wine
1 pinch ground Cloves
15 mL (1/2 oz) maraschino liqueur
garnish:
2 thin slices Cucumber
1 pinch cinnamon
cracked ice

Method
Shake ingredients except
Cucumber. Strain into a 6 oz
Tumbler glass, garnish with
Cucumber and serve.

RED EYE

150 mL cold beer
150 mL tomato juice

Method
Place tomato juice in a 10 oz
highball glass, add beer and serve.

RED LIGHTS

20 mL gin
15 mL (1/2 oz) Cointreau
15 mL (1/2 oz) Galleon Liverno
60 mL (1 oz) orange juice

Method
Shake and strain into a 10 oz
highball glass and serve.

RED RAY

60 mL (1 oz) gin
60 mL (1 oz) white crème de
menthe
30 mL (1 oz) grenadine
cracked ice

Method
Shake and strain into a Old
Fashioned glass filled with ice.
Garnish with and orange wheel
and serve.

RED SHADOW

30 mL (1 oz) Scotch whiskey
1 tsp lemon juice
15 mL (1/2 oz) apricot brandy
cracked ice
15 mL (1/2 oz) cherry brandy

Method
Shake and strain into a 3 oz
cocktail glass and serve.

R

REFLECTIONS

30 mL (1 oz) Frangelico
cracked ice
2 tbsp white crème de cacao
garnish:
2 maraschino Cherries
1 tbsp Cheri-Suisse
1 red Straw

Method
Shake and strain into a 3 oz Martini glass. Cut 5 mm off a red Straw and use it to join 2 maraschino cherries. Place one of the Cherries in the glass, the other above the liquid creating a reflection effect and serve.

REMARKABLE COW

30 mL (1 oz) gin
juice 1 lemon
30 mL (1 oz) Van der Hum
1 dash sugar syrup
1 dash grenadine

Method
Shake and strain into a 5 oz champagne saucer and serve.

RENDEZVOUS

30 mL (1 oz) Cointreau
30 mL (1 oz) vodka
15 mL (1/2 oz) Rubis
lemonade (top up)

Method
Shake and strain into a flute glass, top with lemonade and serve.

RHETT BUTLER

30 mL (1 oz) Southern Comfort
5 mL lime cordial
30 mL (1 oz) orange curaçao
soda water (top up)
15 mL (1/2 oz) lemon juice
garnish:
1 orange wheel

Method
Build ingredients over ice in a 10 oz highball glass, top with soda water. Garnish with orange wheel and serve with straws.

RHYTHM OF LOVE

10ml Midori
small piece of kiwifruit
10ml Creme de Cassis
float cream

Method
Squeeze kiwifruit onto Midori into glass, then layer in order.

RICK O'SHEA

10ml Galliano
10ml Bacardi
10ml orange juice

Method
Layer in order.
Comments: One shot and you'll be bouncing back over the Irish Sea for more.

RIO LADY

30 mL (1 oz) white cream de cacao
50 mL cream
15 mL (1/2 oz) goldwasser

Method
Shake and strain into a 5 oz
champagne saucer and serve.

RITZ

30 mL (1 oz) brandy
chilled champagne (top up)
15 mL (1/2 oz) Cointreau
cracked ice
15 mL (1/2 oz) orange juice

Method
Shake and strain into a 5 oz Epsom
glass, top with champagne and
serve.

ROB ROY

60 mL (1 oz) Scotch whiskey
garnish:
1 maraschino cherry
15 mL (1/2 oz) sweet vermouth
cracked ice
1 dash Angostura bitters

Method
Stir and strain into a 3 oz cocktail
glass, garnish with cherry and
serve.

ROCK LOBSTER

45 mL Grand Marnier
30 mL (1 oz) cream (float)
15 mL (1/2 oz) amaretto
garnish:
cinnamon
milk (top up)

Method
Build over ice in a 10 oz margarita
glass, top with milk, float cream.
Sprinkle with cinnamon and serve.

ROCKET FUEL (AUSTRALIAN)

15 mL (1/2 oz) white rum
15 mL (1/2 oz) gin
15 mL (1/2 oz) vodka
lemonade (top up)
15 mL (1/2 oz) tequila
cracked ice

Method
Build ingredients over ice in a 10 oz
highball glass, top with lemonade,
add straws and serve.

ROCKET FUEL (BLACK)

10 mL each Spirit behind the bar
cracked ice

Method
Shake and strain into a 10 oz
highball glass and serve.

ROCKET FUEL (MULTICOLOURED)

10 mL each white Spirit behind the bar

one of the following:

20 mL crème de menthe for green

20 mL grenadine for red

20 mL advocaat for yellow

20 mL blue curaçao for Blue

Method
Shake and strain into a 10 oz highball glass and serve.

ROCKET FUEL (WHITE)

10 mL all white Spirits behind the bar

Method
Shake and strain into a 10 oz highball glass and serve.

ROLLS ROYCE

30 mL (1 oz) dry gin

10 mL Benedictine

15 mL (1/2 oz) dry vermouth

cracked ice

15 mL (1/2 oz) sweet vermouth

Method
Stir and strain into a 3 oz cocktail glass and serve.

ROMAN DRIVER

30 mL (1 oz) Galleon Liverno

1 dash grenadine

15 mL (1/2 oz) vodka

20 mL cream

20 mL almond syrup

cracked ice

Method
Shake and strain into a champagne saucer and serve.

ROMAN THE GLOMAN

60 mL (1 oz) Scotch whiskey

1 tbsp orange juice

30 mL (1 oz) Cointreau

cracked ice

Method
Shake and strain over ice in a rocks glass and serve.

ROMULAN ALE

30 mL (1 oz) blue curaçao

15 mL (1/2 oz) gin

15 mL (1/2 oz) vodka

15 mL (1/2 oz) tequila

15 mL (1/2 oz) white curaçao

1 splash dry vermouth

15 mL (1/2 oz) Bacardi rum

lemonade (top up)

Method
Shake and strain over ice in a 10 oz highball glass, top with lemonade, add straws and serve.

ROSE

30 mL (1 oz) gin
15 mL (1/2 oz) lemon juice (GLASS RIM)
15 mL (1/2 oz) dry vermouth
1 tbsp castor sugar
15 mL (1/2 oz) apricot brandy
1 maraschino cherry
1 dash grenadine
cracked ice

Method
Rim a 3 oz cocktail glass with sugar. Shake the rest of the ingredients and strain into the Rimmed glass and serve.

ROSE AND FAMMO SPECIAL

30 mL (1 oz) Bacardi rum
10 mL blue curaçao
30 mL (1 oz) white crème de cacao
garnish:
1 twist lemon peel
15 mL (1/2 oz) dry vermouth

1 maraschino cherry
10 mL orange gin
cracked ice

Method
Stir and strain into a 5 oz champagne saucer, garnish with lemon peel, cherry and serve.

ROSE NO. 2

15 mL (1/2 oz) cherry brandy
cracked ice
15 mL (1/2 oz) kirsch
garnish:
1 maraschino cherry
45 mL dry vermouth

Method
Stir ingredients and strain into a 3 oz cocktail glass, garnish with cherry and serve.

ROSE NO. 3

45 mL apricot brandy
20 mL dry vermouth
45 mL gin
1 dash grenadine

Method
Shake and strain into a 3 oz cocktail glass and serve.

ROYAL FLUSH

30 mL (1 oz) brandy
60 mL (1 oz) grapefruit juice
60 mL (1 oz) Cointreau
10 mL grenadine
Sparkling white wine (top up)
cracked ice

Method
Shake and strain into a Tumbler glass, top with white wine and serve with straws.

R

ROYAL SNOWCAP

30 mL (1 oz) Bacardi rum
1 egg white
30 mL (1 oz) dry vermouth
garnish:
chocolate Flakes
15 mL (1/2 oz) parfait amour
cracked ice
1 dash lemon juice

Method
Shake and strain into a 3 oz
cocktail glass, garnish with
chocolate Flakes and serve.

RUBY SHY

30 mL (1 oz) Malibu
lemonade (top up)
30 mL (1 oz) raspberry cordial
garnish:
grated coconut

Method
Pour Malibu and raspberry cordial
over ice in a 10 oz highball glass.
Garnish with grated coconut,
straws and serve.

RUM

30 mL (1 oz) white rum
cracked ice
1 tsp sugar syrup
garnish:
1 spiral orange peel
3 dash Angostura bitters

Method
Stir and strain over ice into a 3 oz
cocktail glass, garnish with spiral of
orange peel and serve.

RUM ALEXANDER

30 mL (1 oz) crème de cacao
cracked ice
15 mL (1/2 oz) white rum
garnish:
nutmeg
15 mL (1/2 oz) cream

Method
Shake and strain into a champagne
saucer, cross two straws over top
and sprinkle with nutmeg. Remove
straws and serve.

RUM COOLER

60 mL (1 oz) rum
soda water (top up)
60 mL (1 oz) lemon juice
cracked ice
4 dashes grenadine
fruit or garnish

Method
Shake and strain over ice into a 10
oz highball glass, top with soda,
garnish with fruit. straws and serve.

RUM REBELLION

30 mL (1 oz) Bacardi rum
5 mL cherry brandy
30 mL (1 oz) banana liqueur
75 mL pineapple juice
1 scoop crushed ice

Method
Blend until smooth and pour into
an Old Fashioned glass and serve.

RUM THING

30 mL (1 oz) Bacardi rum

30 mL (1 oz) Galliano Liverno

30 mL (1 oz) orange curaçao

1 twist orange peel

30 mL (1 oz) dry vermouth

Method
Stir and strain into a champagne saucer, garnish with twist of orange peel and serve.

RUMFUSTATION

120 mL beer

1 pinch Ground ginger

75 mL Still white wine

1 pinch cinnamon

1 tsp sugar

1 pinch nutmeg

1 egg yolk

Method
Beat ingredients over a low heat until warmed. Pour into an Old Fashioned glass and serve.

RUNNING HOT

45 mL Bacardi rum

40 mL pineapple juice

30 mL (1 oz) Cointreau

1 dash grenadine

Method
Shake and strain over ice in an Old Fashioned glass and serve.

RUSSIAN

30 mL (1 oz) vodka

30 mL (1 oz) crème de cacao

30 mL (1 oz) dry gin

cracked ice

Method
Shake and strain into a 3 oz cocktail glass and serve.

RUSSIAN (AUSTRALIAN)

45 mL vodka

whipped cream (float)

30 mL (1 oz) Tia Maria

cracked ice

Method
Pour vodka and Tia Maria over ice in an Old Fashioned glass. Float whipped cream and serve.

RUSSIAN (BLACK NO. 2)

30 mL (1 oz) vodka

cracked ice

30 mL (1 oz) Kahlúa

Method
Build in an ice filled Old Fashioned glass and serve.

R

RUSSIAN (BLACK NO. 3)

30 mL (1 oz) vodka
Coca-Cola (top up)
30 mL (1 oz) Kahlúa
cracked ice

Method
Build over ice in a 10 oz highball
glass, top with Coca-Cola, add
straws and serve.

RUSSIAN (BLACK)

30 mL (1 oz) vodka
cracked ice
15 mL (1/2 oz) Kahlúa

Method
Build in an ice filled 3 oz cocktail
glass and serve.

RUSSIAN (BROWN)

45 mL vodka
cracked ice
30 mL (1 oz) amaretto

Method
Shake and strain into a 3 oz
cocktail glass and serve.

RUSSIAN (GOLDEN)

45 mL vodka
cracked ice
30 mL (1 oz) Galliano Liverno

Method
Shake and strain into a 3 oz
cocktail glass and serve.

RUSSIAN (WHITE)

40 mL vodka
60 mL (1 oz) cream
15 mL (1/2 oz) coffee liqueur
cracked ice

Method
Shake and strain into a 5 oz
cocktail glass and serve.

RUSSIAN COW

30 mL (1 oz) vodka
10 mL Galliano Liverno
30 mL (1 oz) coconut milk
60 mL (1 oz) milk

Method
Blend with a scoop of ice until
smooth, pour into a 10 oz highball
glass and serve.

RUSSIAN HOLIDAY

30 mL (1 oz) vodka
60 mL (1 oz) pineapple juice
20 mL Grand Marnier
whipped cream (float)

Method
Pour vodka and pineapple juice
over ice in a 10 oz highball glass.
Float whipped cream, add Grand
Marnier and serve.

RUSSIAN ROULETTE

15 mL (1/2 oz) Galliano Liverno
10 mL sugar syrup
15 mL (1/2 oz) banana liqueur
1/2 banana
15 mL (1/2 oz) vodka
15 mL (1/2 oz) lemon juice
30 mL (1 oz) orange juice
1 scoop crushed ice

Method
Blend until smooth and pour into
a brandy Balloon and serve.

RUSTY BUCKET

30 mL (1 oz) port wine
Coca-Cola

Method
Pour into a 5 oz cocktail glass
and serve.

RUSTY NAIL

30 mL (1 oz) Scotch whiskey
cracked ice
30 mL (1 oz) Drambuie

Method
Fill an Old fashioned glass with
cracked ice. Add ingredients
and serve.

RUSTY NAIL NO. 2

45 mL Scotch whiskey
garnish:
1 twist lemon peel
45 mL Drambuie
cracked ice

Method
Pour ingredients over ice in an
Old Fashioned glass, garnish with
lemon peel and serve.

RUSTY SPADE

1 mango
1 dash cream
30 mL (1 oz) strawberry liqueur
ice
pulp 1 passionfruit
garnish:
1 strawberry

Method
Blend until Smooth and pour into
a margarita glass, garnish with
strawberry and serve.

RYAN'S RUSH SHOOTER

10 mL Kahlúa
10 mL Bacardi rum
10 mL Bailey's Irish cream

Method
Layer in order in a shot glass
and serve.

SAIL AWAY

30 mL (1 oz) Midori
30 mL (1 oz) lime juice
15 mL (1/2 oz) peach liqueur
1 dash lemon juice
30 mL (1 oz) vodka
garnish:
1 lime wheel

Method
Shake ingredients and strain into a
5 oz cocktail glass. Garnish with a
lime wheel and serve.

SAINT MORITZ

30ml Schnapps

Method
Build with ice. Garnish with a layer
of heavy cream.

SAINT PETERSBURG

30 mL (1 oz) vodka
lemonade (top up)
30 mL (1 oz) blue curaçao

Method
Shake vodka and curaçao and
strain into a 5 oz cocktail glass. Top
with lemonade and serve.

SAINT VINCENT

30 mL (1 oz) gin
30 mL (1 oz) cream
30 mL (1 oz) Galliano Liverno
cracked ice
1 dash grenadine

Method
Shake and strain into a champagne
glass and serve.

SAKETINI

30ml Gilbey's Gin
5-10ml Gekkeikan Sake

Method
Shake over ice and pour. Garnish
with an olive.

SAKI SPECIAL

30 mL (1 oz) saki
2 dashes Angostura bitters
60 mL (1 oz) gin
cracked ice

Method
Mix ingredients in a mixing glass,
strain into a 3 oz cocktail glass and
serve.

SALTY DOG

45 mL vodka

cracked ice

grapefruit juice (top up)

Method
Place ingredients in a 10 oz highball glass, top with grapefruit juice and serve with straws.

SALUBRIOUS SALUTATIONS

15 mL (1/2 oz) Galliano Liverno

15 mL (1/2 oz) Benedictine

15 mL (1/2 oz) Drambuie

30 mL (1 oz) fresh cream

15 mL (1/2 oz) gin

cracked ice

Method
Shake and strain into a 3 oz cocktail glass and serve.

SAMBUCA SHAKER

30ml Romana Sambuca

Method
Pour Sambuca then light. Cup your hand entirely over the rim while it flames, creating suction. Shake the glass, place under your nose, take hand from glass to inhale the fumes, then shoot.

SAN FRANCISCO

45 mL gin

1 dash Angostura bitters

10 mL sweet vermouth

cracked ice

10 mL dry vermouth

garnish:

1 maraschino cherry

1 dash orange bitters

Method
Stir ingredients in a mixing glass, strain into a 5 oz cocktail glass, garnish with cherry and serve.

SANGRIA

Spanish Red Wine

20ml Cointreau

20ml Milne Brandy

20ml Bacardi

orange, lime, lemon and strawberry pieces

sugar syrup

Method
Pour in order.

Ready, Set, Go!

Rocket Fuel

Screwdriver

South Pacific

Stars and Stripes

Strawberry Blonde

S

SATIN PILLOW

5 mL strawberry liqueur
15 mL (1/2 oz) Tia Maria
10 mL Cointreau
20 mL pineapple juice
15 mL (1/2 oz) Frangelico
garnish:
1 strawberry
20 mL cream

Method
Blend with ice and pour into a 5 oz cocktail glass. Garnish with cut strawberry and a dash of cream and serve.

SATURDAY NIGHT

15 mL (1/2 oz) banana liqueur
60 mL (1 oz) lemon juice
30 mL (1 oz) gin
garnish:
1 maraschino cherry
15 mL (1/2 oz) blue curaçao

1 lime wheel
60 mL (1 oz) cream

Method
Shake and strain into a colada glass, garnish with lime wheel, cherry and serve.

SAYONARA

30 mL (1 oz) Midori
75 mL cream
30 mL (1 oz) advocaat
cracked ice

Method
Shake well, strain into a 5 oz cocktail glass and serve.

SCANDINAVIAN GLÖGG

30ml Smirnoff Vodka
60ml red wine
3 blanched almonds
3 raisins
grated orange peel
1 dried fig
4 cardamon seeds
1 cinnamon stick
1 clove
1 sugar cube per serve

Method
Simmer all ingredients in a saucepan for a few minutes except for sugar cubes, then pour.

SCARLET O'HARA

45 mL Southern Comfort
45 mL cranberry juice
30 mL (1 oz) lime juice
garnish:
1 maraschino cherry

Method
Shake and strain into a champagne glass. Garnish with cherry and serve.

SCORPION

15ml Coruba Dark Rum
15ml Courvoisier Cognac
15ml Romana Sambuca
15ml Orgeat
45ml orange juice
15ml lemon juice

Method
Blend with ice. Garnish with a lime wheel with cherry.

SCOTCH MIST

60 mL (1 oz) Scotch whiskey
garnish:
1 twist lemon peel
cracked ice

Method
3/4 fill an Old Fashioned glass with ice. Pour Scotch whiskey into a shaker with lemon peel and pour unstrained into glass and serve.

SCOTCH FROG

60 mL (1 oz) vodka
15 mL (1/2 oz) lime cordial
30 mL (1 oz) Galliano Liverno
garnish:
1 maraschino cherry
1 dash Angostura bitters

Method
Shake and strain into a champagne saucer, garnish with cherry and serve.

SCOTCH SOLACE

30 mL (1 oz) Scotch whiskey
150 mL milk
15 mL (1/2 oz) Cointreau
30 mL (1 oz) cream
1 tsp honey
1 tsp grated orange peel

Method
Fill a 10 oz highball glass with cracked ice, add whiskey, Cointreau, honey and stir. Add milk, cream, orange peel and serve with straws.

SCOTCH MATE

45 mL Scotch whiskey
30 mL (1 oz) sweet vermouth
30 mL (1 oz) Galliano Liverno
30 mL (1 oz) orange juice
cracked ice
garnish:
1 strip orange peel

Method
Shake and strain into a champagne saucer, garnish with orange peel and serve.

SCREAMING LIZARD

30 mL (1 oz) crème de menthe
1 dash soda water
30 mL (1 oz) Chartreuse
cracked ice

Method
Pour ingredients over ice in an Old Fashioned glass and serve.

S

SCREWDRIVER

45 mL vodka
cracked ice
orange juice (top up)
garnish:
1 orange wheel

Method
Place ice in a 10 oz highball glass
and add vodka, top with orange
juice. Garnish with orange wheel,
straws and serve.

SEA BREEZE

15 mL (1/2 oz) Malibu
60 mL (1 oz) pineapple juice
15 mL (1/2 oz) blue curaçao
cracked ice
30 mL (1 oz) gin
garnish:
1 slice kiwifruit
30 mL (1 oz) cream

Method
Shake and strain into a 5 oz
cocktail glass, garnish with kiwifruit
and serve.

SEDUCTION

20 mL Grand Marnier
30 mL (1 oz) cream
15 mL (1/2 oz) Cointreau
10 mL orange bitters
20 mL banana liqueur
1 banana

Method
Blend until smooth and pour into a
margarita glass and serve.

SEE THROUGH

30 mL (1 oz) Bacardi rum
1 dash blue curaçao
15 mL (1/2 oz) Cointreau
cracked ice
15 mL (1/2 oz) orange gin
garnish:
1 cocktail Onion

Method
Stir ingredients in a mixing glass
and strain into a 3 oz cocktail glass.
Garnish with Onion on a Toothpick
in the glass and serve.

SENORITA

20 mL tequila
20 mL cream
20 mL crème de noyaux
20 mL orange juice
20 mL Galliano Liverno
garnish:
cinnamon

Method
Shake and strain into a
champagne saucer, sprinkle with
cinnamon and serve.

SENTRY DELIGHT

30 mL (1 oz) Midori
15 mL (1/2 oz) lemon juice
15 mL (1/2 oz) strawberry liqueur
15 mL (1/2 oz) lime juice
15 mL (1/2 oz) mango liqueur
garnish:
1 strawberry

Method
Blend and pour into a 3 oz cocktail
glass, garnish with Fanned
strawberry and serve.

SERPENTS STING

30 mL (1 oz) Bacardi rum
30 mL (1 oz) cream
30 mL (1 oz) Galliano Liverno
cracked ice
30 mL (1 oz) almond liqueur
1 maraschino cherry
30 mL (1 oz) orange juice

Method
Shake and strain into a 5 oz
cocktail glass, garnish with cherry
and serve.

77 SUNSET STRIP

15 mL (1/2 oz) vodka
1 dash grenadine
15 mL (1/2 oz) gin
60 mL (1 oz) lemonade
15 mL (1/2 oz) triple sec
60 mL (1 oz) pineapple juice

Method
Pour ingredients over ice in a 6 oz
tulip glass, add straws and serve.

SEX ON THE BEACH

15 mL (1/2 oz) Kahlúa
60 mL (1 oz) cream
30 mL (1 oz) Malibu
garnish:
1 pineapple wedge
30 mL (1 oz) pineapple juice

Method
Shake and strain into a 5 oz
cocktail glass, garnish with
pineapple wedge and serve.

SHADY LADY

30 mL (1 oz) Midori
garnish:
1 slice lemon
30 mL (1 oz) tequila
1 slice lime
90 mL grapefruit juice
1 maraschino cherry

Method
Shake and pour over ice in a 10 oz
highball glass, garnish with lemon,
lime, cherry and serve.

SHAMROCK SHOOTER

10 mL crème de cacao
10 mL Bailey's Irish cream
10 mL crème de Menthe

Method
Layer in order in a shot glass and
serve.

SHANDY

150 mL beer
150 mL lemonade

Method
Half fill a 300 mL beer glass with
lemonade, top with beer and serve.

SHANGHAI PUNCH

30ml Courvoisier Cognac

30ml Coruba Rum

40ml orange juice

20ml Cointreau

20ml lemon juice

almond extract

fresh tea

grated orange and lemon peels

cinnamon sticks

Method
Boil tea and add ingredients then
stir.

SHEEP'S HEAD

15 mL (1/2 oz) sweet vermouth

garnish:

1 maraschino cherry

40 mL bourbon

1 Piece lemon peel

1 tsp Benedictine

cracked ice

Method
Stir and strain into a small Tumbler
glass, garnish with lemon peel.
cherry and serve.

SHERIDAN SHOOTER

20ml Black Sheridan's

10ml White Sheridan's

Method
Layer in order.
Comments: Try this newest shooter
straight from the bottle.

SHERRY

30 mL (1 oz) gin

30 mL (1 oz) lemon juice

30 mL (1 oz) sweet sherry

cracked ice

Method
Shake and strain into a 3 oz
cocktail glass and serve.

SHERRY NO. 2

30 mL (1 oz) sweet sherry

1 egg yolk

15 mL (1/2 oz) cream

1 tsp sugar

Method
Blend ingredients and pour into a
champagne saucer and serve.

SHIRLEY TEMPLE

15ml Grenadine

ginger ale or lemonade to top-up

Method
Build over ice. Garnish with slice of
orange, serve with swizzle stick and
two straws.

SHOCKING BLUE

30 mL (1 oz) blue curaçao
30 mL (1 oz) lemonade
30 mL (1 oz) Midori
garnish:
1 lime wheel
30 mL (1 oz) banana liqueur

Method
Fill a 10 oz highball glass with ice and gently layer ingredients. Garnish with lime wheel and serve.

SHOOTING STAR

30 mL (1 oz) Midori
30 mL (1 oz) cream
30 mL (1 oz) peach liqueur
30 g Rockmelon
15 mL (1/2 oz) orange curaçao

Method
Blend until smooth and pour into a colada glass.

SHY MARIA

30 mL (1 oz) Tia Maria
10 mL Frangelico
15 mL (1/2 oz) Cointreau
60 mL (1 oz) cream

Method
Shake with ice and strain into a champagne saucer and serve.

SICILIAN KISS

20ml Southern Comfort
20ml Amaretto di Galliano

Method
Build with ice.

SIDECAR

30 mL (1 oz) brandy
garnish:
1 maraschino cherry
15 mL (1/2 oz) Cointreau
cracked ice
15 mL (1/2 oz) lemon juice

Method
Shake and strain into a 3 oz cocktail glass, garnish with impaled cherry and serve.

SILVER STREAK

30 mL (1 oz) kümmel liqueur
cracked ice
30 mL (1 oz) gin

Method
Shake and strain into a 3 oz cocktail glass and serve.

S

SILVER THREAD SHOOTER

15 mL (1/2 oz) crème de menthe
15 mL (1/2 oz) Tia Maria
15 mL (1/2 oz) banana liqueur

Method
Layer in order in a shot glass and serve.

SIMON'S BALL BUSTER SHOOTER

30 mL (1 oz) Jack Daniel's whiskey
garnish:
1 coffee Bean
30 mL (1 oz) Frangelico

Method
Layer in a shot glass, float coffee Bean and serve.

SIMPLY PEACHES

45 mL peach liqueur
2 peach halves
30 mL (1 oz) Cointreau
2 scoops ice cream
75 mL peach nectar
1 scoop ice

Method
Blend until smooth and pour into a colada glass. Float a small scoop of ice cream, add straws and serve.

SING SING

60 mL (1 oz) Scotch whiskey
cracked ice
30 mL (1 oz) sweet vermouth
garnish:
1 twist orange peel
30 mL (1 oz) orange curaçao

Method
Stir and strain into a 5 oz cocktail glass, garnish with twist of orange peel and serve.

SINGAPORE ISLAND

45 mL gin
5 mL sugar syrup
20 mL Peter Heering
5 mL lemon juice
5 mL grenadine
lemonade (top up)
70 mL pineapple juice

Method
Shake and strain into a 10 ox highball glass.
Top with lemonade, add straws and serve.

SINGAPORE SLING

60 mL (1 oz) gin
soda water (top up)
30 mL (1 oz) cherry brandy
garnish:
1 strip lemon peel
30 mL (1 oz) lemon juice

1 sprig mint

Method
Place ingredients with ice in a 10 oz
highball glass, top with soda water.
Garnish with lemon peel, mint,
straws and serve.

SINKING SUN

80 mL Scotch whiskey
garnish:
1 strip lemon peel
180 mL dry apple cider (top up)
cracked ice

Method
Stir ingredients and strain into a
rocks glass.
Top with apple cider, garnish with
lemon peel and serve.

69ER

15 mL (1/2 oz) Kahlúa
90 mL cream
15 mL (1/2 oz) Malibu
1 banana
15 mL (1/2 oz) Tia Maria
crushed ice

Method
Blend until smooth and pour into a
brandy Balloon and serve.

SKY WALKER

45 mL Bacardi rum
20 mL advocaat
30 mL (1 oz) Cointreau
60 mL (1 oz) cream

Method
Shake and strain into a champagne
saucer and serve.

SLIDE YOUR THIGH

20 mL banana liqueur
15 mL (1/2 oz) white crème de
cacao
20 mL Midori
45 mL cream

Method
Shake and strain into a 5 oz
cocktail glass and serve.

SLIPPERY NIPPLE

60 mL (1 oz) sambuca
60 mL (1 oz) Bailey's Irish cream

Method
Float sambuca over Bailey's in a 5
?? cocktail glass and serve.

SLOW COMFORTABLE SCREW No.1

30 mL (1 oz) vodka
orange juice (top up)
15 mL (1/2 oz) sloe gin
cracked ice
15 mL (1/2 oz) Southern Comfort

Method
Build over ice in a 10 oz highball
glass, top with orange juice and
serve with straws.

SLOW COMFORTABLE SCREW No.2

30 mL (1 oz) gin
garnish:
1 orange wheel
60 mL (1 oz) Southern Comfort

1 maraschino cherry
120 mL orange juice
cracked ice

Method
Shake and strain into a 10 oz highball glass, garnish with orange wheel, cherry, straws and serve.

SMARTIE SHOOTER

15 mL (1/2 oz) grenadine
5 mL tequila
10 mL Kahlúa

Method
Layer in order in a shot glass and sieve.

SMOG CITY

30 mL (1 oz) tequila
60 mL (1 oz) cream
30 mL (1 oz) crème de cacao
Coca-Cola (top up)

Method
Half fill a highball glass with cracked ice, add liquid ingredients and lop with Coca-Cola. Add straws, swizzle stick and serve.

SMOOTH LADY

30 mL (1 oz) Midori
30 mL (1 oz) coconut cream
15 mL (1/2 oz) Tia Maria
30 mL (1 oz) cream
70 mL pineapple juice
garnish:
Orchids

Method
Shake and strain into two 3 oz cocktail glasses. Garnish with Orchids (if available) and serve.

SMUGGLER'S GOLD

60 mL (1 oz) Scotch whiskey
1 dash lemon juice
1 dash goldwasser
cracked ice
30 mL (1 oz) Forester liqueur

Method
Shake and strain into a 5 oz cocktail glass and serve.

SNAKE IN THE GRASS

30 mL (1 oz) gin
30 mL (1 oz) lemon juice
30 mL (1 oz) sweet vermouth
garnish:
1 twist lemon peel
30 mL (1 oz) Cointreau

Method
Shake and strain into a champagne saucer, garnish with lemon peel and serve.

SNAKEBITE

60 mL (1 oz) gin
60 mL (1 oz) crème de menthe

Method
Shake and strain into a 3 oz
cocktail glass and serve.

SNAKEBITE SHOOTER

45 mL Galliano Liverno
20 mL crème de menthe

Method
Layer in a shot glass and serve.

SNOOPY'S GLEAM

30 mL (1 oz) bourbon
15 mL (1/2 oz) orange soda (float)
10 mL orange curaçao
garnish:
1 orange wheel
10 mL grenadine

1 maraschino cherry

Method
Shake and strain into a 3 oz
cocktail glass, garnish with orange
peel, cherry and serve.

SNOWBALL

30 mL (1 oz) advocaat
cream (float)
190 mL lemonade (top up)
garnish:
1 maraschino cherry

Method
Pour advocaat over ice in a 10 oz
highball glass and top with
lemonade. Float cream, garnish
with cherry and serve with straws.

SNOWDROP

60 mL (1 oz) Scotch whiskey
30 mL (1 oz) orange juice
30 mL (1 oz) Benedictine
garnish:
1 twist lemon peel
2 dashes green ginger wine

Method
Shake and strain into a champagne
saucer, garnish with lemon peel
and serve.

SNOWFLAKE

30 mL (1 oz) vodka
10 mL advocaat
15 mL (1/2 oz) Galliano Liverno
1 dash cream
15 mL (1/2 oz) Southern Comfort
lemonade (top up)
20 mL orange juice

Method
Shake and strain into a 10 oz
highball glass, top with lemonade
and serve with straws.

S

SOCK IT TO ME, BLUEY

60 mL (1 oz) vodka
cracked ice
60 mL (1 oz) white crème de
menthe
garnish:
1 maraschino cherry
10 mL blue curaçao

Method
Shake and strain into a
champagne saucer, garnish with
cherry and serve.

SOMBRERO SPINNER

30 mL (1 oz) tequila
45 mL strawberry liqueur
20 mL Rubis
4 strawberries
30 mL (1 oz) Cointreau
1 scoop crushed ice

Method
Blend until smooth and pour into a
champagne saucer and serve.

SOMETHING SWAMPY

90 mL blue curaçao
30 mL (1 oz) parfait amour
90 mL vodka
1 scoop crushed ice
30 mL (1 oz) tequila
garnish:
3-4 jelly frogs
30 mL (1 oz) Midori
lemonade (top up)

Method
Shake and pour over crushed ice
in a very large brandy Balloon.
Top with lemonade, add frogs,
straws and serve.

SONJA

30 mL (1 oz) yellow Chartreuse
fresh cream (float)
15 mL (1/2 oz) blue curaçao
garnish:
nutmeg
15 mL (1/2 oz) Galliano Liverno
garnish:
1 maraschino cherry

Method
Stir Chartreuse, curaçao and
Galleon Liverno and strain into a 3
oz cocktail glass. Float cream and
sprinkle with nutmeg, garnish with
cherry and serve.

SOUTH PACIFIC

30 mL (1 oz) gin
15 mL (1/2 oz) Galleon Liverno
30 mL (1 oz) blue curaçao
lemonade (top up)

Method
Place ingredients in a 10 oz
highball glass. Top with lemonade
and serve.

SOUTH SEAS

30 mL (1 oz) Frangelico
60 mL (1 oz) orange juice
20 mL mango liqueur
1/2 banana

Method
Blend until smooth. Pour into a
champagne glass and serve.

SOUTH YARRA SAMURAI

30 mL (1 oz) Midori
1/2 banana
30 mL (1 oz) banana liqueur
1 scoop crushed ice
30 mL (1 oz) lemon juice
garnish:
1 strawberry

Method
Blend until smooth and pour into a
brandy Balloon, garnish with
strawberry and serve.

SOUTHERLY BUSTER

30 mL (1 oz) brandy
dry ginger ale (top up)
15 mL (1/2 oz) dry vermouth
garnish:
1 slice lemon
15 mL (1/2 oz) lime cordial
cracked ice

Method
Half fill a 10 oz highball glass with
cracked ice. Add liquid ingredients.
Top with ginger ale. Garnish with
slice of lemon and serve.

SOUTHERLY KISS

10 mL gin
champagne (top up)
30 mL (1 oz) parfait amour
1 sugar Cube

Method
Add gin to sugar cube in a
champagne glass. Top with
champagne. Pour parfait amour
down the side of the glass and
serve.

SOUTHERN FLAME SHOOTER

Method
Fill a shot glass with Southern
Comfort, ignite and serve while
flaming.

S

SOUTHERN PEACH

30 mL (1 oz) Cointreau
15 mL (1/2 oz) lemon juice
15 mL (1/2 oz) brandy
garnish:
grated chocolate
15 mL (1/2 oz) cherry brandy

1 Twirl cream
15 mL (1/2 oz) pineapple juice

1 strawberry

Method
Shake and strain into a 3 oz
cocktail glass. Garnish with a
strawberry, grated chocolate and a
twirl of cream and serve.

SOUTHERN STRAWBERRY

30 mL (1 oz) Southern Comfort
90 mL pineapple juice
30 mL (1 oz) Campari
30 mL (1 oz) sugar syrup
90 mL orange juice
4 strawberries

Method
Blend with crushed ice until
smooth. Pour into a wine glass and
serve.

SOVIET COCKTAIL

30ml Smirnoff Vodka
10ml Cinzano Dry Vermouth
10ml Amontillado

Method
Shake over ice and pour. Garnish
with a twist of lemon.

SPANISH MOSS

30ml Chambord
10ml Kahlúa
5ml Green Creme de Menthe

Method
Shake with ice and strain over a
cube of ice. Garnish with a green
cherry.

SPECIAL CREAM CHOCOLATE

60 g Plain chocolate
1/2 tsp cinnamon
20 mL brandy
150 mL whipped cream (float)
300 mL milk

Method
Heat chocolate, milk and
cinnamon, add brandy and pour
into a 10 oz highball glass. Float
cream and serve with straws.

SPLICE

30 mL (1 oz) Cointreau
15 mL (1/2 oz) tequila
30 mL (1 oz) Malibu
cracked ice
30 mL (1 oz) Midori
1 scoop ice cream
15 mL (1/2 oz) Margimix

Method
Blend until smooth and pour into a colada glass and serve with straws.

SPRINGBOK

20ml Passionfruit Syrup
10ml Green Creme de Menthe
5ml Aphrodite Ouzo

Method
Layer in order.

SPRITZER

60 mL (1 oz) Still white wine
cracked ice
soda water (Top Up)

Method
Place white wine in a 10 oz highball glass over ice. Top with soda water and serve with straws.

SPUTNIK

75 mL vodka
10 mL lemon juice
30 mL (1 oz) Fernet Branca
cracked ice
1/2 tsp sugar

Method
Shake and strain over ice in a 5 oz cocktail glass and serve.

SPUTNIK NO. 2

30 mL (1 oz) vodka
Sangrita
15 mL (1/2 oz) brandy
1 shake cayenne pepper
15 bourbon
cracked ice

Method
Shake and strain into a Tumbler glass and serve with straws.

SQUASHED FROG

30 mL (1 oz) Midori
30 mL (1 oz) Bailey's Irish cream
15 mL (1/2 oz) advocaat
15 mL (1/2 oz) cherry advocaat

Method
In a 90 mL port glass, place Midori. Stir in advocaat and cherry advocaat. Float Midori and serve.

STARS AND STRIPES

10 mL blue curaçao

30 mL (1 oz) strawberry liqueur

30 mL (1 oz) Southern Comfort

4 strawberries

30 mL (1 oz) Frangelico

Method

Pour blue curaçao in a 10 oz cocktail glass. Blend Southern Comfort and Frangelico with a scoop until frozen of ice and add to glass. Blend strawberry liqueur and 4 strawberries with ice Until frozen and add to top. Garnish with grated chocolate over top, add a strawberry with an American flag sticking out of it to the lip of the glass and serve.

STEROID BLAST

30 mL (1 oz) O.P. rum

30 mL (1 oz) vodka

15 mL (1/2 oz) tequila

1 dash soda water (LAST)

30 mL (1 oz) Benedictine

Method

Shake and strain into a 5 oz cocktail glass, top with soda water and serve.

STIMULATION

30 mL (1 oz) Bailey's Irish cream

30 mL (1 oz) Cointreau

30 mL (1 oz) Malibu

15 mL (1/2 oz) cream

Method

Layer in order in a 5 oz cocktail glass and serve.

STINGER

60 mL (1 oz) brandy

30 mL (1 oz) white crème de menthe

Method

Shake with ice and strain into a 3 oz cocktail glass and serve.

STRAWBERRY BLONDE

30 mL (1 oz) crème de cacao

Coca-Cola (top up)

1 splash grenadine

garnish:

1 maraschino cherry

fresh cream (float)

Method

Build over ice in a 10 oz highball glass, garnish with cherry and serve with straws.

STRAWBERRY COLADA

30 mL (1 oz) white rum
30 mL (1 oz) cream
30 mL (1 oz) coconut cream
4 strawberries
30 mL (1 oz) pineapple liqueur
1 scoop ice
90 mL pineapple juice
garnish:
1 pineapple wedge

Method
Blend ingredients and pour into a
colada glass and serve with a
pineapple wedge as a garnish.

STRAWBERRY FANTASIA

30 mL (1 oz) strawberry liqueur
30 mL (1 oz) cream
30 mL (1 oz) crème de Grand
Marnier

Method
Shake and strain into a 5 oz
cocktail glass and serve.

STRAWBERRY MARGARITA

30 mL (1 oz) tequila
5 mL egg white
15 mL (1/2 oz) Cointreau
2-4 strawberries
15 mL (1/2 oz) strawberry liqueur
ice

Method
Blend until smooth, pour into a salt
rimmed glass with a half 1/2
strawberry as garnish. Serve.

STRAWBERRY PASSION

30 mL (1 oz) Bailey's Irish cream
60 mL (1 oz) orange juice
30 mL (1 oz) strawberry liqueur
30 mL (1 oz) cream
30 mL (1 oz) vodka
cracked ice
garnish: 1 strawberry

Method
Shake and strain into a Tumbler
glass, garnish with a strawberry
and serve.

STRAWBERRY ROYAL

30 mL (1 oz) strawberry liqueur
2-3 strawberries
chilled champagne (top up)

Method
Blend strawberry liqueur and
strawberries with ice and pour into
a flute glass.
Top with champagne and serve.

STRAWBERRY SHORTCAKE

30 mL (1 oz) strawberry liqueur
60 mL (1 oz) cream
15 mL (1/2 oz) Malibu
4-5 strawberries
15 mL (1/2 oz) white crème de
cacao
1 scoop ice
garnish: grated chocolate

Method
Blend until smooth and pour into
a brandy Balloon. Garnish with
grated chocolate and serve.

S

STRAWBERRY TANGO

30 mL (1 oz) Tia Maria
10 mL milk
30 mL (1 oz) Kahlúa
2 strawberries
1 dash Grand Marnier
ice
30 mL (1 oz) lemon juice

Method
Blend and pour into a 5 oz cocktail glass and serve.

STRAWGASM

15 mL (1/2 oz) Malibu
3 strawberries
15 mL (1/2 oz) strawberry liqueur
1/4 small banana
15 mL (1/2 oz) Galliano Liverno
45 mL cream
30 mL (1 oz) crème de cacao
1/2 scoop ice

Method
Blend until smooth, pour into a colada glass and serve.

SUDANI'S SADNESS SHOOTER

10 mL sambuca
10 mL advocaat
10 mL cherry advocaat
10 mL Tai Maria
10 mL blue curaçao

Method
Layer in a shot glass and serve.

SUMMER BREEZE

30 mL (1 oz) mango liqueur
45 mL orange juice
15 mL (1/2 oz) Bacardi rum
45 mL pineapple juice
30 mL (1 oz) peach liqueur
20 g mango
15 mL (1/2 oz) gin
20 g peach
garnish: 1 pineapple wedge

Method
Blend and pour into a colada glass. garnish with a pineapple wedge and serve.

SUMMER PASSION

30 mL (1 oz) mango liqueur
60 g fresh mango
30 mL (1 oz) peach liqueur
1 tsp passionfruit pulp (float)
30 mL (1 oz) cream

Method
Blend ingredients except passionfruit pulp. Pour gently into a champagne saucer, float passionfruit pulp over lop and serve.

SUMMER SHERBET

30 mL (1 oz) mango liqueur
30 mL (1 oz) lemon juice
30 mL (1 oz) Galliano Liverno

Method
Shake and strain into a 5 oz cocktail glass and serve.

SUNBURST

45 mL mango liqueur
orange juice (top up)

Method
Build over ice in a 10 oz highball
glass and serve.

SUNDANCER

20 mL Bundaberg 0 P rum
1 dash egg white
20 mL Bundaberg U P rum
15 mL (1/2 oz) lemon juice
30 mL (1 oz) amaretto
30 mL (1 oz) orange juice
30 mL (1 oz) pineapple juice
cracked ice

Method
Shake and strain into an Old
Fashioned glass and serve.

SUNKEN TREASURE

30 mL (1 oz) gin
1 strawberry
15 mL (1/2 oz) peach liqueur
apricot Conserve
champagne (top up)

Method
Place a dab of apricot Conserve in
the bottom of a champagne saucer
and push strawberry into it. Stir gin
and peach liqueur with ice and
strain over strawberry. Top with
champagne and serve.

SUNKISSED

30 mL (1 oz) Rubis
50 mL blackcurrant juice
15 mL (1/2 oz) Cointreau
1 tbsp Raspberries

Method
Blend until smooth and pour into a
champagne saucer and serve.

SUNSET

30 mL (1 oz) cherry brandy
30 mL (1 oz) fresh cream
30 mL (1 oz) advocaat
lemonade (top up)

Method
Pour ingredients over ice in a 10 oz
highball glass, top with lemonade
and serve with straws.

SUNSET NO. 2

30 mL (1 oz) Cointreau
5 mL lemon juice
30 mL (1 oz) peach tree
champagne (top up)
20 mL peach nectar
garnish:
1/2 peach
5 drops grenadine

Method
Pour grenadine into bottom of a
10 oz highball glass and add other
ingredients over ice. Top with
champagne, garnish with sliced
peach half, straws and serve.

S

SUNSET SPECIAL

40 mL sweet vermouth

garnish:

1 slice orange

40 mL Cointreau

crushed ice

80 mL gin

Method
Shake and strain into a 5 oz cocktail glass, garnish with orange slice and serve.

SUNSHINE SURPRISE

30 mL (1 oz) Midori

30 mL (1 oz) orange juice

30 mL (1 oz) Kahlúa

30 mL (1 oz) pineapple juice

15 mL (1/2 oz) Cointreau

garnish:

1 pineapple wedge

1 dash cream

Method
Blend until smooth and pour into a colada glass, garnish with pineapple wedge and serve with straws.

SUNTORIAN STAR

30 mL (1 oz) Midori

pulp 1/2 a passionfruit

15 mL (1/2 oz) banana liqueur

4 strawberries

4 pineapple Pieces

Method
puree strawberries and pour a swirl in a 5 oz cocktail glass. Blend Midori, banana liqueur, pineapple Pieces and pour into glass. Top with passionfruit pulp and serve.

SURFERS PARADISE

60 mL (1 oz) vodka

10 mL blue curaçao

40 mL dry vermouth

1 maraschino cherry

20 mL Galliano Liverno

Method
Stir and strain into a champagne saucer, garnish with cherry and serve.

SURPRISE

30 mL (1 oz) gin

20 mL apricot brandy

60 mL (1 oz) orange juice

cracked ice

Method
Shake and strain over ice in an Old Fashioned glass and serve.

SURPRISE KISS

30 mL (1 oz) Galliano Liverno
15 mL (1/2 oz) orange curaçao
20 mL gin
30 mL (1 oz) orange juice
15 mL (1/2 oz) ouzo
1 dash egg white

Method
Shake and strain into a 5 02
cocktail glass and serve.

SWAMP WATER

30 mL (1 oz) green Chartreuse
20 mL lime juice (float)
pineapple juice (top up)

Method
Pour Chartreuse over ice in a 10 oz
highball glass, top with pineapple
juice. Float lime juice, add straws
and serve.

SWEET LADY JANE

30 mL (1 oz) strawberry liqueur
30 mL (1 oz) fresh cream
15 mL (1/2 oz) Grand Marnier
15 mL (1/2 oz) coconut cream
15 mL (1/2 oz) orange juice
garnish:
chocolate Flakes
15 mL (1/2 oz) Cointreau
1 sprig mint

Method
Shake and strain into a champagne
saucer, garnish with chocolate
Flakes, mint and serve.

SWEET SIXTEEN

30 mL (1 oz) gin
1 dash pineapple juice
15 mL (1/2 oz) Malibu
1 dash coconut cream
15 mL (1/2 oz) white crème de
cacao
1 slice pineapple

Method
Blend until smooth and pour into a
5 oz cocktail glass and serve.

SWEDISH SNOWBALL

30ml Advocaat
15ml lemon juice
top up with soda

Method
Build over ice then top up with
soda. Garnish with a lemon slice.

SWISS CHOCOLATE

30 mL (1 oz) anisette
fresh cream (float)
30 mL (1 oz) cherry brandy
garnish:
1 maraschino cherry
30 mL (1 oz) green tea

Method
Pour ingredients into a 3 oz
cocktail glass, float cream, garnish
with cherry and serve.

T

T.K.O. SHOOTER

10 mL Kahlua
l0 mL ouzo
10 mL tequila

Method
Layer in order in a shot glass and serve.

T.N.T.

60 mL (1 oz) brandy
2 dashes Pernod
30 mL (1 oz) orange curaçao
garnish:
1 twist orange peel
2 dashes Angostura bitters

Method
Shake and strain into a champagne saucer, garnish with orange peel and serve.

TOBLERONE

30 mL (1 oz) Frangelico
60 mL (1 oz) cream
15 mL (1/2 oz) Kahlúa
1/2 tsp honey
15 mL (1/2 oz) white crème de cacao
garnish:
almond Flakes
5 mL Bailey's Irish cream

nutmeg

Method
Blend with ice and pore into a 5 oz cocktail glass. Garnish with almond Flakes, nutmeg and serve.

TALISMAN

30 mL (1 oz) Midori
15 mL (1/2 oz) lime juice
30 mL (1 oz) orange juice
1 slice lime

Method
Build ingredients in an Old Fashioned glass. Garnish with a lime slice in the glass and serve.

TAMOGOZAKE

180 mL saki
1 tsp sugar
1 egg

Method
Bring saki to the boil and ignite with a match. Allow to burn for one minute and remove from heat. Add egg and sugar, whisk and serve in a cup.

TEDDY BOY SHOOTER

30 mL (1 oz) Kahlúa
30 mL (1 oz) Midori
30 mL (1 oz) Bailey's Irish cream

Method
Layer in order in a shot glass and serve.

TEMPTATION

60 mL (1 oz) rye whiskey

15 mL (1/2 oz) Dubonnet

15 mL (1/2 oz) Pernod

15 mL (1/2 oz) white curaçao

garnish: 1 twist orange peel

Method

Stir and strain into a champagne saucer. Garnish with a twist of orange peel and serve.

TEN FURLONGS

30 mL (1 oz) vodka

Bitter lemon drink (top up)

30 mL (1 oz) apricot brandy

garnish:

1/2 slice pineapple

15 mL (1/2 oz) white curaçao

1 maraschino cherry

3 dashes lime juice

Method

Stir ingredients except Bitter lemon drink, pineapple and cherry. Strain into a highball glass and top with Bitter lemon. Garnish with pineapple slice and cherry and serve.

TENNESSEE MANHATTAN DRY

45 mL Tennessee whiskey

garnish:

1 twist lemon peel

20 mL dry vermouth

cracked ice

2 dashes Angostura bitters

Method

Stir and strain into a 3 oz cocktail glass. Garnish with twist of lemon peel and serve.

TENNESSEE SNIFTER

Warm a brandy Balloon by pouring warm water over it. dry the glass, add 90 mL Tennessee whiskey and serve.

TENNESSEE SOUR

60 mL (1 oz) Tennessee whiskey

garnish:

1/2 slice lemon

juice 1/2 lemon

1 maraschino cherry

1/2 tsp sugar

cracked ice

soda water (top up)

Method

Shake ingredients except soda water. Strain into a 5 oz cocktail glass, top with soda. Garnish with lemon slice and cherry and serve.

TEQUILA

60 mL (1 oz) tequila
1 dash egg white
juice 1/2 lemon
garnish:
1 maraschino cherry
4 dashes grenadine
cracked ice

Method
Shake vigorously and strain into a 5 oz cocktail glass and serve.

TEQUILA CALIENTE

40 mL tequila
15 mL (1/2 oz) lime juice
15 mL (1/2 oz) crème de cassis
soda water
2 dashes grenadine
cracked ice

Method
Stir ingredients and strain into a Tumbler glass. Add a shot of soda water and serve.

TEQUILA SLAMMER SHOOTER

30 mL (1 oz) tequila
30 mL (1 oz) ouzo

Method
Place ingredients in a shot glass and serve.

TEQUILA SLAMMER SHOOTER NO. 2

30 mL (1 oz) tequila
20 mL dry ginger ale

Method
Place ingredients in a shot glass and serve.

TEQUILA SPARKLE

20 mL tequila
75 mL milk
30 mL (1 oz) coffee liqueur
75 mL cream

Method
frost the rims of a margarita glass with salt. Stir ingredients and strain into prepared glass and serve.

TEQUILA SUNRISE

60 mL (1 oz) tequila
soda water
30 mL (1 oz) lemon juice
garnish:
1 slice lime
30 mL (1 oz) grenadine
cracked ice

Method
Shake and strain into a 10 oz
highball glass. Garnish with slice of
lime and serve with straws.

TEQUILA SUNRISE NO. 2

30 mL (1 oz) tequila
5 mL lemon juice
15 mL (1/2 oz) Galleon Liverno
cracked ice
15 mL (1/2 oz) banana liqueur
garnish:
1 orange slice
5 mL grenadine

1 maraschino cherry

Method
Shake and strain over crushed ice in
an Old Fashioned glass. Garnish
with a slice of orange and serve.

TEQUILA SUNRISE NO. 3

30 mL (1 oz) tequila
orange juice (top up)
10 mL grenadine
cracked ice
garnish: 1 orange slice

Method
Half fill a 10 oz highball glass with
ice. Add tequila and top with
orange juice. Float grenadine on
top. Garnish with an orange slice
and serve with straws.

TEST-TUBE BABY SHOOTER

30 mL (1 oz) amaretto
30 mL (1 oz) tequila
30 mL (1 oz) Bailey's Irish cream

Method
Layer in a shot glass or test tube
and serve.

THE BIG CHILL

30 mL (1 oz) Midori
30 mL (1 oz) Bacardi rum
15 mL (1/2 oz) banana liqueur
90 mL pineapple juice

Method
Build ingredients over ice in a 10 oz
highball glass and serve with
straws.

T

THE DICK HEWETT

30 mL (1 oz) cognac
glass water (on the side)
30 mL (1 oz) Benedictine

Method
Shake with ice and strain into a 3
oz cocktail glass. Serve with glass of
water and serve.

THE ENFORCER SHOOTER

30 mL (1 oz) Southern Comfort
30 mL (1 oz) tequila
30 mL (1 oz) grenadine

Method
Layer in order in a shot glass and
serve.

THE TIME WARP

20 mL Midori
5 mL blue curaçao
15 mL (1/2 oz) Malibu
cracked ice
15 mL (1/2 oz) pineapple juice
garnish:
1 maraschino cherry
5 mL raspberry cordial

Method
Shake Midori, Malibu, pineapple
juice and strain into a 5 oz cocktail
glass. Add raspberry cordial and
blue curaçao, garnish with cherry
and serve.

THIRD DEGREE

90 mL dry gin
8 mL Pernod
30 mL (1 oz) dry vermouth
garnish:
1 twist lemon peel

Method
Shake and strain into a champagne
saucer, garnish with lemon peel
and serve.

THIRD RAIL

30 mL (1 oz) rum
20 mL orange juice
20 mL dry vermouth
cracked ice
20 mL sweet vermouth

Method
Shake and strain into a 3 oz
cocktail glass and serve.

THREE ORBIT

30 mL (1 oz) Drambuie
30 mL (1 oz) vodka
30 mL (1 oz) Cointreau

Method
Shake and strain into a 3 oz
cocktail glass and serve.

THREE SISTERS

45 mL brandy
1 dash grenadine
45 mL Galliano Liverno
garnish:
1 maraschino cherry
45 mL orange juice

Method
Shake and strain into a champagne
saucer, garnish with cherry and
serve.

TIDAL WAVE

30 mL (1 oz) Cointreau
30 mL (1 oz) mango liqueur 30 mL
(1 oz) peach liqueur
30 mL (1 oz) cream

Method
Layer in order in a 5 o/. cocktail
glass and serve.

TOBLERONE

5ml Baileys Irish Cream
15ml Kahlúa
15ml White Creme de Cacao
30ml Frangelico
60ml cream
1/2 teaspoon honey

Method
Blend with ice and pour.
Garnish with sprinkled nut flakes
and ground nutmeg over top.

TIKI

30 mL (1 oz) vodka
1/4 kiwifruit
30 mL (1 oz) Midori
1 scoop ice
90 mL pineapple juice
garnish:
1 pineapple spear

Method
Half fill a 10 oz highball glass
with cracked ice, blend the above
ingredients except the pineapple
spear and pour into glass. garnish
with pineapple spear, straws
and serve.

TIME BOMB

30 mL (1 oz) vodka
30 mL (1 oz) lemon juice
30 mL (1 oz) Aquavit
garnish:
1 strip lemon peel

Method
Stir and strain into a 3 ?/ cocktail
glass, garnish with lemon peel
and serve.

TITANIC

30 mL (1 oz) Scotch whiskey
30 mL (1 oz) Drambuie
30 mL (1 oz) Grand Marnier
30 mL (1 oz) green Chartreuse

Method
Layer in order in a 5 oz cocktail
glass and serve.

T

TOKYO JOE

45 mL vodka
45 mL Midori

Method
Layer in a 3 oz cocktail glass
and serve.

TOKYO ROSE

10ml tomato juice
10ml Smirnoff Vodka
10ml Gekkeikan Sake

Method
Layer in order.

TOM COLLINS

60 mL (1 oz) gin
garnish:
1 maraschino cherry
60 mL (1 oz) lemon juice

1 lemon wheel
1 tsp sugar
cracked ice soda water (top up)

Method
Place ingredients in a 10 oz
highball glass and top with soda
water. Garnish with cherry, lemon
wheel, straws and serve.

TOP OF THE CROSS

30 mL (1 oz) Pernod
ginger beer (top up)
30 mL (1 oz) blue curaçao
cracked ice

Method
Quarter fill a 10 oz highball glass
with cracked ice. Add Pernod and
curaçao, top with ginger beer, add
straws and serve.

TOPPING

30 mL (1 oz) gin
cracked ice
30 mL (1 oz) dry vermouth
1 maraschino cherry
15 mL (1/2 oz) crème de Violette

Method
Shake and strain into a 3 oz
cocktail glass, garnish with cherry
and serve.

T.Q. TORNADO

30ml T.Q. Hot Tequila
15ml Midori
5ml Blue Curacao
90ml pineapple juice

Method
Blend together T.Q. Hot and
pineapple juice with ice. Pour Blue
Curacao into bottom of glass, pour
blended mix on top, then float
Midori last. Garnish with a
pineapple leaf, lime wheel and
cherry.

TRADER VIC'S RUM FIZZ

30ml Whole Hog Rum
30ml lemon juice
10ml sugar
15ml cream soda
1 raw egg

Method
Shake over ice and pour. Garnish
with an orange spiral.

TRAFFIC LIGHT SHOOTER

10 mL strawberry liqueur
25 mL green Chartreuse
10 mL Galliano Liverno

Method
Layer in order in a shot glass and
serve.

TRAFFIC STOPPER SHOOTER

30 mL (1 oz) banana liqueur
30 mL (1 oz) blue curaçao
30 mL (1 oz) Bailey's Irish cream

Method
Layer in order in a shot glass and
serve.

TRANSPLANT

30 mL (1 oz) Bacardi rum
orange juice (top up)
1 dash Galliano Liverno
garnish:
1 spiral orange peel
1 dash crème de menthe
cracked ice

Method
Place ingredients into a 10 oz
highball glass and top with orange
juice.garnish with orange peel,
straws and serve.

TRAVELEX

20 mL kümmel liqueur
15 mL (1/2 oz) lemon juice
15 mL (1/2 oz) Galliano Liverno
garnish:
1 pineapple spear
10 mL vodka
cracked ice
10 mL crème de banana

Method
Shake and strain into a 3 oz
cocktail glass, garnish with
pineapple spear and serve.

TRIPLE BY-PASS

20ml Creme de Cassis
20ml White Creme de Menthe
20ml Cherry Brandy

Method
Layer liqueurs in order then float
with cream.

Tequila Sunrise

Toblerone

Traffic Light

Voodoo Child

Test Tube Baby

Water-Bubba Shooter

T

TROPICAL

30 mL (1 oz) vodka
60 mL (1 oz) pineapple juice
30 mL (1 oz) peach tree
1 dash cream
15 mL (1/2 oz) Rubis
5 strawberries

Method
Blend and pour into a 10 oz highball glass, add straws and serve.

TROPICAL AMBROSIA

1 mandarin orange
1 apple
150ml coconut milk
15ml lemon juice

Method
Blend over ice and pour. Garnish with an apple slice.

TROPICAL DELIGHT

30 mL (1 oz) dark rum
cracked ice
30 mL (1 oz) cream
garnish:
nutmeg
20 mL orange juice

Method
Shake and strain into a 3 oz cocktail glass, sprinkle with nutmeg and serve.

TROPICAL FIELD

30 mL (1 oz) strawberry liqueur
cracked ice
15 mL (1/2 oz) cherry brandy
garnish:
1/2 strawberry
30 mL (1 oz) pineapple juice

1 maraschino cherry
30 mL (1 oz) cream

Method
Shake and strain into a 5 oz cocktail glass, garnish with strawberry, cherry and serve.

TROPICAL PARADISE

45 mL Bacardi rum
5 mL lemon juice
45 mL peach tree
1 slice mango
20 mL mango liqueur
1 dash mango nectar

Method
Blend and pour into a 3 oz cocktail glass and serve.

TROPICAL SMIRNOFF

30 mL (1 oz) Smirnoff vodka
90 mL orange juice
15 mL (1/2 oz) Grand Marnier
1 peach

Method
Blend and pour into a 5 oz cocktail glass and serve.

TROPICAL SUNSET

30 mL (1 oz) Bacardi rum
60 mL (1 oz) orange juice
20 mL Grand Marnier
1 egg yolk
30 mL (1 oz) pineapple juice
garnish:
1 pineapple slice
1 dash grenadine

Method
Shake and strain into a 10 oz
highball glass, garnish with
pineapple slice, straws and serve.

TRUE BLUE

15 mL (1/2 oz) Bacardi rum
fresh cream (float)
15 mL (1/2 oz) crème de cacao
garnish:
1 maraschino cherry
15 mL (1/2 oz) maraschino
crushed ice

Method
Half fill a champagne saucer with
crushed ice. Shake remaining
ingredients except cream and pour
over ice. Float cream and serve.

TROPICAL SURPRISE

30 mL (1 oz) peach tree
30 mJs coconut cream
15 mL (1/2 oz) vodka
5 mL lemon juice
30 mL (1 oz) Midori
30 mL (1 oz) orange juice
30 mL (1 oz) pineapple juice
cracked ice

Method
Shake and pour into a 10 oz
highball glass, add straws and
serve.

TURKISH DELIGHT

30 mL (1 oz) Sabra
5 mL grenadine
15 mL (1/2 oz) parfait amour
cracked ice
30 mL (1 oz) cream
garnish:
chocolate Flakes
120 mL milk

Method
Shake and strain into a 14 oz colada
glass, sprinkle with chocolate
Flakes, add straws and serve.

T-U

TWILIGHT ZONE

60 mL (1 oz) Bacardi rum
15 mL (1/2 oz) fresh cream
30 mL (1 oz) crème de menthe
garnish:
1 maraschino cherry
15 mL (1/2 oz) parfait amour
cracked ice
15 mL (1/2 oz) lime cordial

Method
Shake and strain into a champagne
saucer and serve.

U.S.S. ARIZONA

30 mL (1 oz) Kentucky bourbon
15 mL (1/2 oz) Bianco vermouth
30 mL (1 oz) Malibu
Coca-Cola (top up)

Method
Pour ingredients over ice in a 10 oz
highball glass, top with Coca-Cola.
Add straws and serve.

TWO STROKE

30ml chilled Smirnoff Vodka
cracked pepper

Method
Layer in order.

TZEN WITH ENVY

15 mL (1/2 oz) crème de menthe
15 mL (1/2 oz) parfait amour
15 mL (1/2 oz) sambuca
lemonade (top up)

Method
shake and strain into a 5 oz cocktail
class, top with lemonade and serve.

VALENCIA SMILE

30 mL (1 oz) apricot brandy
30 mL (1 oz) orange juice
4 dashes apricot brandy
champagne (top up)

Method
Shake and strain into a flute glass,
top with champagne and serve.

VELVET HAMMER

30 mL (1 oz) Cointreau
30 mL (1 oz) cream
30 mL (1 oz) Galliano Liverno
crushed ice

Method
Half fill a 5 oz cocktail glass with
crushed ice. Shake ingredients,
pour over ice and serve.

VAMPIRE

90 mL Americano vermouth
30 mL (1 oz) banana liqueur

Method
Shake and strain into a champagne
saucer and serve.

VELVET HAMMER NO. 2

30 mL (1 oz) Cointreau
30 mL (1 oz) cream
30 mL (1 oz) Kahlúa
crushed ice

Method
Half fill a 5 oz cocktail glass with
crushed ice. Shake ingredients and
strain over ice and serve.

VAMPIRE'S PASSION

30 mL (1 oz) red crème de menthe
30 mL (1 oz) Opal Nera
30 mL (1 oz) sambuca
30 mL (1 oz) Bailey's Irish cream
15 mL (1/2 oz) strawberry liqueur

Method
Layer in order in a 5 oz cocktail
glass and serve.

VELVET HUE

30 mL (1 oz) brandy
30 mL (1 oz) Tia Maria
30 mL (1 oz) Cointreau
60 mL (1 oz) cream

Method
Shake and strain into a champagne
saucer and serve.

V

VERMOUTH CASSIS

90 mL dry vermouth
soda water (top up)
40 mL crème de cassis
garnish:
1 strip lemon peel

Method
Place a few cubes of ice in a Goblet glass along with vermouth and crème de cassis. Top with soda water, garnish with lemon peel and serve.

VIBRATOR SHOOTER

10 mL Bailey's Irish cream
20 mL Southern Comfort

Method
Layer in a 1 oz cordial glass and serve.

VICIOUS VERNON SHOOTER

30 mL (1 oz) banana liqueur
30 mL (1 oz) Bailey's Irish cream
30 mL (1 oz) Kahlúa

Method
Layer in a shot glass and serve.

VIKING II

20ml Galliano
20ml Aquavit

Method
Layer in order.

VIOLET SLUMBER SHOOTER

15 mL (1/2 oz) Malibu
10 mL orange juice
15 mL (1/2 oz) parfait amour

Method
Layer in a shot glass and serve.

VIRGIN

30 mL (1 oz) gin
20 mL Forbidden fruit
20 mL white crème de menthe
garnish:
1 maraschino cherry

Method
Shake and strain into a 3 oz cocktail glass, garnish with cherry and serve.

VIRGIN MARY

150ml tomato juice

15ml lemon juice

teaspoon Worcestershire sauce

Tabasco sauce

salt and pepper to taste

Method
Blend all ingredients together, then serve in salt-rimmed glass with ice, garnished with celery stalk, mint sprig and slice of lemon.

VIRGIN'S DELIGHT

20 mL Cointreau

20 mL cream

20 mL Galliano Liverno

garnish:

1 maraschino cherry

20 mL orange juice

Method
Shake and strain into a champagne saucer , garnish with cherry and serve.

VIRGIN'S PARADISE

20 mL gin

20 mL cream

20 mL Galliano Liverno

20 mL orange juice

20 mL almond liqueur

garnish:

1 maraschino cherry

Method
Shake and strain into a champagne saucer, garnish with cherry and serve.

VIRGIN'S PRAYER

30 mL (1 oz) dark rum

80 mL orange juice

30 mL (1 oz) Bacardi rum

cracked ice

30 mL (1 oz) Kahlúa

garnish:

1 lime wheel

40 mL lemon juice

Method
Shake and pour unstrained into a 10 ?/. highball glass, garnish with lime wheel and serve.

VIVID RESOLUTION

30 mL (1 oz) Rosso Antico

10 mL lemon juice

30 mL (1 oz) vodka

cracked ice

Method
Pour ingredients over ice in an Old Fashioned glass and serve.

VODKA COLLINS

30 mL (1 oz) vodka

cracked ice

1 tsp sugar

1 slice lemon

juice 1 lime

garnish:

1 maraschino cherry

soda water (top up)

Method
Shake and strain into a 10 oz highball glass and top with soda water. Garnish with lemon slice, cherry and serve with straws.

V

VODKA GIBSON

30 mL (1 oz) vodka
cracked ice
15 mL (1/2 oz) dry vermouth
garnish:
1 cocktail Onion

Method
Shake and strain into a 3 oz cocktail glass, garnish with Onion and serve.

VODKA MIST

45 mL vodka
1 twist lemon peel
cracked ice

Method
Shake and pour unstrained into an Old Fashioned glass and serve.

VODKATINI

30 mL (1 oz) vodka
cracked ice
1 dash dry sherry
garnish:
1 strip lemon peel

Method
Stir and strain into a 3 oz cocktail glass, garnish with lemon peel and serve.

VODKATINI NO. 2

40 mL vodka
cracked ice
10 mL dry vermouth
garnish:
1 twist lemon peel

Method
Shake and strain into a 3 07 cocktail glass, garnish with lemon peel and serve.

VOLCANO

15 mL (1/2 oz) Bacardi rum
15 mL (1/2 oz) blue curaçao
15 mL (1/2 oz) Bundaberg rum
garnish:
green Chartreuse
orange juice

1/2 slice lime
pineapple juice

Method
Soak 1/2 lime wheel in a small amount of green Chartreuse. Shake Bacardi and rum with ice and strain into a 10 oz Hurricane glass. Top up with equal parts of orange and pineapple juices. Add blue curaçao and float the lime slice. Ignite the lime and serve with straws beside the glass.

VOLTAGE

30 mL (1 oz) Midori
30 mL (1 oz) Cointreau
30 mL (1 oz) vodka

Method
Shake and strain into a 3 oz
cocktail glass and serve.

VOODOO

15 mL (1/2 oz) Frangelico
15 mL (1/2 oz) Opal Nera
15 mL (1/2 oz) strawberry liqueur
cracked ice
30 mL (1 oz) cream
garnish:
grenadine
15 mL (1/2 oz) Midori

3 jelly Babies

Method
Shake Frangelico, strawberry
liqueur and cream and strain into
a 3 oz cocktail glass. Layer Midori
and Opal Nera on top. Garnish
with jelly Babies dabbed in
grenadine on Toothpicks and serve.

VOODOO CHILD

15 mL (1/2 oz) Midori
15 mL (1/2 oz) Tia Maria
15 mL (1/2 oz) Opal Nera
15 mL (1/2 oz) cream
15 mL (1/2 oz) Bailey's Irish cream
garnish:
green & black jelly Babies

Method
Layer Midori over Opal Nera in a
3 oz cocktail glass. Shake remaining
ingredients and carefully strain
over the top. Garnish with green
and black jelly Babies on a skewer
placed across the glass and serve.

VOODOO CURE

30 mL (1 oz) Bacardi rum
1/2 banana
20 mL banana liqueur
60 mL (1 oz) orange juice
15 mL (1/2 oz) Malibu

Method
Blend until smooth and pour into a
champagne saucer and serve.

W

WALDORF

30ml Jim Beam Bourbon
5ml Pernod
5ml Cinzano Sweet Vermouth
2 dashes of Angostura Bitters

Method
Shake over ice and strain. Garnish
with an orange twist.

WARD

45 mL Canadian whiskey
15 mL (1/2 oz) Powdered sugar
30 mL (1 oz) lemon juice
cracked ice
7 mL grenadine

Method
Shake and strain into a 3 oz
cocktail glass and serve.

WARD EIGHT

45 mL rye whiskey
10 mL grenadine
15 mL (1/2 oz) orange juice
cracked ice
15 mL (1/2 oz) lemon juice

Method
Shake and strain into a 3 oz
cocktail glass and serve.

WATER BUBBA SHOOTER

15 mL (1/2 oz) cherry advocaat
12 mL blue curaçao
10 mL advocaat

Method
Pour advocaat into cherry advocaat
in a 1 oz cordial glass. Layer blue
curaçao an serve.

WEST INDIES YELLOW BIRD

30 mL (1 oz) white rum
30 mL (1 oz) pineapple juice
15 mL (1/2 oz) banana liqueur
1 1/2 scoops ice
30 mL (1 oz) lemon juice
garnish:
1 pineapple wedge
30 mL (1 oz) orange juice

1 maraschino cherry

Method
Blend until smooth, pour into a
brandy Balloon, garnish with a
pineapple wedge and cherry and
serve.

WESTMOORELAND

90 mL bourbon
garnish:
2 sprigs mint
1 tbsp sugar
crushed ice

Method
Crush half the mint with half the sugar and ice. Place in a 7 oz Old Fashioned glass, add bourbon. Place remaining mint and ice into glass and serve with straws.

WET SPOT

30 mL (1 oz) Midori
30 mL (1 oz) cream
15 mL (1/2 oz) Frangelico
30 mL (1 oz) passionfruit pulp (float)
30 mL (1 oz) apple juice
cracked ice

Method
Shake and strain into a 5 oz cocktail glass. Float the passionfruit and serve.

WHISKEY BOMB

60 mL (1 oz) Scotch whiskey
5 mL sugar syrup
1 dash Angostura bitters
cracked ice

Method
Stir and strain into a 3 oz cocktail glass and serve.

WHISKY SOUR

30ml Ballantine's Scotch Whisky
30ml lemon juice
15ml sugar syrup
1/2 egg white

Method
Shake with ice and strain. Garnish with a red cherry at bottom of glass and slice of lemon on side.

WHITE LADY

30ml Gilbey's Gin
15ml lemon juice
15ml sugar syrup
1/2 egg white

Method
Shake with ice and strain. Garnish with a Twist of lemon.

WHITE MAGIC

bitter almonds
20ml Cherry Brandy
10ml vanilla ice cream

Method
Pour Cherry Brandy onto bitter almonds then float vanilla ice cream.

W

WIDOW'S KISS

30ml Apple Brandy

10ml Benedictine

10ml Yellow Chartreuse

5ml Angostura Bitters

Method
Shake over ice and strain. Garnish with a floating strawberry.

WOODSTOCK

30ml Gilbey's Gin

10ml lemon juice

10ml maple syrup

2 dashes Angostura Bitters

Method
Shake over ice and strain then add cubed ice. Garnish with a straw.

YORKER

30 mL (1 oz) Midori
30 g Avocado
30 mL (1 oz) cream
garnish:
1 strawberry
60 mL (1 oz) milk

Method
Blend ingredients and pour into a colada glass. Garnish with a strawberry and serve.

ZANDARIA

30 mL (1 oz) brandy
cracked ice
30 mL (1 oz) Tia Maria
garnish:
1 Pinch nutmeg
120 mL fresh cream

Method
Shake and strain into a 6 oz cocktail glass. Sprinkle with nutmeg and serve.

ZED

30 mL (1 oz) gin
1 tsp sugar
30 mL (1 oz) Mandarin Napoleon
garnish:
1/2 slice lemon
90 mL pineapple juice

1 sprig mint

Method
Shake and strain into a 3 oz cocktail glass. Garnish with mint sprig and lemon.

ZIPPER SHOOTER

15 mL (1/2 oz) tequila
15 mL (1/2 oz) Grand Marnier
15 mL (1/2 oz) Bailey's Irish cream

Method
Layer in order in a shot glass and serve.

ZOMBIE

30 mL (1 oz) light rum
30 mL (1 oz) apricot nectar
30 mL (1 oz) Golden rum
15 mL (1/2 oz) O.P. rum
30 mL (1 oz) dark rum
5 mL sugar syrup
30 mL (1 oz) lemon juice
cracked ice
30 mL (1 oz) pineapple juice
fruit for garnish

Method
Fill a Zombie glass 3/4 full with ice. Shake and strain ingredients except 0 P rum into the glass. Gently add rum. Garnish with fruit and serve.

Y-Z

ZOMBIE NO. 2

30 mL (1 oz) dark rum

4 dashes passionfruit soda

30 mL (1 oz) Jamaican rum

30 mL (1 oz) lemon juice

4 dashes apricot brandy

garnish:

1 slice orange

30 mL (1 oz) white rum

green and red Cherries

4 dashes cherry brandy

cracked ice

15 mL (1/2 oz) Proof rum (top up)

Method

Fill Zombie glass with cracked ice.
Add the above ingredients except
151 Proof rum. Stir and top with
151 Proof rum. Decorate with
Cherries and orange slice. Serve
with straws.

ZOOM

40 mL brandy

20 mL cream

15 mL (1/2 oz) honey

cracked ice

Method

Shake and strain into a 5 oz
cocktail glass and serve.

ZORBA THE GREEK

60 mL (1 oz) Bacardi rum

30 mL (1 oz) orange juice

15 mL (1/2 oz) ouzo

15 mL (1/2 oz) grenadine

Method

Shake and strain into a 5 oz
cocktail glass and serve.

ZULU WARRIOR

30 mL (1 oz) Midori

garnish:

1 slice Rockmelon

30 mL (1 oz) strawberry liqueur

3 strawberries

30 mL (1 oz) lemon juice

1 1/2 scoops ice

Method

Blend until smooth. Pour into a
brandy Balloon. Garnish with a slice
of Rockmelon and serve.

Index

Index

Index

Index

Index

Index

Index

Index